BURN THE TOWN and SACK THE BANKS!

BURN THE
TOWN and
SACK THE
BANKS!

★ ★ ★ ★ ★ ★ ★ ★ ★ ★ ★ ★ ★ ★ ★ ★ ★ ★ ★

Confederates Attack Vermont!

Cathryn J. Prince

CARROLL & GRAF PUBLISHERS

NEW YORK

BURN THE TOWN AND SACK THE BANKS
Confederates Attack Vermont!

Carroll & Graf Publishers
An Imprint of Avalon Publishing Group, Inc.
245 West 17th Street
11th Floor
New York, NY 10011

AVALON
publishing group incorporated

Copyright © 2006 by Cathryn J. Prince

First Carroll & Graf edition 2006

Library of Congress Cataloging-in-Publication Data is available.

ISBN-13: 978-0-78671-751-4
ISBN-10: 0-7867-1751-3

9 8 7 6 5 4 3 2 1

Printed in the United States of America
Interior design by Bettina Wilhelm
Distributed by Publishers Group West

For Pierre

Contents

Acknowledgments

★ ★ ★ ★ ★ ★ ★ ★ ★ ★ ★ ★ ★ ★ ★ ★ ★ ★ ★

Several people offered help and encouragement in the writing of this book.

First, the staffs at the St. Albans Historical Society in St. Albans, Vermont; the Bailey/Howe Library at the University of Vermont in Burlington; and the Filson Historical Society in Louisville, Kentucky.

Richard Z. Chesnoff, thank you for acting as my mentor for so many years in a field that can often be most difficult to negotiate.

Eric Lupfer, a trusted agent and editor, whose tireless work and thoughtful comments on even the earliest and roughest of drafts helped bring this book about.

At Carroll & Graf Publishers: Will Balliett, Shaun Dillon, and Keith Wallman, whose thoroughly attentive and constructive editing helped polish this work. Phil Gaskill for his methodical copyediting.

In addition, I have been blessed with a family who has supported and encouraged my writing from the beginning. My parents, Marvin and Norma Prince, are role models of the highest caliber, who instilled in me the values of hard work, dedication, and curiosity. My children Nathan and Zoë were tremendously excited about this book. Their inquisitiveness about the past, and about our nations history, truly inspires me.

Finally, Pierre: twelve years into our adventure and still your certainty in me gives me sustenance.

Prologue

★ ★ ★ ★ ★ ★ ★ ★ ★ ★ ★ ★ ★ ★ ★ ★ ★ ★ ★

Cyrus Newton Bishop likely rose early on October 19. He wanted to get to the bank with time to spare before the first customers came to do business. There was just always so much to do the morning after Market Day and, as usual, the banks would be full with cash. Bishop would begin his workday bundling and marking the stacks of bills deposited by the vendors and farmers. Naturally, he would want to finish this chore as soon as possible.

The washed-charcoal sky showed no signs of letting so much as a splinter of sunshine through. Yes, it would be another dull, bone-chilling day. The first thing Bishop would do when he got to the bank, where he was proud to work as the chief teller, was to stoke the wood-burning stove and allow the warmth to fill the building. Autumn had nearly departed the serene village, and winter would soon come to camp. With the advent of colder weather, many of the townspeople liked to keep company with Bishop, read the newspapers, and chat. Particularly now with so many of the town's men and boys down South, fighting their way through what must seem like a foreign country.

As Bishop turned onto Main Street, he would have passed any number of merchants getting their storefronts in order for the day. Business went on, despite the war. On his way to the bank, Bishop passed the milliner and the apothecary, and he would have seen the town's first young pupils march up the steps of their school, which stood just across from the bank. The town green—a swatch of grass just starting to turn russet—separated the two buildings.

Once Bishop ducked inside, he hung his hat and coat; rain threatened again today. If he was the first to arrive, Martin A. Seymour would join him soon. Seymour would be eager to begin the day's bookkeeping.

Sometime around noon, or just after, the two men would pause for a spot of lunch. They might catch up on the news of their townsmen who were moving from one battle to another. The tragedy hit close to home when wounded soldiers or those on furlough came home. Certainly Bishop and Seymour would have agreed that they were lucky to be spared, by their ages, from the fear and devastation this crusade was bringing to bear on so many.

While the day went on in the manner to which Bishop was accustomed, his afternoon was disrupted as two armed men barreled through the doors as he stood behind the counter sorting money. At first, he believed the rough-looking men were customers, but their drawn pistols quickly changed his mind. Bishop hurried into the back office to warn Seymour, who was poring over the ledgers. Suddenly, one of the robbers threw open the door, striking Bishop smack in the middle of his forehead. "If you stir or make any resistance, we will blow your brains out."

Unaware of the commotion stirring in the bank, Samuel Breck, a merchant in the enterprise of Weatherbee and Breck, walked over to make a deposit. He noticed that the doors to the St. Albans Bank were locked. He knocked on the door. There was no answer. He knocked again. This time an unfamiliar face opened the door and pushed his gun into Breck's face.

"I take deposits," he said, grabbing Breck by the shoulder, pulling him inside, saying: "Give me money, or I'll shoot you," and then something that defied possibility: "I am a Confederate soldier."

Bishop, tied up in the back, heard this and called out: "Breck, we are caught; you had better give it for."

Breck knew many of the St. Albans boys fighting their way at this moment through the Shenandoah Valley under the leadership of the legendary General Phil Sheridan. People kept close watch of the news in the local papers, from the *St. Albans Daily Messenger* to the *Burlington Free Press*. Even the governor's wife, who lived in St. Albans, had a brother who had been fighting. But this kind of thing wasn't supposed to happen here. They were supposed to be safe up here in their tiny kingdom in Vermont.

"Not a word," the menacing soldier breathed. "We're Confederate soldiers detailed from Gen. Early's army to come north and to rob and plunder, as your soldiers are doing in the Shenandoah Valley."

1

Autumn in Vermont

★ ★ ★ ★ ★ ★ ★ ★ ★ ★ ★ ★ ★ ★ ★ ★ ★ ★ ★

At the outbreak of the Civil War, patriotism coursed through the veins of Vermonters as syrup ran through the trunks of the state's maple trees. "Don't Tread on Me" was more than a slogan. It may have taken two days for Vermonters to learn that the Confederates had taken Fort Sumter on April 12, 1861, but it then took them perhaps two minutes to raise the Stars and Stripes in nearly every town, village, and city of the state.

As one of the smallest states in the Union, Vermont measures only about 9,609 square miles. But as a contributor of troops to the Union cause, it measured the largest. It sent more than 30,000 men into the service of the Union Army. All told, about one in ten Vermonters fought in the war, and the state lost a higher proportion of its men than any other. Towns across Vermont poured their sons into the conflict, towns like Woodstock, population 3,062 during the war, which sent 284 men to fight, thirty-nine of whom would die as soldiers in Company C of the 6th Vermont, a regiment in the First Vermont Brigade. All told, Vermont delivered seventeen infantry regiments, three sharpshooter companies, and one cavalry regiment to the war, and more than six hundred Vermonters served in the United States

Navy. Of all its units to serve, the greatest was perhaps the First Vermont Brigade, which remains one of the hardest-fighting brigades in American military history.

Yet more than being known just for a commitment to the Union, the state also had firm traditions rooted in abolition. Chapter One, Article One of the state's constitution (written in 1777) outlawed slavery. Time and again, the citizens elected anti-slavery congressmen. There were numerous anti-slavery societies in the state, and a Sunday sermon might well preach the evils of slavery as much as the value of hard work.

The state of Vermont also passed laws that protected slaves who were able to reach her borders, decreeing that slave-owners could not have their fugitive slaves back, even though that contradicted the Federal law. In 1786, Vermont had made it illegal for slave-catchers to remove slaves from the state without a trial.

The famous Underground Railroad ran through Vermont. There were two main routes for the Railroad, and they worked for decades. One of the routes passed through Woodstock to Montpelier and up along the western side of the state, eventually winding on to Canada. The other hugged the eastern border and went from Brattleboro. There are records indicating that some slaves chose to remain in Vermont, but most were taken to Canada.

Abolition was part of the culture, of the upbringing experienced by many a Vermonter. Ezra Brainerd, for one, helped runaway slaves escape when he was growing up there. Born in 1844, Brainerd graduated from Middlebury College in 1864 and would later become president of the school. "Often these fugitive slaves were kept overnight at our house, and I was told to be up early and take them in our carryall. . . . The poor creatures seemed to suffer badly from the cold, and I recall hearing one of them pray 'Lord, don't let me freeze to death so near freedom!'"

This thinking infused many Vermonters with the courage and conviction they would need on the battlefield. Yet, although ready for a fight in their hearts, the state was hardly prepared for what the war would demand from its boys. For many years, long before the war, all able-bodied men in Vermont had participated in the state's militia, and on the first Tuesday of June, every year, when the leaves were turning a darker shade of green and the afternoons were stretching into evening, the men would drill on town greens across the state while the women would watch. Afterward, there would be celebrations and feasting. But the training day had been eliminated some years before, in 1846; by the time of the Civil War, most Vermont men had not even a smattering of military service.

Lincoln needed troops, but there were very few that could accurately be said to be ready. At the beginning of the war, about 16,000 men served in the U.S. Army, most of them not stationed on the East Coast but rather spread throughout the West.

"Washington is in grave danger. What may we expect from Vermont? A. Lincoln," read the telegram to Governor Erastus Fairbanks, who served from 1860 to 1861. "Vermont will do its full duty," went the reply. The Confederate guns had just forced Union soldiers to surrender Fort Sumter in the harbor of Charleston, South Carolina.

Fairbanks, then sixty-eight years old, was in the middle of his second one-year term as Vermont's governor. He had previously served a term from 1852–1853. Fairbanks was also a businessman. He, along with his brothers and father, had started E & T Fairbanks & Company. Vermont elects a governor every two years, so the state had three wartime governors. After Fairbanks, Frederick Holbrook was elected to serve from 1861 to 1863, and then J. Gregory Smith from 1863 to 1865.

After answering Lincoln, Fairbanks summoned the state legislature to a special session. Within eight days, all the legislators had assembled in Montpelier and a thirty-four-gun salute welcomed their arrival and the solemn reason for their presence.

According to state lore, the lawmakers felt moved to sing "The Star-Spangled Banner," but unfortunately no one knew the words to the song. That evening, while their work continued, a twenty-five-person choir holding small American flags sang to the legislators from the gallery.

Four days after the meeting, Vermont voted to contribute two regiments, exceeding Lincoln's request for one regiment of 780 officers and privates. Governor Fairbanks had effectively appealed to the necessity to save the Union, the capital, the government, and everything they stood for, from the South's destructive forces. In addition, the legislature voted to appropriate one million dollars so that each private would receive $7 a month in addition to the $13 offered by the Federal government.

Men could enlist for terms between three months and five years. One could become an officer if he had the proper political and social connections. A man might get the rank of colonel if he was a prominent member of a town or city. A man might expect the rank of captain if he was friends with a local politician and could be counted on to raise a certain number of troops.

Persuasion was still needed to raise troops, notwithstanding the rush to enlist in the opening days of the conflict. The fairer sex was employed in propaganda campaigns, as it was widely said that they preferred soldiers as their sweethearts. When the First Vermont went from Bradford to New York in May 1861, they were met at Bellows Falls by ladies, refreshments, and sweet talk, while grand speeches, spectacles, and bands played in the background.

After Fairbanks and the state legislators concluded their emergency meeting, Horace H. Baxter, the state's adjutant general, sent Vermont's quartermaster general to the Federal armory in Springfield, Massachusetts. Gen. George F. Davis had the task of securing rifled muskets. The Massachusetts armory wouldn't open its doors, so Davis was sent to Boston and, by appealing directly to Massachusetts Governor John A. Andrews, was able to secure about three hundred. During the war, Gen. Davis earned a reputation for ensuring that Vermont's soldiers were well cared for and were supplied with the proper equipment. He also often traveled to the front to personally assess battlefield situations.

By the late spring of 1862 Vermont had already given eight infantry regiments, one cavalry regiment, and two artillery batteries to the Union cause; it would ultimately deliver seventeen infantry regiments. The state's only recruiting concern, in the midst of a war engulfing the entire country, seemed to be whether or not it would suffer the indignity of resorting to a draft.

"Notwithstanding my appeals to their love of country, of glory, and of universal liberty, the young men will not come forward and 'list' except slowly and by gradual approaches, and hence I mourn in spirit, still trusting that the disgrace of drafting will never rest upon the fair name and fame of Vermont, when engaged in a holy cause," wrote one recruiter, Alfred C. Ballard, in the *Rutland Herald,* on June 6, 1862.

Yet however hesitant the decision could be for young men at the time, going to war often had the feel of a festival. Bands played while women sewed uniforms and men drilled on town greens. There were feasts, tents, songs, and cheering crowds.

"Sometimes the patriotism of such a gathering would be wrought up so intensely by waving banners, martial and vocal music, and burning eloquence, that a town's quota would be filled in less than an hour," wrote John D. Billings in his 1887 book *Hardtack and Coffee, or The Unwritten Story of the Army Life.* "It needed only the first man to step forward, put down his name, be patted on the back, placed upon the platform, and cheered to the echo as the hero of the hour, when a second, a third, a fourth would follow, and at last a perfect stampede set in to sign the enlistment roll, and a frenzy of enthusiasm would take possession of the meeting."

Whatever the fanfare, however, recruiting could be quite difficult, especially as total war became the strategy as the conflict endured. "Grant's scheme required that regiments remain filled, manpower quotas filled . . . would need a draft again, more men needed . . . would have more war widows and orphans . . . north was losing patience."

Nevertheless, Green Mountain Boys of every age stepped forward, even those discouraged from doing so because of their young age, like five-foot-five, sixteen-year-old Dunham G. Burt, born in Castleton, Vermont, who won permission from his father to join up (some weeks later, Dunham's fifteen-year-old brother Charles Burt would join the same unit).

There was no minimum age at first for Northern troops, so there were drummer boys and cavalry buglers of about twelve years old, and some as young as nine. On March 3, 1864, only about a year before the end of the war, Congress made it official that one had to be sixteen, but of course that didn't stop some from lying about their age—or getting their parents to lie about their age.

Of the exceptionally young recruits, quite a few made names for themselves through their conduct and bravery. Willie Johnston of St. Johnsbury enlisted in Company D, Third Vermont Infantry in 1861 after persuading his father to allow him to join. The twelve-year-old drummer boy first saw combat at Lee's Mills, Virginia on April 16, 1862, which was soon thereafter followed by the Seven Days' Fighting and Peninsula Campaign from June 25 to July 1, 1862, when events unfolded that proved the boy's bravery. During the retreat from that campaign, while many soldiers dropped their weapons and equipment to lighten their loads, young Johnston held on to his drum and brought it to Harrison's Landing, where he drummed for the division parade.

President Lincoln heard the story and suggested that Willie Johnston be given a medal. Secretary of War Stanton agreed and on September 16, 1863, Willie Johnston received the Medal of Honor.

Letters from the early months of the war show the magnitude of pride that Vermonters felt for the uniform and for their country. The letters also show how sincerely the Green Mountain Boys believed they were fighting to protect the serenity and freedom of their loved ones at home. Never would they think their homes would be, or could be, directly touched by the violence of this conflict.

"When this great national crisis came—when I felt that I must go to my country's rescue, among my first thoughts were we would go together, side by side, and if needs be die in each other's defense," wrote Joseph L. Perkins to his brother on April 23, 1861. "Would it not be much easier to die in the arms of one we loved? Would not the death struggle be mitigated if we felt a heart near our own that shared all our joys and sorrows? . . . In answer to whether it is dear to me I would refer you to my hopes of the future . . . to the love I bear her whose life is two fold dearer than my own and perhaps that stimulates me to action— What would be the pleasure of homes without Liberty? Twould not be home—we were born free let us die freemen."

Those too old to join up did what they could to help supply the young, while students at the University of Vermont and Middlebury College formed their own militia companies, tirelessly drilling in the school yards. The state's railroad and steamboats offered to provide free transport for troops and munitions. Each of the two Montpelier banks loaned an estimated $25,000 to equip the troops. The state was sure to give its all for the boys who left it for the battlefields to the south.

"On our journey from the Green Mountain State we were treated with the greatest respect and hospitality. Everybody upon the way seemed to be out waving handkerchiefs and banners as we passed, and scores of young ladies even threw kisses at us," wrote Judson A. Lewis of the 11th Vermont to the *Rutland Herald.*

All the pomp and circumstance nourished the troops' morale and helped soothe the nerves of their loved ones as they bid them adieu for parts unknown.

Saving the Union was paramount for the citizens of this state; but for all that the state did to prepare its men and boys to fight, it hadn't given much thought to its own defense. The war was, after all, hundreds of miles away. It's true that late in the war, on October 12, 1864, Governor John Gregory Smith addressed the legislature about organizing and equipping a militia: "Vermont stands today utterly destitute of any arm of defense or any effective power to resist or prevent invasion. The dangers to our frontiers are by no means inconsiderable." These strong words might as well have been whispered, for those left behind in Vermont, and those already fighting down South, couldn't fathom the report of combat rifles sounding in their villages and hills.

"I am as safe here as I would be at home and if bad should come to worse I can return home at almost any time," wrote Samuel Sumner to his father in Troy, Vermont on April 27, 1861.

New recruits to Union forces could expect to wear wool uniforms and belt sets that included a cartridge box and cap box. They would each receive a bayonet and scabbard, a haversack for rations, a canteen, a blanket roll, or a knapsack, which had inside a wool blanket, a shelter, and perhaps even a rubber blanket or poncho that could double as ground cover. If they could, soldiers also carried an extra pair of socks, comb, papers, ink, pens, and razors.

Union uniforms were dark blue in the early days of the war; later, the trousers were dyed a lighter blue. Their uniforms were of far better quality than those of the Southerners, in large part because the North had access to their own mills and to material from Europe. Federal soldiers wore floppy-crowned forage caps, adorned with brass letters of regiment and company until around 1863, when corps badges were made.

Once outside the fanfare of their farewells, and far beyond the comfort of the hills that they knew so well, army life proved to be extraordinarily harsh for the new recruits. Two-by-four tents and ramshackle wooden shelters replaced home and hearth, with six men assigned to tents with only room enough for four. The troops complained that the tents were good enough only for a dog and accordingly nicknamed them "dog shanties" and "pup tents."

The tent, which the Union started using with regularity in 1862, was fashioned from a rectangular piece of canvas, buttoned to another. It was the perfect shelter for armies on the move; soldiers could easily pitch them by tying each end to a rifle stuck in the ground by the bayonet or by stringing the tent to sticks or even fence rails. On the other side, Confederates usually made lean-tos. However, as the war went on, it was quite common to see Union tents in Confederate camps, as well as Union rubber blankets, which the South didn't make. After any Confederate victory and Union retreat, "butternut" soldiers (from the color of their uniforms late in the war) would forage in Union camps for supplies.

Union camps looked like canvas towns lit by hundreds of campfires. In the winter, they would make quarters from log huts that could fit several soldiers. The tent often served as a roof to the hut, which soldiers were fond of naming after restaurants and inns from home.

The menu consisted mostly of salt pork, beans and peas, and hardtack, a thick biscuit prepared with flour, water, and occasionally a bit of salt. Soldiers ate hardtack alone or sometimes crumbled it into their coffee. Coffee itself was a highly prized delicacy. The soldiers, of course, had to learn how to grind and roast it, but it was worth every bit of work.

Wrote Billings: "What a Godsend it seemed to us at times! How often after being completely jaded by a night march . . . have I had a wash, if there was water to be had, made and drunk my pint or so of coffee and felt as fresh and invigorated as if just arisen from a night's sound sleep!"

Oftentimes weevils infested the biscuits; when soldiers went about preparing their morning coffee, the insects would rise to the top to be skimmed. Once in a while, a soldier would break up the biscuit and fry it together with fat to make a dish known as skilligalee. The lucky few who had a bit of sugar ration left over would spread it on the hardtack for a rare battlefield treat. Fresh food was a memory left on the tables of their homes.

When not performing their military drills or otherwise engaged, soldiers wrote letters home and sent pay home to loved ones in need. While family and friends in Vermont might be experiencing a degree of economic hardship due to the war, soldiers were at least comforted by the knowledge that those left behind were not touched by the direct horror and violence of war. Union soldiers could spend the money they kept for themselves in the sutler's store, similar to today's post exchange, where they could purchase canned fruit, pocketknives, and other extra creature comforts. (Confederate soldiers didn't have that privilege.)

Soldiers also filled the space between battle and drills with card games, horseshoes, and even baseball. In fact, many a troop stuffed a copy of the rules for this relatively new sport in their haversacks. And of course, many soldiers kept pets like dogs, cats, squirrels, and raccoons. Though officially against the rules, even officers like Gen. George Armstrong Custer of the Army of the Potomac had dogs.

Training was poor, the equipment was inferior, and the medical treatment most often came from barber-surgeons. And although it would later join the fight, discipline hadn't answered the bugle's call at the start of the war. Aside from West Point, the United States boasted no serious officer-candidate schools. Troops learned how to march and to follow commands from men as green as they. Regiments practiced their marches on country roads in columns of fours as they learned to fight elbow to elbow during battle.

Every day, new soldiers drilled as squads and in company formations. As military tactics hadn't changed all that much since the American Revolution, the drill was exceedingly important. Soldiers fought in close-knit formations of two rows of soldiers with single-shot, muzzle-loading muskets that were not known for their high rate of accuracy. And although smoothbore muskets became obsolete fairly early on during the war and rifled muskets were coming into action, it still took a long time for tactics to change accordingly. Officers believed close formations would ensure continuous firepower, but it also meant heavy casualties.

The basic weapon for Union soldiers was the above-described single-shot, muzzle-loading percussion musket. Most of these were the Springfield, manufactured at the U.S. Armory in Springfield, Massachusetts. Production of weapons had to be ramped up because, when the war started, there wasn't much in the way of extensive stores of arms and ammunition. In October 1860, there were maybe a little more than five hundred thousand muskets in arsenals across the country.

Still, the shots fired on the battlefield would be but one hazard for the troops. Diseases such as typhoid and typhus ran unchecked in many camps; in the Deep South, a mosquito's bite might bring on death faster than any shell. About 250,152 Federals and 164,000 Confederates died from disease. Among the tonics were quinine and a strange mixture known as "Blue

Mass"; and of course these were in addition to the standards of whiskey and brandy.

Each Vermont regiment that marched into service would see their ranks decimated by bullets and disease. The Seventh Vermont had three hundred soldiers die from disease in the first year of duty alone.

The pages of the calendar had turned slowly as the conflict unfolded, with newly minted men sent to the front year after year. By 1864, the war was three years old, testing the political and emotional resolves on both sides of the Mason–Dixon Line. Casualties had seemed to grow exponentially; neither side seemed destined for decisive victory; and many had begun to question whether the war was worth the price paid in homes torn asunder, limbs ripped from bodies, and lives lost on the fields of battle.

The year 1864 promised tumult off the field as well. More than ever, the Union required a sure victory. With the presidential election just months away, Lincoln and his administration needed a battlefield triumph to secure their next four years. His mandate of 1860 no longer held—there were enough voters in the North who vehemently opposed his war policies, and a fracture was running through the Union between those who agreed that force was necessary to hold the Union together and those who felt that reunification through compromise could offer a better solution.

But amidst the doubts they heard cast throughout the states and the daily hardships they endured, the soldiers of Vermont told a different story. The Civil War was the last major war where neither the national press nor letters home were censored. Troop levels and positions, casualty counts, troop movements, battle reports, and subordinates' views of officers were all fodder for readers back home. For many readers in Vermont, soldiers' letters more often than not read as reflections of an unwavering sense of pride.

"I am just struck with the idea that the Fourth of July is an obtrusive animal. Go where you will, even among the swamps and sand of Florida or Louisiana, the Fourth of July wakes you up with an alarm clock that strikes thirteen and absolutely demands your attention for the day," wrote John Q. Dickinson of the 7th Vermont. "My curiosity is excited to know how they regard this anniversary just over the lines ten miles from us. Do they do honor to this day which can remind them of naught save the liberty which they are denying and the Independence they are fast pawning for despotism?"

The citizens of Vermont had little choice but to simply carry on in the autumn of 1864. Vermont women in particular became ever more industrious. Their fingers had been flying throughout the conflict as they fashioned uniforms for soldiers-to-be. Women were thrust into jobs they hadn't had before, such as farm chores, and they continually found new ways in which they could contribute with groups like the Ladies Aid Society of Cornwall, Vermont and the Ladies Relief Association, who sent boxes of hospital stoves, haversacks, woolen shirts, towels, sewing kits, and other essentials down south. Many of the items would first go to Washington, D.C., where Vermont Senator Justin Smith Morrill's wife, Ruth Barrell Swan, would assemble the goods and ensure that they reached troops in the field.

Industry also continued with vigor. During the war, Windsor, Vermont manufactured about a hundred thousand rifles for the Union, while gunpowder came from the Bennington Powder Company. The mills of Felchville produced cloth for uniforms, and tailors in Rutland and Brattleboro turned that fabric into uniforms.

In truth, the war meant steady, and even profitable, business for Vermont. In Brattleboro and St. Johnsbury, where troops encamped before heading to battle, shops and inns made consistent money. Anyone with a hand in lumber, dry goods, and other stuffs also did quite well. Even the families of governors Fairbanks and Smith found opportunity. Gov. Fairbanks filled his coffers from his harness hardware business. And during the war, the need for supplies and information meant that railroads and telegraph lines sprouted all across the state, which benefited the family of J. Gregory Smith.

From far away, the people of Vermont prayed and worked for their boys, gone but still full of spirit, who were carried proudly by the famous Morgan horses for which the region had become known. The Morgan horse was yet another point of pride for the Green Mountain state, born out of rural legend.

Justin Morgan, a singing teacher from Vermont, had once been given a small colt by his cousin who owed him but had only a tiny horse to offer. Eventually the colt grew quite strong from hard work in the fields. In time, the colt came to be known as Justin Morgan's Horse, and then, when the owner died, the horse was simply called Justin Morgan. The horse lived to be thirty-two, and breeders realized that his descendants had strength, speed, intelligence, and a gentle nature. The Morgan horses used after that by the U.S. Army were on average between five and nine years old and, as the Federal government required, were between fifteen and sixteen hands high and bore a "US" brand on their forefoot and fore shoulder. It was perhaps the smallest of contributions, but the Morgan horses brought gratitude and fame to Vermont, and indeed it was said that the great Gen. Sheridan himself rode one.

★ ★ ★

Though autumn's brilliant colors were being tarnished by the news of ceaseless fighting in Spotsylvania, Cold Harbor, and

Antietam unfolding hundreds of miles away, 1864 would ultimately come to define the waning power of the Confederacy,
as total war became the battle hymn for the North. The South
was facing an economic drain from an ever-tightening
blockade; and the cessation of the prisoner exchange which
had occurred in 1862, coupled with desertions, had left it fast
running out of men.

With the fall of Vicksburg on July 4, 1863, the Union controlled the Mississippi from St. Louis to the Gulf of Mexico. West
of the Mississippi River, Texas, Arkansas, and Louisiana were
separated from the other Confederate states, and Mississippi and
northern Alabama already found themselves in the Union's grip.
Kentucky and Tennessee had essentially fallen, too. Of the eleven
states that had seceded, only six remained whole and fully free
of Union occupation.

However, even that wasn't a situation destined to last long.
General William Tecumseh Sherman was readying his campaign
through Georgia, and Gen. Ulysses S. Grant had begun to press
toward Richmond.

Gloom for the Confederacy sat on the horizon like a fog, but
the citizens of Vermont couldn't yet see the momentous trend of
the time. For their attention in October 1864 was understandably
drawn very narrowly to Virginia, to the Shenandoah Valley, and
to the looming battle of Cedar Creek into which their volunteers,
led by Gen. Sheridan and his fine Morgan, would soon plunge.

2

The Army of the Shenandoah

★ ★ ★ ★ ★ ★ ★ ★ ★ ★ ★ ★ ★ ★ ★ ★ ★ ★

On October 10, 1864, a significant Union Army force, including the Eighth Regiment Vermont Volunteers, crossed the north side of Cedar Creek in the Shenandoah Valley of Virginia to set camp after weeks of slow and costly fighting. The rapid creek, thirty yards wide, runs shallow and is surrounded on both sides by hills three hundred feet high, sweeping in tortuous curves across the upper valley before emptying into the lower lands below.

The Shenandoah Valley itself fits into the Great Valley of Virginia. The Blue Ridge Mountains rise on the east and the Alleghenies protrude through the surface of the earth on the west. The valley, a 125-mile tableau of ravines, rivers, grazing land, and rocks, extends northeastward from Rockbridge County in the south to the Potomac River in the north.

By the time the Union soldiers had camped at Cedar Creek, boots and horses had already tramped and galloped across the valley floor in countless battles from America's earliest days, from the fall of 1775 when Washington had defended the region known as Winchester from Native Americans, to the earlier years of the Civil War during which the gorges and hollows had become a Confederate arena of victory for the likes of Johnston,

Jackson, Ashby, Lee, Breckenridge, Mosby, Elwell, and Early. Indeed, until the battles of Opequon, Winchester, and Fisher's Hill in the summer and early fall of 1864, the Shenandoah had been a valley of shame for the Blue, and no one had yet been able to push back the Confederates.

As the Federals set their positions, the Shenandoah seemed to have more soldiers than trees. The Union Army of the Shenandoah boasted more troops than any previous force in the Valley—about 35,000 infantry and artillery, about 8,000 cavalry, nearly 29,000 troops from the Department of Washington's Middle Military Division, 2,700 troops from the Department of Susquehanna, and about 5,900 Federals from the Middle Department.

The Union camps nestled across a series of ridges between Cedar Creek and the village that shared its name, walled in on the sides by the high hills and mountains. Infantry units and artillery batteries manned the ridges east to west, and the Union line stretched five miles from flank to flank. It would be tough fighting ground for attackers and defenders alike, for if any part of any line were to fall into trouble, reserves would find extreme difficulty in filling the holes. Despite the challenging terrain, Union Gen. Philip Sheridan still felt certain in his choice of camp. "Our position was a good one, and as far as human foresight could reach, a safe one."

Days before camping, Sheridan had faced Confederate Gen. Jubal Early at Winchester, a battle that Sheridan won handily. Certain that he was close to conquering the valley once and for all after months of campaigning, Sheridan decided to hunker down along Cedar Creek, fifteen miles south of Winchester, following advice from the reports of his scouts and those of the impossibly young Gen. George Armstrong Custer. At the time, the Confederates were said to be camping in the heights south of Strasburg, approximately five miles beyond Cedar Creek.

Sheridan knew only too well about the Union's previous debacles in the Shenandoah Valley, and Gen. Grant had instructed him to follow Jubal Early "to the death." For at least six weeks, Sheridan had fought with Early's army, but he had never succeeded in moving them any farther south than Winchester. Now, after Winchester, the end of Sheridan's mission was, at the very least, in sight.

The next few months would settle the course of the war and—most probably—the terms of its finish. The earlier spring offensive had placed unrelenting pressure on the South, and the human toll was staggering while the material costs were skyrocketing. Yet victory on the battlefield wouldn't be enough. The Union troops would have to squeeze the life out of the Shenandoah as the Confederates clung to it with increasing desperation. Grant intended to see the South so crippled that surrender and reunification would be the only paths to recovery, and control of the Shenandoah was an essential element of his strategy.

Whoever controlled the valley would control both the fertile land that yielded the lush harvests that fed the bellies of northern Virginia and the natural highway that ran straight through to Washington, D.C., the heart of the Union. Sheridan's Shenandoah campaign thus had two aims—to defeat the Confederate defenders and to destroy the fertile valley of Virginia.

Most of the troops felt that victory would secure Lincoln's re-election, and that there was no hope for reconciliation not precipitated by surrender. "The character of the war has very much changed within the last year. There is now no possible hope of reconciliation with the Rebels. . . . There can be no peace but that which is forced by the sword. We must conquer the Rebels or be conquered by them."

But Lincoln had had to contend with generals who weren't afraid to publicly voice their own political and military philosophies. On July 7, 1862, Gen. George B. McClellan wrote to Abraham Lincoln suggesting ways in which to conduct the war. He said: "It should not be, at all, a War upon population; but against armed forces and political organizations. . . . In prosecuting the War, all private property and unarmed persons should be strictly protected; subject only to the necessities of military operations."

Lincoln went through a seemingly endless stream of generals before finally finding Grant, and any hesitancy was discarded when Sheridan set himself to burn his way through the Shenandoah and when Sherman began his march through Atlanta on the orders of Grant—when total war became the way.

When Gen. Philip Sheridan assumed control of the Army of the Shenandoah in August 1864, it had been called the Sixth Corps. It was below strength, with one division of the Nineteenth Corps, two small infantry divisions, and two small cavalry divisions. To say the least, the Corps was in need of an invigorating leader to shape it and to push it forward.

Thickset and broad-shouldered, Sheridan, the cavalryman, stood on short legs. He reached just less than five feet four inches and weighed between 115 and 120 pounds, earning him the nickname "Little Phil." He had a misshapen head, slightly flattened, and some thought that he resembled a brawling bulldog. While Grant personally loved the cigar-smoking general, Lincoln held his opinion in reserve, for, at the time of his appointment, Sheridan had yet to command an entire army.

Sheridan was born to John and Minah Sheridan, who came to America in 1830 from County Cavan, Ireland with two children, Patrick and Rosa (Rosa died en route and was buried at sea). Biographers don't agree on Sheridan's birthplace—putting it in

Albany, Boston, or Somerset, Ohio. But he did go to school in Somerset until he was fourteen, earning his appointment in 1848 to West Point from Thomas Ritchie, a congressman who knew his father. The would-be general didn't exactly make a name for excellence while studying in the highlands above the Hudson River, once earning himself a year-long suspension for attacking a cadet sergeant with a bayonet. He graduated thirty-fourth out of fifty-two in 1853 and was first assigned to the 1st Infantry at Fort Duncan, Texas as a second lieutenant.

He was sent to the 4th Infantry in the Pacific Northwest in 1855, and in April 1856 was assigned to Grand Ronde Indian Reservation in Yamhill County, Oregon and promoted to first lieutenant.

His true warrior self didn't emerge until he actually fought in the field, and he nimbly climbed the ranks thereafter. After Sheridan served eight years on the frontier, including time during which he was the chief quartermaster and commissary of the Army of Southwest Missouri, his star soon shot upward on a rapid rise with the outbreak of the War Between the States. On March 25, 1862, he was promoted to colonel of the 2nd Michigan Cavalry and then, on September 13 of the same year, he rose to brigadier general, assuming command of an infantry division at Perryville, Kentucky and then another at Stone's River, Tennessee.

Skillful and aggressive, Sheridan was promoted to major general on March 16, 1863. He stumbled a few months later in September of that year, losing more than a third of his division at Chickamauga, Georgia but rebounded by the following March when he and his men, without orders but with implicit approval, charged up Missionary Ridge on the outskirts of Chattanooga, Tennessee. The charge solidified Sheridan's reputation for daring and competence, and by March 1864 Grant had moved Sheridan east to command the cavalry. When he became Chief of Cavalry,

Army of the Potomac, Sheridan chose his brother Michael, Lt. T. W. C. Moore, and an old friend, Captain James W. Forsyth, as his aides-de-camp.

Sheridan's sway over his soldiers stemmed, in large part, from the fact that his men knew that he would never issue an order that he wouldn't follow himself. He pushed his men beyond their limits, believing that the Army lived to fight and to bring war to the opponent rather than to wait for war to arrive on its own lines. Households across the country spoke of Little Phil as his legend grew, and he was fast becoming a popular icon. People hung his picture in their homes, his victories rubbed off on those around him, Grant became more popular, and even Lincoln's reelection became more likely because of the lift the small general had provided. A good many officers concurred that Grant's best move had been to put Sheridan in command of Washington, Baltimore, and the Maryland and Pennsylvania borders.

"What was perhaps most important of all . . . the conversion of the whole army to the belief that Gen. Philip H. Sheridan is not only a brilliant cavalry rider, an impetuous fighter, and the impersonation of warlike energy, but that he is also a careful, deliberate, painstaking soldier, thoroughly versed in tactics and strategy, whose fiery zeal is controlled by most unusual discretion, and whose masterly skill curbs a spirit of the hottest mettle. In short that he is, as Gen. Grant has frequently declared, competent to command all the armies of the United States against any enemy," wrote Aldace F. Walker in his book *The Vermont Brigade in the Shenandoah Valley*.

Sheridan's qualities and the force of his reputation were essential for the painstaking work Grant had laid out for him in the Shenandoah. Grant's grand strategy called for the purging of the Confederates from the territory, and the only means to that end were harsh tactics that would require a leader with a stomach strong enough for the tasks at hand.

"In pushing up the Shenandoah Valley, as it is expected you will have to go, first or last, it is desirable that nothing should be left to invite the enemy to return. Take all provisions, forage, and stock wanted for the use of your command; such as cannot be consumed, destroy. It is not desirable that the buildings should be destroyed; they should rather be protected. . . . Bear in mind the object is to drive the enemy south, and to do this you want to keep him always in sight. Be guided in your course by the course he takes."

Autumn colors dotted the Virginia tree line while Sheridan carried out his orders with increasing severity. Between October 6 and October 8, the Union burned and appropriated all food reserves and livestock along the warpath, robbing Gen. Early's Rebels of any available vital sustenance. The Army of the Shenandoah distinguished between neither troops nor those civilians claiming a newfound loyalty to the Union; all food and feed were destroyed with equal determination.

Civilians suffered extensively through the turmoil and later remembered Sheridan's campaign as "The Burning," where parties of soldiers arrived at farms with instructions to set them ablaze, moving on upon the sound of a whistle blast to torch the next. These work details may have moved methodically, but not always without compassion: Farms of widows were to be left alone, and most officers and enlisted troops abided by these orders, even in some cases going a step further by helping families salvage their goods before igniting their storehouses.

Federal troops showed Joseph and Abigail Coffman, owners of eleven slaves, some mercy after Abigail Lincoln Coffman explained that she was the president's first cousin, once removed. Although the troops slaughtered the Coffmans' swine and burned their barn to a crisp, they let the house alone.

However, aside from these periodic acts of grace, the civilians of the Shenandoah were caught up in some of the most devastating circumstances of the war. Terror dominated their days and seized their nights. It wasn't unheard of for a farmer to head out to his fields just after dawn, only to find Federal troops on his property by midmorning preparing to send his home and barn up in blazes.

For example, as Sheridan's troops fanned out through South River, near Waynesboro, Virginia, farmers watched as onyx-colored smoke curled toward the sky. They knew that their farm might be next to fall, so they packed all their essentials, gathered their families, and tried to get as far ahead of the rampaging troops as possible.

"The army again began a march down the valley amid a cloud of smoke, arising from burning barns, mills, storehouses, stacks of hay and grain—in fact everything felt the torch that could in any way give aid and succor to the enemy as the valley had done heretofore," wrote Lt. Moses McFarland, a volunteer in the Eighth Vermont Regiment who later, as Captain of Company A, wrote a history of the Eighth in Cedar Creek. Smoke billowed into the sky, ash rained down, and the evenings glowed.

That people up North had thus far escaped the indignities of war was not lost on the people of the Shenandoah. Letters from Confederate troops to their loved ones showed the fierceness with which they hated their foe. One soldier wrote to his brother expressing his innermost desire to "drive a Bayonet to the heart's Blood of some of the Hell bound invaders of the North. They resort to every mean trick that can be conceived of to Whip us." These sentiments would naturally prompt some Confederate soldiers to seek their vengeance on the hated Yankees.

In early October, Sheridan filed a report to Grant outlining how the valley, from the Blue Ridge to the North Mountain, had been rendered untenable for the Rebel army. According to the report, Sheridan's men had burned more than two thousand barns stocked with grain and implements, and more than seventy mills filled with wheat and flour. The army took more than four thousand head of livestock, butchered about three thousand sheep for food, and commandeered many of the region's horses.

The division of Gen. Wesley Merritt, a graduate of West Point's class of 1860 who had rapidly ascended to his rank, reported that it alone had torched 630 barns, forty-seven flour mills, four sawmills, one woolen mill, three iron furnaces, two tanneries, one railroad depot, one locomotive, and three boxcars. The troops had also put matches to about four thousand tons of hay, straw, and fodder and perhaps half a million bushels of wheat and oats, 515 acres of corn, and 560 barrels of flour, and had driven off 3,300 head of livestock.

"I therefore, on the morning of the sixth of October, commenced moving back, stretching the cavalry across the Valley from the Blue Ridge to the eastern slope of the Alleghenies, with directions to burn all forage and drive off all stock, &c, as they moved to the rear, fully coinciding in the views and instructions of the lieutenant-general [Grant], that the Valley should be made a barren waste. The most positive orders were given, however, not to burn dwellings," wrote Sheridan.

However, in the gray area between the war on the Confederates in the valley and the collateral war on the civilians of Virginia, the Union often found itself on guard against an enemy who was, at times, unknown. One of the darker days for Sheridan's troops came on October 3 as Lt. John R. Meigs, Sheridan's engineer officer, and two assistants were scouting the woods in an attempt to verify enemy brigade positions. During their reconnaissance, they came upon three Confederates from Gen. William Carter Wickham's brigade (Wickham would resign two days later to take a seat in the Confederate Congress), who were on a similar scouting mission; there was an inevitable confrontation.

Though exactly what transpired will never be known, according to the diary of one of the Confederate scouts, Benjamin Franklin Shaver of the First Virginia Cavalry, when the Southern scouts realized that the Federal troops were going to discover them, they chose to fight rather than to flee. One of Shaver's fellow soldiers, George Martin, demanded that Lt. Meigs surrender, and amidst the shouts and threats, a trigger was pulled and a bullet discharged. Some accounts point to Meigs, oldest son of Union Quartermaster General Montgomery C. Meigs, as the first to fire, while other accounts contend that Martin shot first. But in the end, it was Meigs who lay dead in the road with a gaping hole in his face.

One of Meigs's assistants escaped and hastened to Sheridan with the news. Having known Meigs's father well, Sheridan had a soft spot for the lieutenant and bore the news with anguish. The pugnacious general refused to classify it as a circumstance of war; he saw it as murder and demanded retribution.

Sheridan ordered that all homes in Dayton, Virginia and within a five-mile radius be burned. General Custer executed the terrible orders and oversaw the mission as the troops set fire to seventeen homes, five barns, and numerous outbuildings. Everything was to be destroyed. Some residents had time to salvage furnishings and photographs from their generations-old homes, but most stood paralyzed outside, watching as the flames licked their homes like hungry dogs, looking on as their village, which would soon become known as the "Burnt District," was reduced to ash.

Perhaps no one in the town had been directly involved in the Meigs killing, but that was a detail of small consequence for Custer and his men, who knew that the irregulars often hid among the general population. Perhaps drawing from the frustration of the uncertainty that accompanied the combat in the valley, the belief among the soldiers was widespread that Confederate guerrillas had murdered Meigs. To Custer and his comrades, these men were no different from those who had been harassing Federal troops night after night, attacking Union wagon trains, and capturing and killing their occupants.

The Union troops were convinced that this was the work of the so-called bushwhacker-guerrilla. Who among the Vermont troops had ignited the flames in these retribution fires may never be known, but clearly they were as affected as anyone. Even the chaplain of the Tenth Vermont Infantry, normally a spiritual man, revealed the depths of his anger as he himself was caught in the storm of war: "This, every living soldier who was in this campaign knows to be true. The people were meek-faced citizens by day, and in the presence of any considerable body of Union troops; but as soon as the troops were out of sight, when darkness came on, they became desperate and bloodthirsty guerrillas; and in this character they stole upon our men like savages, and shot them down or dragged them away to the woods where some of them were found hung up by their heels with their throats cut," said Chaplain Edwin M. Haynes of the Tenth Vermont Infantry.

While laboring under the threat of bullets fired from hidden guns and enduring the tiring toll of total war on the Valley, the Union was reaping success from its efforts, winning such fights as mid-September's battle at Opequon against increasingly beleaguered Confederate lines. The month of campaigning between Fisher's Hill on September 22 and camping at Cedar Creek had also further seasoned the troops, especially those from Vermont, many of whom had been green at Gettysburg, no small matter as there was yet a final push to be made.

The South had dug its nails into the Virginia earth.

"Although we had at last successfully quieted the demonstrations of the enemy, which had excited so great apprehensions
at time during the last three months, it had also become apparent
that the Rebels would not leave the Valley nor abandon their
still threatening attitude toward Maryland and Pennsylvania
until they were driven away," wrote George N. Carpenter.

While Grant likely felt satisfied up to this point (after all, he
had ordered turning "the Shenandoah Valley into a barren waste
. . . so that crows flying over it for the balance of this season will
have to carry their provender with them"), Sheridan understood
that complete victory was the expectation. However, with the
Confederates on their heels and his soldiers weary from continuous fighting, Sheridan took the mid-October break in fighting
as an opportunity to camp at Cedar Creek and on October 15 left
his men briefly for Washington to attend a strategy conference
at the behest of Secretary of War Stanton.

Edwin M. Stanton wore spectacles and had a bushy beard
worthy of a squirrel's tail. Born in Steubenville, Ohio in 1814,
Stanton worked as a lawyer in Pittsburgh for almost a decade
before going to Washington, where he grew a large practice in
the Federal courts. President James Buchanan appointed Stanton
attorney general in December of 1860. After Lincoln's election,
Stanton was appointed secretary of war in 1862.

As he prepared to meet with the secretary in Washington,
Sheridan was well aware that Lee had sent two more divisions as
reinforcement for Gen. Early's men, who were camped a few
miles away, but he dismissed the idea of a frontal offensive,
"believing that the enemy at Fisher's Hill could not accomplish
much." In his absence, Sheridan left Maj. Gen. Horatio G.
Wright in charge.

While in Washington, Sheridan received from couriers messages of rumblings and maneuvers along the front and was
mindful to react to those that warranted response. Wright kept

him informed as to the position of his men and general conditions with respect to the enemy.

"General—I enclose a dispatch which explains itself. If the enemy should be strongly re-enforced in cavalry, he might, by turning our right, give us a great deal of trouble. I shall hold on here until the enemy's movements are developed, and shall only fear an attack on my right, which I shall make every preparation for guarding against and resisting," wrote Wright in a letter to Sheridan.

The time away from the men in the valley was disquieting to Sheridan, a condition exacerbated by a steady stream of intelligence with unknown origins. During his stay in the capital, he received an intercepted Confederate dispatch, purportedly from Confederate Gen. James Longstreet: "Lieutenant-General Early: Be ready to move as soon as my forces join you and we will crush Sheridan. Longstreet." Sheridan's instincts rightly told him that the Longstreet dispatch was a ruse; but, not willing to take any chances, he made sure to verify Longstreet's position at Petersburg. Sheridan planned to return to Cedar Creek by October 18, a matter of days, and could find little reason for anything more than orders for continued vigilance and judicious reinforcement: "The cavalry is all ordered back to you; make your position strong. If Longstreet's dispatch is true, he is under the impression that we have largely detached. . . . If the enemy should make an advance I know you will defeat him. Look well to your ground and be well prepared. Get up everything that can be spared."

However, as October 18 dawned and then drew to a close, Sheridan, having decided to stop his return twenty miles short of Cedar Creek in Winchester, had not yet returned to his men. With little action stirring, the commanders on the line found nothing to worry about in the absence of their leader and continued their routines as they had in the previous days. That evening, a courier presented Gen. Wright with word that all was quiet.

"So we all went to bed," Gen. George A. Forsyth, who served on Gen. Sheridan's staff as a major and then colonel, wrote later, "without any thought of what awaited us."

On the night of October 18, not everyone in the Union camp at Cedar Creek went to bed so secure in his position. Having just come off duty as corps officer, Col. Stephen Thomas moved about the area unable to sleep. Thomas had received his commission as colonel and commander of the 8th Vermont Volunteer Infantry in 1862 and had seen a fair amount of action, including the repulsion of Gen. Jubal Early's July 1864 attack on Washington, D.C., before landing at his post as a brigade commander in the XIX Corps in the Shenandoah.

While on watch, he had seen through his binoculars a cluster of men pointing to the lines while engaged in discussion, their disposition suggesting to him that Early's forces had designs on the Union lines. He reported his observations to Gen. William H. Emory, and Emory consequently asked Thomas to relay the information to Gen. Wright. Although Wright didn't think the information gave much cause for concern, he did send out Gen. George Crook, who also served in the Apache Wars, with a reconnoitering force all the same.

Ever vigilant, Thomas decided to double-check the picket lines under his command and from that point on refused to dismount from his steed for the rest of the night. Just after midnight, Thomas rode beyond the picket line directly into a ravine where the voices of Confederate soldiers suddenly challenged him.

"Surrender, you damned Yankee!"

"No, sir, it's too early in the morning! Besides, your request was not respectful," Thomas replied before turning and galloping up the bank under a flurry of bullets.

While Thomas rode hurriedly away from the gunfire, the rest of the Union men, with a false sense of security in Sheridan's absence, slept more soundly than they had in a long time. Thomas's encounter and misgivings aside, Wright, and the other officers left under his command, simply believed that Early was too far away to do anything, even if his scouts were but hundreds of yards away. But Wright and the other officers simply did not know Gen. Early.

★ ★ ★

General Jubal Early was an attorney, a veteran of the Mexican War, and a graduate of West Point, class of 1837. A classic career infantry soldier who lacked an understanding of cavalry, the solemn but foul-mouthed general hated listening to the suggestions of ranking subordinates and, similarly to Sheridan, relished aggressive and offensive warfare. An effective leader who shared with his men a popular taste for apple brandy and whiskey, Early became known among the soldiers as "Old Jube" and "Old Jubilee."

But opinions about Old Jube could vary, particularly when coming from the Union, as some felt that his pride often clouded his better judgment. "Jubal A. Early, was a soldier unused to defeat, a bitter enemy and a desperate foe, and as later events went to show, an officer willing to risk his all on the mere possibility of regaining, by a sudden and unexpected blow, the lost prestige of himself and army," wrote Major (later to become General) George A. Forsyth.

Whatever his lesser traits, in the latter stages of the war Early had been facing challenges known to every Confederate leader of the time as the South's war apparatus began to crumble. By the summer of 1864, Early's army had a shortage of decent weapons, horses, and equipment, and their material losses in September had been immense. From Winchester to New Market, Confederate hospitals were pregnant with the wounded and the dead, and abandoned wagons, ambulances, and carcasses littered the roadside. Each day, between two and three dozen Southern soldiers deserted and surrendered.

By all accounts, after having earlier lost at Winchester and Fisher's Hill, Early and his men should have remained fatigued. Yet Early, perhaps egged on by Lee, was resolved to stop Sheridan from cleaning out the valley.

While Sheridan's men had been settling into Cedar Creek on October 13, Early was marching his starving, poorly equipped army of seventeen thousand men to Fisher's Hill to reorganize and to lay out his next moves. Early's supplies were nearly depleted, so he "threw himself with his accustomed energy into the development of those plans of attack which were to materialize so brilliantly in the early morning not many days thereafter." While Sheridan was riding off to Washington, his Confederate counterpart was busy plotting.

Early and his officers began carefully scrutinizing and mapping the positions of Federal camps from the summit of Three Top Mountain for several days, and what they saw from that elevated view were camps that would be completely exposed in the event of a surprise charge up the ridge. Three Top Mountain offered the highest vantage point in the area, and tenacious Confederates had held on to the valuable ground throughout the Shenandoah Valley campaign. The advantage was one upon which Early could not help but capitalize. The spying on Union positions required only the same effort as that needed to read a giant map. From on high, Early saw that the Eighth Vermont waited at the left of the pike in two divisions; the Nineteenth

Corps stood just to the right of the Eighth; the Sixth held the right flank; and the cavalry and artillery stood nearby.

Early knew that Cedar Creek constituted one of the last chances to preserve the Confederates' weakening prospects for victory, and he was personally intent on regaining his reputation, which had suffered so severely in the Union push through the valley. For Early, with his army pressed to the breaking point and with the Union preparing for a continuance of their campaign, it was a question of immediate attack or ultimate retreat.

As night fell on October 18, Early committed to a bold assault that he hoped would break a Union line still caught in the dreams of a good night's sleep.

Circumstances for the morning combat favored the black-eyed, bearded Early. Utter darkness had hidden the movements of his men during the night. The morning of October 19 broke chilly and raw, owing to a dense fog that lingered until at least nine o'clock.

Early had deployed his men in three columns and had marched them in perfect silence. By dawn, all were in place.

The sound of musketry cracked through the early hours to the right of the Eighth Vermont. Appearing through the heavy mist like ghost soldiers, Early's army attacked the Blue as four Confederate brigades initiated the charge. There were about three thousand veterans from South Carolina, Georgia, and Mississippi in the ranks. The Rebel yell filled the air, sounding like a wildcat from hell, sending shivers up Northern spines as Early's men poured over the entrenchments. Volleys exploded in the morning air as panicked Union soldiers tried to fend off the attack.

"Everything is confusion and dismay. Added to the consternation of being driven from bed and sleep to meet an unknown foe, comes the astounding intelligence that Crook is surprised and his men, the Eighth corps, in panic stricken fight," wrote Moses McFarland. "Soon the flying fugitives come in sight, half dressed, shoeless and hatless—all in the wildest confusion."

In a matter of minutes, the Confederates smashed two thirds of the Union infantry and drove the rest of the soldiers back at least three miles. The whole Army of the Shenandoah retreated: thirteen hundred prisoners and eighteen guns gone.

"The enemy captured the pickets who did not fire a shot, rushed upon the main line, which was first made aware of the attack by a full volley poured into their camp, and it was rapidly crowded towards the west. The men sprang from their tents and fled without boots or clothing save what they had worn through the night; the very tents were pulled off from some as they lay in their blankets; many with soldierly instinct placed themselves without orders behind the breastworks, only to find themselves flanked and taken in reverse file by file, each successively by the whole Rebel column; and in simply time enough for the enemy in his impetuous charge to pass over the ground covered by the 'Army of Western Virginia' that whole command was a disorganized, routed, demoralized, terrified mob of fugitives, their camp equipage left behind, officers and men all rushing to the rear in reckless dishabille," wrote Walker.

Before the Union lines crumbled, hand-to-hand combat reigned. Point-blank shootings, bayonet charges, and fists felled troops wearing both uniforms.

"My comrades! Who shall attempt to describe that wild tumult of war, that hand-to-hand conflict in the gloom of that fateful October morn, when bayonets actually dripped blood, when skulls were broken by clubbed muskets, and faces burned by the powder's flash? The hand is palsied, and the lips are dumb," wrote Col. Herbert E. Hill.

"I do not expect to give you any news, although on the 19th we fought on this ground one of the bloodiest battles of the war," wrote James Barrett, "J. B.," the six-foot-tall, twenty-two-year-old Company G bugler of the First Vermont Cavalry. "At three o'clock on the morning of the 19th, we were awakened by the bugles sounding 'Boots & Saddles,' and the sharp report of carbines. Soon we heard heavy firing along our infantry lines, and then we knew Early had pitched in for a big fight. The 8th Corps was completely surprised and soon came running back upon the 19th Corps in confusion. The Rebels had marched all night and were ready when the signal was given to charge in upon our infantry almost in a body."

Crook's Corps streamed through the lines of the Eighth Vermont like runaways. Four Rebel divisions closed in from behind, many wearing blue overcoats they had lifted from Union camps.

McFarland reported how a Lt. Cooper lost his life. "He was lying a little at my left, where he could see some distance ahead down a wood road. Seeing men approaching, dressed in blue, he rose and said to me, 'Captain, we are firing on our own men.' I replied, 'I think not.' Just at that moment he fell, exclaiming, 'I am shot by our men!' Surgeon Ross, who helped bury Lt. Cooper said that he was hit by six bullets inside a five inch circle."

"That these men were brave no one doubts; their previous brilliant conduct had amply shown it; but a night surprise, total and terrific, is too trying for the morale of the best troops in the world to survive," wrote Walker.

Sheridan would later describe the events as best he could. "During my absence the enemy had gathered all his strength, and, in the night of the 18th and early on the 19th, moved silently at Fisher's Hill, through Shenandoah, on the road from Strasburg to Front Royal, and again re-crossed the river at Bowman's Ford, striking Crook, who held the left of our line, in flank and rear, so unexpectedly and forcibly as to drive in his outposts, invade his camp, and turn his position. This surprise was owing, probably, to not closing in Powell, or that the cavalry divisions of Merritt and Custer were placed on the right of our line, where it had always occurred to me there was but little danger of attack."

Early had pulled it off. He had moved four gray divisions in near-silence and launched a brilliant predawn attack on the two left-flank Union divisions.

★　★　★

In spite of the carnage, morale and bravery held up through those violent hours, and the Green Mountain Boys in particular displayed their mettle. During the darkest moments of the fight, the Vermont soldiers provided what was perhaps the only inspiration to which the routed Union troops could turn.

The Vermonters considered the flag in its entire silken splendor as worthy of protection as if it had been a living, breathing soul. There can be no other explanation for their willingness to die like dominoes in a line for the interest of its preservation.

"For the Eighth Vermont, carrying a flag meant death or maiming," wrote McFarland. "But not even in that vortex of hell was it necessary to remind men to look after the flag."

The Eighth, together with the Twelfth Connecticut and the 116th New York, had occupied one of the more exposed positions that day. Most had stood their ground when the first bullets zipped through the chill.

As the fighting erupted, Cpl. John Petre held the colors before a musket ball smashed through his thigh. Petre, fallen, called out "Boys, leave me. Take care of yourselves and the flag!" Petre would die later that night, but his comrades honored his words.

As Petre lay bleeding, Cpl. Lyman F. Perham picked up the flag. A Confederate soldier close enough to grab it demanded that he surrender the colors, but Sgt. Ethan P. Shores from the unit quickly "placed his musket at the Rebel's breast, fired and killed him," McFarland wrote. Yet in the instant following Shores's shot, another butternut-clad soldier fired at Perham and killed him.

Corporal George F. Blanchard then took the standard, only to die a few seconds later, as half the regiment now lay killed or wounded. Just a foot away from Blanchard stood Lt. A. K. Cooper, who called for the flag, but he too was killed upon grabbing Old Glory. Sgt. Seth C. Hill of Company A saw Blanchard fall and shot the responsible Confederate soldier before moving to help his wounded comrade. As he knelt down, a bayonet slid between his body and arm, and, springing up, Hill clubbed the Rebel whose arm had guided the steel, refusing to surrender and carrying on despite the wound.

Corporal Leonard C. Bemis then grabbed the flag but fell after being struck down by a wall of fire from three Confederates who were once more demanding its surrender. Sergeant Shores bayoneted one of the three Rebels, and Sgt. Lemuel Simpson shot another, both men drawing nearer to the flag. The relay continued with a Sgt. Moran now holding the flag as the third Rebel retreated upon losing his numbers.

Despite the heroic efforts of the Vermonters on behalf of the flag, however, the ground had given way to Early.

The Southern soldiers had driven Sheridan's men back several miles. "It was indeed a dark look for the Army of the Shenandoah. We had been driven far from our camp the day before. Our artillery, such as had not been captured, had gone to the rear, while before us was an exultant, victorious foe," McFarland wrote.

Confusion and dismay greeted the troops. "Wagons and ambulances lumbering hither and thither in disorder; pack horses led by frightened bummers, or wandering at their own free will; crowds of officers and men, some shod and some barefoot, many of them coatless and hatless, few without their rifles, but all rushing wildly to the rear . . . and added to the confusion and consternation the frequent sight of blood, ambulances, wagons, men, stained and dripping, with here and there a corpse; while the whistling bullets and the shrieking shell told that the enemy knew their advantage and their ground. It was a sight that might well have demoralized the Old Guard of the first Napoleon," wrote Walker.

Early thrilled in his morning victory. His jubilant soldiers broke ranks and descended upon the Union camps, harvesting food and supplies from the pockets and haversacks of dead and wounded soldiers. Disciplined at this point they were not, but Early paid no mind. It was now only ten o'clock in the morning.

News of the attack quickly spread to Winchester, where Sheridan had spent the night. The picket duty, Col. Oliver Edward's VI Corps, heard the distant storm of fighting and reported to Sheridan early in the morning of the 19th. At first the general didn't pay it much heed; rather he went about his morning ablutions, supposing that the artillery he heard in Winchester was coming from a reconnaissance that had been sent out in the morning.

Around nine o'clock, after breakfast, Sheridan mounted his black horse Rienzi, which he would later rename Winchester, and rode through the town. During the ride, Sheridan took Lt. Col. James W. Forsyth, his chief of staff, along with two other aides and two engineer officers. As they reached the end of Winchester town, they heard the louder rumble of the guns. Near Mill Creek, they witnessed the first signs of what was occurring at Cedar Creek—a jumble of wagons—and quickly learned from West Virginian troops that the Union position had been overrun.

"The sound of the artillery made a battle unmistakable, and on reaching Mill Creek, half a mile south of Winchester, the head of the fugitives appeared in sight, trains and men coming to the rear with appalling rapidity," Sheridan reported. Sheridan picked up the pace, tightened the reins of his bridle, and "with a slight touch of the spur he dashed up the turnpike and was off."

The army supply—trains, ammunition, wagons, and artillery—had gouged deep ruts in the once-decent road. "Everywhere the dust lay thick and heavy on its surface, and powdered the trees and bushes that fringed our sides, so that our galloping column sent a gray cloud swirling behind us," wrote Maj. Forsyth. The small group found the wounded and dead strewn everywhere, hastily placed in front of houses-turned-hospitals, and passed rows of their comrades, now corpses, laid out near the field hospital. "Then we came suddenly upon indubitable evidence of battle and Federal retreat while galloping over the open field," recalled Forsyth.

Sheridan, overwhelmed at the sight of his retreating men, ordered a halt. He commanded the brigade at Winchester to form a wall across the road to prevent stragglers from leaving. Sheridan thundered past the retreating troops shouting, "Face the other way, boys! We are going back!"

"Taking twenty men from my escort, I pushed on to the front, leaving the balance under Gen. Forsyth [who was then a Major] and Colonels Thom and Alexander to do what they could in stemming the torrent of fugitives," Sheridan wrote in his official report. "I am happy to say that hundreds of the men, when of reflection found they had not done themselves justice, came back with cheers . . . still none behaved more gallantly or exhibited greater courage than those who returned from the rear determined to reoccupy their lost camp."

Sheridan waved his hat as if it were the battle colors and pointed to the front, pressing on, passing scores of men in the midst of their retreat. One glance at his face and his stately horse changed many a mind, and the "fainting heart takes new hope, for under Sheridan the army knows no defeat. Up and down the lines he rides, inspiring confidence by his encouraging words," wrote Forsyth.

The poem "Sheridan's Ride" by Pennsylvania poet and artist Thomas Buchanan Read immortalized those twenty miles. Sheridan's ride became analogous to Paul Revere's ride: "Up from the South at break of day / Bringing to Winchester fresh dismay / The affrighted air with a shudder bore / Like a herald in haste, to the chieftain's door / The terrible grumble and rumble and road / Telling the battle was on once more / And Sheridan twenty miles away. . . ."

As Sheridan rode on, Union troops were expecting a second Rebel charge, but the cheers they heard from down the road were those of the stragglers, the wounded, and the gunless artillerymen for Sheridan. In the words of G. G. Benedict, "Sturdy, fiery Sheridan on his sturdy fiery steed, flaked with foam from his two hours mad galloping." The astounded troops watched as their general wheeled from the pike and hurried down the line, inspiring the divisions to break forth into deafening applause.

"No more doubt or chance for doubt existed; we were safe, perfectly and unconditionally safe, and every man knew it," wrote Walker.

"When the men saw the General coming they flung their caps into the air and with a cheer all started for the front," wrote Barrett. "Now came the time that tried the courage of a soldier—to turn defeat upon an excited, victorious army. Slowly did our line of battle advance, and then faster until the deafening roar rolled onward towards Cedar Creek."

When Sheridan finally reached the battlefield around 10:30, chaos still reigned and reorganization was the priority. Wright's Corps was solid and Emory's Corps could be fixed and bolstered by returning troops. Slowly the Union officers regained control over their men so that by the middle of the day, a sense of order had descended upon the scene.

All the while, Sheridan infused his men with courage. As he passed the badly beaten troops, he said: "Boys, if you don't want to fight yourselves, come back and look at the others fighting. We will whip them out of their boots before four o'clock."

Now newly redeployed and reorganized, the Federal troops still waited for a second attack. Some skirmishing erupted, but little more than that, and Forsyth recommended to Sheridan that he ride the line so his men could see him, telling him to take off his hat so that he'd be instantly recognizable.

As he rode past each unit, holding his hat in his hand, the men roared and cheered. The soldiers on the line began to think that they, the Army of the Shenandoah, would win the day and that he, Sheridan, had already shown them victory and would now do it again.

As Julius Caesar had done in 52 B.C.E. in Alesia, so was Sheridan doing now. As described by Grant, "Caesar put on speed to get there in time for the fight. The enemy knew he was coming by the scarlet cloak that he always wore in action. . . . The Romans dropped their spears and fought with their swords. Suddenly the Gauls saw the cavalry in their rear and fresh cohorts coming up in front. They broke and fled, but found their retreat cut off by the cavalry."

A Vermont soldier wrote that victory "was simply Sheridan's personal magnetism, and all-conquering energy. He felt no doubt, he would submit to no defeat, and he took his army with him as on a whirlwind." Invigorated by the command, the corps wheeled about and took the fight directly to Early and his men.

At around four o'clock, Sheridan ordered the advance and exposed the vital difference between Little Phil and Old Jube—Sheridan finished what he started. "This attack was brilliantly made, and as the enemy was protected by raid breast-works, and at some portions of his line by stone fences, his resistance was very determined."

Emory's troops cracked the line, and George Custer hurled his entire cavalry division through the gap, splitting the Rebels. Order broke down and Southern soldiers ran to save themselves while Sheridan pursued. The escape was cut short when the Union cavalry destroyed a bridge in the Confederate rear, trapping wagons and artillery.

The afternoon attack drove the Confederates from the field faster than they'd swept the Federals away earlier in the morning. It happened so quickly that the Eighth hadn't yet had time to remove all its dead from the battlefield. The Union took approximately a thousand Gray prisoners, and they recaptured the eighteen guns they'd lost and twenty-three more.

Save for one last-ditch effort to push the Yankees back, Early failed to act. Perhaps he had worried about his right flank, or perhaps he had been too content in the morning, satisfied with what he mistook for victory. Whatever the reason, caution prompted Early and he lost his attack footing by the afternoon.

The Union triumphed before nightfall.

Sheridan's promotion to lieutenant general gave him a place in history alongside Grant and Sherman. "Sheridan showed consummate generalship here, for he plucked glory from calamity: his crown was Cedar Creek," said Hill at a Cedar Creek reunion.

Cedar Creek ended the campaign in the Shenandoah Valley for all intents and purposes. When it had opened, the Gray was confident, even unwilling to acknowledge that the soldiers of the Union were their equals in courage; but, when closed, the Blue had successfully erased this misguided impression. The victory also served to solidify resentment for the North by the South. Stories of what Southerners had interpreted as atrocities continued to spread throughout the region and would later be used to try to explain the actions of a few Southern gentlemen.

And while praise was heaped on Sheridan, Early was left to harsher assessments for his failure to see through what he'd started early in the morning with his daring raid. "The blame rests upon himself, for it was truly a sad state of discipline which could not keep together, in the flush of victory, a sufficient number of men to follow up a disorganized retreat; his gallant army was not alone in fault for this shameful state of affairs which he reprobates so bitterly," says Walker.

The victory was an important one for the Union, though undoubtedly it came at a high cost. "The very best troops of the Confederacy had not only been defeated, but had been routed in successive engagements, until their spirit and esprit were destroyed. In obtaining these results, however, our loss in officers and men was severe," Sheridan said. Of the 175 Vermonters who fought, 106 were killed, wounded, or captured. One of the regiments, the Vermont Eighth Regiment, suffered 68 percent casualties.

The Eighth Vermont won recognition for its performance that day. As Sheridan stated, "The Eighth Vermont fought with conspicuous gallantry at the battle of Cedar Creek." Colonel Newhall of Sheridan's staff wrote that the Eighth Vermont performed exceptionally all the time, but in particular on the morning of October 19, "when, in the confusion and din, one firm regiment was worth its weight in gold. Your men, standing by the colors, and making that desperate fight with the battle clashing around them, showed as much morale as Sheridan did when he came up later, and in the same spirit led on to victory."

If the Vermont Eighth's casualties showed anything, it was that the soldiers from the Green Mountains threw themselves into the thick of the fighting at Cedar Creek with disregard for their own well-being. Thirty-six-year-old Maj. Lewis Addison Grant, who before the war had worked as an attorney, was severely outnumbered and shelled as he led his unit to hold off two Confederate divisions on the Union flank before eventually calling for the withdrawal of his battered force.

Burlington-born Charles Henry Blinn of the First Vermont Cavalry Volunteers, who had enlisted on August 21, 1861 and had seen action during the battles of Gettysburg, Spotsylvania, Cold Harbor, Winchester, and the Wilderness, led his regiment during Sheridan's counterattack and captured forty-two cannon at Cedar Creek, the most taken by any regiment during the war.

Even those who may be said to have been the lesser of the Vermont troops displayed the characteristic determination of the others. One such soldier, Maj. Templeton, a gallant officer in the Eleventh Vermont, "had during the previous campaign excited considerable amusement in the Brigade by constantly carrying in his hands on the march a camp-chair, from the comfortable elevation whereof he was wont at the halts to smile serenely, in his rather boisterous way, at the ungainly rest obtained by other officers who were forced to sprawl themselves out upon the ground for rest. The exigencies of his retreat from the ditch, mentioned above, proved too great for the Captain's equanimity and he reluctantly abandoned his cherished chair to the tender mercies of the foe. When we formed, his loss was at once seen and he was ridiculed unmercifully, but he successfully redeemed himself by recapturing his furniture in the subsequent advance," wrote Walker.

Of all Vermonters, Col. Thomas, who had been fired on by the Confederate scouts the night before Early's attack, was most highly praised, ultimately receiving the Congressional Medal of Honor years later on July 25, 1892 for bravery at Cedar Creek and "distinguished conduct in a desperate hand-to-hand encounter, in which the advance of the enemy was checked."

In all, Cedar Creek claimed 5,665 Union casualties: 644 killed, 3,430 wounded, and 1,591 missing. Of the 2,910 Confederate casualties, there were 320 killed, 1,540 wounded, and 1,050 missing.

Though they had lost so many of their brothers-in-arms, for the Union troops still standing, battered but victorious, there remained a reliable and fitting companion in the flag under which they stood. At the end of the day, the very flag for which many Vermonters had given their lives, full of bullet holes and bayonet tears, flew proudly over her fierce defenders.

Sheridan rejoiced in the victory with a quiet manner, telling his officers and troops that their victory was nothing more than their duty to a fractured nation, something their country expected of them.

Newspapers were less humble.

"Hurrah for Phil. Sheridan! And for his gallant army!" proclaimed the *New York Tribune*. "Thank God for the great victory which they won! We care not to repress the grateful exultation, which we can but feel over this splendid success. It went with a thrill to the heart of every loyal man who heard it yesterday morning, and with a chill to the heart of every traitor in Richmond and New York. Consciously or unconsciously it struck everyone as the turning point of the great Virginia campaign, and it flashes upon us as the First Victory in the valley of the Shenandoah, which hitherto has been to us a Valley of Humiliation, and almost of Despair. We remember no Victory in this War which has more suddenly and joyfully awakened the sympathies of the North; nor one which has been welcomed with a more enthusiastic delight."

News of the victory and of the Vermont soldiers' bravery in battle would scream northward and arrive before nightfall on the 19th of October 1864. But as momentous as the news was, it would not be the biggest story in Vermont that day. A much more shocking event had been brewing there, hundreds of miles removed from the battlefields of the war, for months.

3

A Southern Gentleman

★ ★ ★ ★ ★ ★ ★ ★ ★ ★ ★ ★ ★ ★ ★ ★ ★ ★ ★

Aside from worrying about loved ones on the front lines, and although unaware of the major victory soon to be scored at Cedar Creek, early October 1864 was golden for most of the people of Vermont. But for F. Stewart Stranahan of the bustling township of St. Albans, the same could not be said. Stranahan was home on sick leave, detained from his duties on the staff of Gen. Custer of the Army of the Shenandoah. As war raged in Virginia in the late summer and early fall, all Stranahan could do was wait for word of his compatriots' fates.

But on October 18, 1864, the day before the decisive battle of Cedar Creek, regardless of any anguish his absence from the front may have caused him, there must have been a part of Stewart Stranahan that was pleased to be resting in the picturesque town he called home.

★ ★ ★

Some time before the Revolutionary War, a man named Jesse Welden arrived on the shores of Lake Champlain in what was then the colony of New York, built a log cabin, and became the first settler of St. Albans. Soon following Welden, many souls eagerly tried their hand living on the fertile plot of land tucked into the northwestern folds of Vermont, and, by 1788, a formal settlement was organized. The region of Vermont, claimed by what were now the states of New York, New Hampshire, and Massachusetts, never achieving separate Territory status, was finally admitted into the Union in 1791, the fourteenth state.

Before railroads were introduced to the state in 1848, St. Albans, like many other towns in Vermont, existed in semi-isolation. In the days before the iron horse, visitors, merchants, and others who wanted to travel south had to go by horseback to Troy, Vermont, and then by boat down Lake Champlain. Goods had to be shipped from New York to Troy and then loaded onto sailboats on Lake Champlain. Anyone living in the northern corners of the state had to travel overland to Burlington, where the nearest port lay.

This relative isolation contributed to the smuggling operations that were a large part of St. Albans's early days; there was an active contraband route between the town and Canada. On either side of the line, people felt justified in smuggling, and the activity was earnestly pursued. Goods were scarce, and all foreign goods were very expensive.

In these early days, most people from St. Albans and other Vermonters from the area traveled by steamer on Lake Champlain, which was a significant link to Canada and to the West.

During their workday, if they had a moment, the men working in the St. Albans foundry could walk near Lake Champlain, which covers almost half of Vermont's western border. The lake played a major role in both the affairs of the state and the many military conflicts that made up Vermont's early history. When President Thomas Jefferson halted foreign trade in the early 1800s due to the troublesome Barbary Coast pirates, Vermonters decided they would continue to act as their spirit moved them, which meant embarking on a long period of smuggling goods to Canada via lake transport. During the War of 1812, a war which many in Vermont actually opposed, Lake Champlain became a site of some rather explosive action where, despite fortifications along the lake, British forces sank American ships and bombarded Burlington.

Things had gotten a bit easier in 1828, when a steam ferry to Plattsburgh was founded. But still, access to the markets of Boston and other large manufacturing centers in the east was not available to the majority of northern Vermonters. So although the rest of the country was enjoying a great deal of trade with that region, St. Albans was not. Naturally, when a railroad that could provide easy and uninterrupted communication with the rest of the nation was suggested, the state heartily welcomed the idea. And in 1843, the state legislature granted several railroad charters, the Rutland & Burlington and Vermont Central railroads included. The Vermont Central Railroad had been established in 1830, and by 1848, when the first passenger train in Vermont traveled from White River Junction to Bethel, it was a Vermont Central train.

The first roads in Vermont were post roads, followed by private toll roads (called turnpikes). The number of routes in Franklin County grew, with foryt-six in 1828 and sixty-six in 1833; in the 1850s, a plank road was constructed between St. Albans and the nearby town of Enosburg, covering a distance of twelve miles.

Dotted along these roads were covered bridges, which soon became social centers all their own, providing shelter from the hot sun in the summer and from the rains in the spring and autumn. For imaginative young boys and girls, they were forts, play houses, and castles. For eager slightly older boys and girls, they were "kissing" or "courting" bridges. For men going off to war, they served as locations for camp meetings and even as drill floors for local militia companies.

Further links with the rest of the country occurred in 1847, when a telegraph line opened between Burlington and Troy, New York. It was extended to Boston and White River Junction the next year.

Whatever their uses, the bridges, the roads, and the railroad had pushed St. Albans into a new era of prosperity. With the northward expansion of the Vermont Central Railroad through St. Albans in 1850, the burgeoning city had begun to grow at a faster clip. The railroad was a tributary of the 20,000-plus-mile railroad network that connected the East Coast to the Midwest breadbasket, and it allowed the north country to support the booming industries of the era.

By 1864, almost four thousand people called St. Albans home. Nearly three hundred houses dotted the area, which extended a half mile east to west and about two miles north to south. Like trimmings on a well-laid table, barns, silos, and fields decorated the rolling hills of St. Albans and the surrounding towns. Franklin County had become one of the largest maple-producing places in the country, and one of the largest dairy-farm areas in New England. On one side, the farmland sloped toward Lake Champlain; on the other, it reached up toward the Green Mountains, the highest point being about 215 feet above the rail depot.

Wide streets intersected the town, with Taylor Park, the town green, at the center. North of the park was North Main Street; and south of it, South Main Street. Homes stood on the streets running parallel and perpendicular to these two main thoroughfares. Altogether, St. Albans boasted sixty-one stores and many mechanic shops, including the machine shops of the railroad company and foundry.

Over the course of the preceding decades, the modern era had crept into town. The stern brick facades of the Victorian era supplanted the wood of the clapboard buildings, the log structures, the frame stores, and the hotels. Gas lamps lined the main streets, and people greeted their lighting each evening with a touch of wonder, while wooden side- and crosswalks added to the sense of sophistication. New construction flourished, and at the north end of the green, the soon-to-be completed Welden House would join Tremont House, American House, and St. Albans House as another inn for long- and short-term boarders.

St. Albans became a stop on the way for trains, tradesmen, and journeymen traveling between the United States and Canada, soon establishing itself as the northern headquarters for the railroad's administrative offices, which consisted of the switching yard and the home of its president, the Governor of Vermont, John Gregory Smith.

John Gregory Smith was born in St. Albans on July 22, 1818. His parents were John, a lawyer, and Maria (Curtis) Smith. After attending the University of Vermont and Yale Law School, Smith was admitted to the Vermont bar in 1842. His father was involved in the railroad expansion of Vermont, and J. Gregory Smith joined his father's law and railroad management firm, ascending to its presidency when his father died in 1858.

Anna Eliza Brainerd Smith, Governor J. Gregory Smith's wife, was the daughter of a leading anti-slavery leader, Lawrence Brainerd, a noted abolitionist who was so involved in the Underground Railroad that his house in St. Albans was reportedly one of the stops along the way to Canada. Anna Smith could trace her ancestors back to the original Plymouth Rock colony and even to Sir Francis Cook. She had eleven brothers and sisters, six of whom died at very young ages.

Anna had been born on October 7, 1819. She was a prolific letter-writer and corresponded often with friends and family, and even managed to sustain a career writing novels in addition to the work she devoted to her family.

An avid traveler, Anna Smith voyaged to Europe five times and to Egypt once. She was deeply committed to bettering women's lives and was involved in goodwill enterprises such as the Warner Home for Little Wanderers. She was also a member of the First Congregational Church and Society, a common affiliation that was a reflection of the religious revival sweeping the nation. In fact, her later novels, *Seola, Selma,* and *Atla,* were all religious in tone and, as a testament to the times, were rather well received. John Gregory Smith married Anna in 1842, and they had six children: George Gregory; Edward Curtis; Lawrence, who died in infancy; Annie; Julia; and Helen.

During the first years of the Civil War, Anna savored the letters she received from her brother Aldis O. Brainerd, who had served as quartermaster of the Fifth Vermont Infantry until he fell ill in 1862. He remained on the front lines, however, as a civilian extending whatever help he could.

"There are many things about the Army that is very unpleasant the Society is so degrading," Aldis wrote to his sister Anna. "I hope that I may soon forget that part . . . but one thing I will say in the praise of the Vermonters, they are as god [sic] Soldiers as there are in the Army and I think no braver men than the Vtrs can be found. When I shall leave I cannot tell as long as I can make it pleasant for myself without making it unpleasant for others."

Yes, the tiny state had sacrificed and would continue to sacrifice to preserve the Union; the family of Rufus Kinsley, who had migrated to St. Albans in the 1840s, saw five of its seven military-aged males off to war.

★ ★ ★

By the time of the Civil War, St. Albans had become the legal center and political beehive for all of Franklin County. The Smith house presided over the village, just as its resident did over the state, just a few blocks above the green on Congress

Street. The town also enjoyed a growing reputation as a center for fishing, hunting, and other outdoor pursuits, and of course it bred the famous Morgan horses.

The residents of St. Albans had rung in 1864, hoping it would remain as uneventful as a year of war possibly could. Loved ones were as eager as ever for letters from their sons, brothers, and husbands fighting down South. Sarah Husband White, who had married in her native Ireland in 1843, waited for letters from her beloved William White.

William White, born in Ireland in 1819, became a naturalized U.S. citizen in St. Albans in 1858. When he was forty-three, he enlisted in Company I of the Tenth Vermont Regiment as a sergeant. On December 5, 1862, he had been promoted to first sergeant, and by April 1864 he was commissioned a second lieutenant. At the age of 45, White was wounded—for the second time—during the battle of Cedar Creek, Virginia.

Visitors still streamed into town. Main Street continued to serve as the traditional trade and travel route between Burlington and Canada. And indeed, October 18 was the kind of day that renewed the community's sense of normalcy, for it was Market Day, and farmers, craftsmen, and vendors of all sorts were gathering on the green to set out their wares and produce.

Among the faces familiar to the townspeople, there were always some new ones appearing in St. Albans for the first time to offer, or to buy, goods. This Market Day would be no different; shuffling between the green and Tremont House and American House was a group of men no one knew too well. They had been there for about a week, some of them more, some of them less. A few of the men had caught the eyes of the women of the town, and the enticing strangers had made fine impressions on many with their gentlemanly airs.

Yet on that market day of October 18, no one in St. Albans had even the slightest inkling—not the resting Stewart

Stranahan, not the innkeepers, not the shop owners, the vendors, nor even the town gossips—that the charming men moving among them in their Union-blue town were Confederates.

Bennett H. Young, a hazel-eyed horseman from Kentucky, stared out over the green and prickled with anticipation, poised to bring the distant war home to the people of St. Albans, Vermont.

★   ★   ★

Bennett Hiram Young was full of swagger and charm, an intoxicating combination for anyone who chanced to meet him. "A Kentuckian born and bred, the pride of his ancestors marks his very stride, the light of the bluegrass meadows and the hemp fields shines from his eyes."

Born in 1843 to devout Presbyterians Robert and Josephine (née Henderson) Young, Bennett came from a proud tradition of service. The family had a military legacy going back to Bennett's great-grandfather, who had served in the Revolutionary War under Gen. Nathanael Greene in the battles of Eutau Springs, Monk's Corner, Guilford Court House, and King's Mountain.

Around the turn of the century, Bennett's grandfather, John Young, left North Carolina and moved his family to Virginia. In subsequent years, Bennett's father, Robert, amassed a small fortune as a hat manufacturer in Nicholasville, Kentucky, before retiring to oversee a sizable plantation where scores of slaves tilled the land. If the fact that his parents were wealthy slaveowners bothered him, Bennett Young never let on.

About 1,150,000 people inhabited the Bluegrass State by 1860. There were about 226,000 slaves and about 10,000 freed slaves, and the slave population was growing at a rate far faster than the white population.

A large farmhouse sheltered the lively Young family of nine, and while all seven of the children might have labored a spell in the fields, Young didn't work the earth for long. He was expected to enter the ministry; before the hostilities between North and South ignited, Young was pursuing his education at the Bethel Academy and then at Centre College, a two-year school, studying to become a Presbyterian clergyman.

With secession, the Young family, like President Jefferson Davis, believed that Southern independence was born at the moment of its declaration. When Kentucky voted not to secede from the Union in November 1861, Bennett quickly built a reputation for himself as a Confederate sympathizer in his first months at Centre College, and he was the first in Nicholasville to raise the Stars and Bars in public.

In an incident at the school, when a fellow student learned of the vote and raised the Union flag on the school's roof, Young pointedly requested that the student either lower the flag or see the Confederate flag raised alongside. Without waiting for an answer, Young climbed the ladder leaning against the building to lower the Union colors. As he climbed, the ladder was pulled from beneath him and a fight broke out as soon as he hit the ground.

Kentucky during the Civil War was a state divided, and the border between North and South—at least at the beginning of the war—ran right through the middle of the state. The state gave each side a president: Abraham Lincoln was born in Hodgenville, Jefferson Davis in Fairview. "Esau and Jacob sprang from the same womb, yet they were characters widely different. . . . Kentucky gave birth to Abraham Lincoln and Jefferson Davis, to General E. H. Hobson and General John Hunt Morgan," wrote Rev. F. Senour.

The Virginia House of Burgesses had created Kentucky in 1776 as a separate county of Virginia. For a few years, people were happy living under the government of the Virginia Commonwealth; but by the 1780s they wanted separate statehood and finally, after ten conventions trying to get their own state, Kentucky was admitted as the fifteenth state of the new Federal Republic on June 1, 1792.

By the time of the Civil War, the Democratic Party, which had been losing ground nationally, still appealed to mountain men and poor yeoman farmers, which was surprising, given that their interests didn't seem to match those of the slaveholders. But Lincoln had failed to win his native state because to many a Kentuckian he stood for abolitionism, coercion of states' rights, and, worst of all, Yankee meddling.

Kentucky was Southern in manners, customs, and traditions. A loyalty to the Union and to Abraham Lincoln pervaded the state to a certain extent, but both Lincoln and the Republicans were pushing the limits of the indigenous goodwill. For that reason, Lincoln's first election aroused fear in many a Kentucky heart, and countless mothers worried equally over the prospect of their sons joining the Blue or the Gray.

At the outbreak of war, many people in Kentucky supported a militia so long as its intent was to protect Kentucky from both the Confederate and Federal armies, and the state legislature voted to remain neutral. "The declaration of neutrality was the outcome of internal dissension. The impossible situation in which the state was projected when she felt that she could not forswear her allegiance to the Union, nor could she take up arms against her sister states of the South," wrote Lorine Letcher Butler.

Lincoln was unsuccessful in his attempt to sway Kentucky to his cause, despite his native roots. When he asked Kentucky Governor Beriah Magoffin to give two regiments of volunteers to help protect Washington, D.C., Magoffin responded: "Your dispatch is received. In answer, I say, emphatically, Kentucky will furnish no troops for the wicked purpose of subduing her sister Southern states."

The thinking was to keep everyone out, and in September 1861 the legislature issued an order that all arms in the state be relinquished for use in maintaining armed neutrality. It wasn't so radical a stance for a Southern state, given the confused loyalties of the time. Most people lived a rural life in the South—no railroad tracks reached the mountains of North Carolina or the grasslands of Tennessee, and neither, for that matter, did the telegraph lines. Farming was the way of life, and there was an affinity for the stability of Unionism, for protecting one's way of life and the future, a future some hoped would include increased manufacturing and demand for goods in the South.

In fact, the very heart of the Confederacy, from western North Carolina to eastern Tennessee, was more pro-Union than Jefferson Davis and his government would have cared for. About nine thousand men from North Carolina wore the Federal uniform, and more than twenty thousand men from Tennessee did the same.

Kentucky was a torn thread along the seam of the nation, and many noted families from the state were divided in the same manner. Reverend Robert J. Breckinridge, a passionate Unionist, had two sons in the Union Army and two sons in the Confederate Army (one of the Confederate sons captured one of his Union brothers at the Battle of Atlanta), and the editor of the *Louisville Journal,* the leading Unionist George D. Prentice, watched as his two sons enlisted in the Confederate Army.

Allegiance among Kentuckians was often tested, and the wrong views expressed in the wrong company could be an invitation for death at the hands of bushwhackers. One could incur wrath from neighbors or kin at any moment, depending on the leanings of the heart. The fluctuating levels of violence, which existed not only in Kentucky, left the hinterlands of many states littered with bodies from this most nasty, bloodthirsty vigilante sensibility.

When war finally called, the internal strife did not prevent the necessary number of Confederate troops from being raised in the South. North Carolina, for one, easily filled its quota for soldiers in April 1861 and contributed 50,000 more troops by May. Abraham Lincoln had called for 75,000 troops from the North to suppress the Rebellion in the Lower South, and Confederate support rushed in to counter with the loudly publicized claim that the South planned to fight until the last man remained standing.

But loyalty to the cause did not supply an adequate and consistent stream of soldiers. As the war ground on, it would become harder and harder to fill the ranks as enlistment fell off. Consequently, the Confederate Congress passed the Conscription Act in April 1862, and men between the ages of eighteen and thirty-five became subject to the draft. But the draft was just as reviled in the South as it was in the North and, as in the Union territories, one could pay another to go in his stead.

The Conscription Act soon forced into hiding many remaining men of age who had avoided service to begin with. Deserters and dodgers roamed the region. Of those who abandoned their posts, most did so because of low morale, or out of fear for the safety of their loved ones at home, or, simply, because they had not been paid. But it was a huge risk to desert, for if a soldier fell into the hands of either his own army or an opposing force, he could face a slow hanging in front of witnesses who would beat his body as it gasped for breath. In some mountain villages in Kentucky, Virginia, and Tennessee, corpses dangled from trees as the people, uncertain as to who had strung the bodies, were too terrified to take them down on account of feared reciprocity. The Confederate Army, seeing early that sustaining adequate manpower would be a principal challenge, was ruthless in enforcing its punishment for desertion.

But Bennett Young warranted no such concern from the Confederate Army, and he proudly counted himself among the fighting men. Once eighteen, the legal age for enlistment, he postponed school, heeded the call to service, and joined the Confederate Eighth Kentucky Cavalry. Young was among the thirty-five to forty thousand Kentuckians who volunteered to the Confederate Army, and when he joined the cavalry he drilled on horseback with a saber and a Sharps, a .52-caliber arm that had been in production since 1850, or a short-barreled carbine, which was the main shoulder weapon for many cavalrymen.

★ ★ ★

As Bennett Young came of fighting age, another of Kentucky's sons found his own reasons to ride off to war. In July 1861, Rebecca Bruce Morgan lay dying. She had been quite ill for two years, and sickness had marked her entire marriage to John Hunt Morgan of Lexington, Kentucky.

After his beloved wife died, John Morgan, with his five brothers, went to war. The Morgan family gave itself to the Confederacy. While brother Richard would serve on A. P. Hill's staff in Virginia, the four other brothers—Thomas, Charlton, Calvin, and Key—would serve under John's command in his notorious unit of raiders.

John Morgan stood about six feet tall and weighed about 180 pounds, and had been born in Huntsville, Alabama on June 1, 1825 and raised in Lexington, Kentucky. Morgan embarked on his military career when he was twenty-one during the Mexican War, raising a company of volunteers and enlisting in June 1846 to serve as a first lieutenant in Col. Humphrey Marshall's regiment. When the Civil War began, he initially supported the State Guard, so long as its intent was to protect Kentucky from both

Confederate and Federal armies but soon decided to support the Confederacy wholeheartedly.

By 1862, John Hunt Morgan's infamous cavalry had become known for specializing in daring raids deep into Union territory, and Morgan himself was known as "The Thunderbolt of the Confederacy." The troops were feared for the destruction they sowed on Union supply lines and garrisons, and Morgan shortly earned a reputation as a superb and awe-inspiring cavalryman.

"General Morgan was a magnetic man, of pleasing address and most genial personality . . . a born gentleman to the tips of his fingers and the ends of his eyelashes. He was blue-blooded, romantic, and chivalry incarnate," wrote James M. Fry.

The cavalry's role in raids, as seen in the glint of Morgan's eye, was based upon the tactics of the old Army in its struggles against the Native Americans—the men were mounted infantry, the methods and arms of the foot soldier complemented by horses held in reserve for quick and long marches.

"I wanted to be a cavalryman / And with John Morgan ride, / A Colt revolver in my belt, / A saber by my side. / I wanted a pair of epaulets / To match my suit of gray, / The uniform my mother made, / And lettered C.S.A.," went a common southern ditty recorded by Lorine Letcher Butler.

Morgan brought the war with him wherever he and his men rode. His meticulous planning ensured that each raid had a purpose, and that their strikes at vital Federal lines of communication could deliver mortal blows to supply lines. To Morgan and his men, each Federal trooper killed, wounded, or captured was one less body to fight on the battlefield.

The tireless rider was quickly garnering attention from friends and foes alike. Among other tactics for which they were known, riders under Morgan's command often wore Union uniforms, a practice that greatly disturbed Federal authorities. Gen. William S. Rosecrans, with Morgan in mind, issued an order that any and all Confederates captured behind Union lines wearing a Union uniform be treated as spies. Morgan and his men, characteristically, considered this a risk well worth taking.

John Hunt Morgan's Raiders eventually absorbed elements of the Confederate Eighth Kentucky Cavalry, and Bennett Young was one of many boys who rushed to join Morgan's men. "From every county in Kentucky the men came—the best blood of Kentucky—to be known as one of Morgan's men became a distinction in Confederate circles," Butler wrote.

Young shared a boldness of spirit with Morgan. Words used to describe his commanding officer applied to him as well; Young undeniably had "a remarkable aptitude for promptly acquiring a knowledge of any country in which he was operating. The celerity with which he marched, the promptness with which he attacked or eluded a foe, intensified the confidence of his followers and kept his antagonists always in doubt and apprehension," wrote Basil W. Duke.

In the early summer of 1863, Gen. John Hunt Morgan, astride Black Bess, his famous horse, began a deep raid into Kentucky and the Northwest that was ordered by Gen. Braxton Bragg as a means to divert Federal troops from east Tennessee, specifically the Union Army of the Ohio, which had begun operations against his Army of Tennessee (this later became known as the Tullahoma Campaign). Morgan himself handpicked about twenty-five hundred Confederate cavalrymen to ride west with him from Sparta, in eastern Tennessee, on June 11, 1863. "Its rank and file was of the mettle which finds its natural element in active and audacious enterprise, and was yet thrilled with the fire of youth; for there were few men in the division over 25 years of age," wrote Thomas H. Hines.

When "the young aristocrats who 'belonged to Morgan' grew ragged and thin, worn hard by riding under short rations, the gallant solders often were forced to stay in their saddles in the presence of ladies for the unromantic reason of their seatless pants—still romance hung about Morgan's men," wrote Butler.

Bennett Young, fresh in the saddle, had the honor of riding along. Although Young seemed to have more *joie de vivre* than Morgan, he was imbued with the spirit of his commander and was confident in his skill. Young deemed no endeavor impossible—or even hazardous, for that matter—and his commanding officer noticed.

"The highest commendation, not only for his courage but for his remarkable physical strength on that long and trying march," read a commendation from Gen. Morgan to Young in the summer of 1863.

For forty-six days, until July 26, 1863, Morgan and his men galloped at a furious pace, covering nearly a thousand miles and terrorizing people from Tennessee to Ohio while disrupting Union communication lines. Morgan crossed into Indiana and Ohio with the hope of inspiring an uprising of like-minded people but achieved little success to that end, instead finding only a measure of tragedy as his younger brother Thomas was killed in a skirmish with Union troops.

As for the great raid, which had now reached into Ohio, John Hunt Morgan and 364 of his men had this time ventured too deep. It had thus far been the longest cavalry incursion of the war, but it was soon to come to an abrupt end.

Spying a vulnerable Union camp, Morgan and his men crossed the Cumberland River at Turkey Neck Bend on a sticky July 1863 day. Swimming their horses to the other side, while ferryboats carried their arms and saddles, Morgan and his men emerged on the northern bank and attacked Federal troops before even bothering to fully dress themselves.

"The curious spectacle of men without clothes engaged in battle so impressed the enemy that they gave up resistance," recounted an eyewitness. But that account of the action was too quickly recorded, for this time victory would vanish as easily as it had come. Federal troops regrouped and captured Morgan, Young, and most of the other men.

Despite the capture, Morgan's diversion appears to have achieved the aims for which it was designed. Later that September, Gen. Bragg and Gen. James Longstreet, together with the First Corps of the Army of Northern Virginia, would win the battle of Chickamauga, and the Confederates would successfully push Gen. William S. Rosecrans all the way back to Chattanooga.

But unable to enjoy news of an outcome yet months in the future, Morgan and his men were now prisoners with little fortune smiling upon them. Finally in the hands of the Union, the authorities hesitated to imprison Morgan and his men in Camp Chase, located on the outskirts of Columbus, Ohio, judging the camp too insecure to confine the notorious unit.

Camp Chase was named for Secretary of the Treasury and former Ohio Governor Salmon P. Chase. Initially it was a training camp for Union volunteers, in addition to its housing of prisoners, mostly political and military, from Kentucky and Virginia.

In the beginning, the camp held Confederate prisoners captured by the Union during its western campaigns and its victories at Fort Donelson, Tennessee on February 16, 1862 and at Mississippi River Island No. 10 on April 8, 1862.

If captured Confederate officers took an oath, they were allowed to meander freely about Columbus, frequent hotels, and receive money and food. Adding to the circus atmosphere of the war's early days, the public actually paid to see the inside of the camp, and it fast became a tourist attraction of sorts. After a time, discipline became so lax that prison officials drastically cracked down.

One result of this change in policy was that most of the officers were sent to Johnson's Island on Lake Erie. Also, officers no longer could roam about the town at will, money was limited, visitors were banned, and mail was heavily censored. By now, most of the prisoners behind the wall of Camp Chase were from the ranks: privates, corporals, and sergeants. Furthermore, the camp soon featured a "dead line," beyond which a prisoner would be shot or would be speared with a bayonet.

As the war continued, the situation worsened a great deal, to the point of becoming inhumane. Prisoners were surrounded with muddy grounds, open cisterns, and open latrines, and during the winter of 1863–1864 a smallpox epidemic swept through the camp.

The prison had been built for thirty-five hundred to four thousand men but was holding up to seven thousand, and some say as many as ten thousand were being held there by the time the war ended. Today there are 2,260 Confederate soldiers buried there, all of whom died right there except for thirty-one of them.

All this prompted the U.S. Sanitary Commission inspectors to demand the reform of the prison. In November 1864, there would be a prisoner exchange between the North and South, but the prison conditions weren't actually improved until the closing months of the war.

★   ★   ★

The Federal Army instead decided to separate Morgan's men and incarcerate them in different camps throughout the territory. General Ambrose Burnside reportedly sentenced the men to prison for the war's duration because of what he termed the heinous nature of their tactics.

Union guards hauled some of the prisoners, including Young, to Camp Douglas, where their heads were shorn upon arrival. At first, Camp Douglas, named for Stephen A. Douglas, was the largest training camp for Illinois soldiers; in all, about thirty-two units were trained at this camp north of Chicago.

In 1862, the first prisoners arrived, about eight thousand from the capture of Fort Donelson. To some Confederate soldiers, Camp Douglas looked like a small town, as it was laid out in a gridlike fashion. Prisoners got rations dispensed from a commissary each morning, and among the prisoners were notables such as Sam Houston, Jr., and Henry M. Stanley, the African explorer.

An estimated eighteen thousand Confederate prisoners would enter the walls of Camp Douglas; six thousand—or one in three—would die. The high mortality rate came from the usual suspects: overcrowding, disease, poor medical treatment, poor nutrition, and brutality.

Sometimes prisoners would be punished by being put in the "white oak," a guardhouse made of white oak logs about twelve or fourteen inches in diameter. There was one small window—and, inside, a dungeon ten feet deep.

Another form of punishment, and supposed escape deterrent, was the confiscation of the prisoners' clothing. It wasn't uncommon for prisoners to wear sacks with holes cut for their heads and arms. There were some winters—that of 1864 in particular—during which inmates froze to death.

A high plank wall, roughly fifteen feet high, surrounded the camp. A walkway was built on top of it for the guards, who had cultivated reputations for being extremely cruel. While Camp Douglas seems to have escaped the notoriety of Andersonville, where nearly thirteen thousand Union soldiers died, it was in many ways equally barbaric. When the Rebel prisoners first arrived in 1862, the camp was relatively clean. However, about nine thousand prisoners were packed inside the camp, with fewer than a thousand guards. The barracks were to hold about

125 prisoners each, with three tiers of bunks standing along every wall of the structures. As the war went on, there would be at least two hundred prisoners jammed into each of the quarters, and when there was no room left there, the men were kept in tents. Food was so scarce that reports later surfaced of inmates trying to catch rats to stuff into pies.

"Sir, the amount of standing water, unpoliced grounds, of foul sinks, of unventilated and crowded barracks, of general disorder, of soil reeking miasmatic secretions, of rotten bones and emptying of camp kettles, is enough to drive a sanitarium to despair," wrote the *Chicago Tribune* on September 22, 1862. "The absolute abandonment of the spot seems to be the only judicious course. I do not believe that any amount of drainage would purge that soil loaded with accumulated filth of those barracks fetid with two stories of vermin and animal exhalations. Nothing but fire can cleanse them."

Morgan, at another facility, and Young, fearsome figures no more, quickly found themselves trading their dusty uniforms for convict clothes.

"Before entering the main prison we were searched and relieved of our pocket knives, money, of all other articles of value, subjected to a bath, the shaving of our faces, and the cutting of our hair," said Hines.

Time in Camp Douglas hardened Young and yet tamed just enough of his impulsiveness. On an occasion when a regiment of Michigan infantry on guard duty fired into the quarters of Confederate soldiers, killing and wounding the prisoners as they slept on bunks, Young demanded that he be permitted to lodge a complaint with the commandant. After Young's protests were heard, the commandant not only rebuked him but also threw him into solitary confinement for his troubles. Not necessarily the outcome desired by the proud Kentuckian; but Young was intent on maintaining his principles while looking for ways to fight another day.

Still being held at a separate location, Young's commander was working to the same end. Morgan was being held in the state penitentiary in Columbus, Ohio, a twenty-five-acre complex on the east bank of the Scioto River. Twenty-two of the prison's acres were behind a wall that, as it happened, contained stretches that bordered flowering plants and shrubs which lay out in front of it. While behind the walls, Morgan, fellow raider Thomas Hines, and four of their captains developed a particular fondness for the decorations nature had donated to the otherwise bleak scene—the shrubbery helped mask the tunnel Hines had been burrowing to freedom.

Undetected, the great raider Morgan slipped out of Union hands yet again.

However, Morgan's career would eventually end in Greenville, in eastern Tennessee, where he and his men were encamped on September 4, 1864. Reports state that a woman named Mrs. Lucy Williams, in whose home he was being entertained, betrayed him to a troop of Federal cavalry. General Morgan, realizing that the enemy was outside the house, attempted to make his escape through the back yard, but while mounting his horse he was shot. His body was seized by his slayers and paraded about town. After a time, the body was sent to Confederate lines under a flag of truce.

Young was no different from his commander, however, when he decided for himself that prison camp was no place to spend the war. On an initial attempted escape, Young was caught, and he spent thirty days in an underground dungeon. But, not a man easily undone, Young tried a second time, succeeded, and quickly made his way to Confederate lines. He slipped into the South expecting that he would soon plunge back into battle in the Deep South, perhaps riding with the cavalry once again. Young did not imagine that his next orders would take him to— of all places—Canada, where he would join other members of the Confederacy to begin the planning of an attack on the Union— in Vermont.

4

A Matter of Recognition

★ ★ ★ ★ ★ ★ ★ ★ ★ ★ ★ ★ ★ ★ ★ ★ ★ ★

The Canadian territory was a means to Rebel ends in the Civil War. By 1864, Montreal and Toronto had become capitals in exile for the Confederacy, buzzing with plots and schemes shaded by Southern accents. The commonwealth would ultimately become a staging ground for Gray guerrilla trade, trafficking, and raids, but initially its engagement was aimed at a much larger prize.

On November 28, 1861, relations between Canada, Great Britain, and the United States very nearly snapped for the third time since 1776. In what became known as the "Trent Affair," the U.S.S. *San Jacinto* stopped the British mail steamer *Trent* on the high seas. The American captain, Charles Wilkes, authorized the removal of two Confederate commissioners, John Slidell of Louisiana and James M. Mason of Virginia, who were then taken back to New England and jailed in Fort Warren in Boston Harbor. While the action may have cast Wilkes in the role of hero in the eyes of many Yankees, it severely aggravated relations between America and Britain.

For a number of weeks, bellicose words flew about on both sides of the Atlantic, as it appeared that Britain was contemplating recognition of the Confederacy and a declaration of war on the Union. The kingdom was aghast that the United States had displayed the gumption to board one of Her Majesty's vessels in international waters. If the conflict continued to escalate, it seemed that Canada would likely be the first target of Union forces, and Canadian volunteers began to mobilize in response, with Britain reinforcing its garrisons there with more than eleven thousand troops.

British regulars were transported, eight men to a sleigh, along the frozen St. Lawrence River—to Halifax, Nova Scotia, and St. John, New Brunswick—traveling for six to ten days. Trying to fight off the frigid temperatures, they put on as many layers as Russian *matrioshka* nesting dolls—covered under their uniforms and greatcoats in woolen underwear and stockings, moccasins filled with straw, flannel shirts, thick sweaters, chamois jackets, fur caps, and woolen scarves, each man with two blankets and each sleigh with two sheepskin coats or buffalo robes.

Fortunately, as tensions rose, newly appointed Viscount Charles Stanley Monck, Governor-General of Canada, stepped in to defuse the situation and helped to persuade the North to free Mason and Slidell. Viscount Monck was known to be reserved and more inclined to spend time with his family and close friends. His wife, Lady Elizabeth Louise Mary Monck, loved horticulture and could often be seen tending to the grounds of Rideau Hall, the official residence in Ottawa.

Under international conventions governing the day, the *Trent* and its passengers should have been brought into port and the matter promptly adjudicated before an admiralty court because it was supposedly carrying contraband. As it happened, the two men gained their liberty in 1862, and British and Canadian troops never traded shots with the United States.

As the events stemming from the Trent Affair unfolded, few of them went unnoticed in President Jefferson Davis's circle. Slidell and Mason's mission on the *Trent* was part of a continuing

Confederate effort to secure European recognition. In the interim, the Davis government had also initiated an aggressive push for relations with Canada, believing this to be another path to British favor. The Confederacy was desperate to compel the nations of the Old World to take notice. With its constitution, established government, standing army, and nearly nine million people, the thinking in Richmond was that Europe would need little convincing to recognize the breakaway states.

The "peculiar institution" of slavery had remained, from the beginning, the ill-mannered guest near which no one wanted to sit. But differences over the matter were not in themselves enough to prohibit recognition. Only a comparatively small percentage of the Southern population owned slaves, and the Confederate constitution prohibited their further importation. Just as the United States had banned the international slave trade in 1808, so ultimately did the Confederacy when it was formed, albeit not for the same reasons. South Carolina, one of the most ardent secessionists, had opposed the ban; however, Virginia and Maryland, both states with a tremendous economic stake in the domestic slave trade, refused to enter the Confederacy without a ban in effect.

Diehard slavery advocate William L. Yancey had led one of the earliest recognition missions to Europe, and Judge Pierre A. Rost, also an advocate of the institution, had traveled along. These two could have posed a personal problem on the matter for British Prime Minister Henry John Temple Palmerston, who was severely against slavery, but Britain had larger worries, namely the avoidance of war. After the Yancey and Rost envoy, Great Britain stopped just short of recognizing Southern nationhood.

Queen Victoria officially declared the Crown neutral in a proclamation issued on May 13, 1861. According to the decree, Great Britain recognized the Confederates as a belligerent power, equal to the Union and entitled to all the rights afforded under international law. The language of the decree left room for the South to purchase arms, commission cruisers, and in effect pursue any course necessary to shore up its war machine. What a difference, to business, a few choice words made: The proclamation kept English manufacturing busy throughout the war, from Laird's Birkenhead shipyard to the Enfield small arms factory north of London.

Of course, the ruling raised the ire of many Federal statesmen. Upon hearing of the decision, Massachusetts Senator Charles Sumner called it "the most hateful act of English history since Charles 2nd." Fiercely antislavery himself, Sumner would go on to introduce the Thirteenth Amendment to the Senate in 1864, but in the meantime he had to contend with this backhanded recognition, which meant, among other things, that, just to the north, Canadian justice would hold anyone scheming on Canadian soil as a legitimate warrior rather than as a traitor to the Federal government of the United States of America.

Secretary of State William H. Seward felt particularly betrayed by Britain's proclamation. Seward had a shock of dark hair that flopped forward on his face, which was dominated by a prominent nose and two considerable ears. Seward was born in 1801 in Orange County, New York. He was an active member of the Whig Party and often took up more progressive politics such as prison reform and education. Seward defended fugitive slaves in court as part of his opposition to the Fugitive Slave Act.

Lincoln offered Seward the position of Secretary of State almost immediately upon his election, and Seward became an extremely valued confidant of the president's. Later known for spearheading the prescient purchase of Alaska from the Russians, Seward favored expansion and a powerful United States.

A man who rarely minced words, Seward reacted with customary fire to Britain's determined course. "We from that hour shall cease to be friends and become once more, as we have twice before been forced to be, enemies of Great Britain." Once again the two cousins across the Atlantic were at odds.

Britain remained unmoved by these outbursts, convinced that its public position of neutrality was the most pragmatic. At the very least, such a stance would rob the Federal Army of any justification for an invasion of Canada for the time being.

President Jefferson Davis decided to recall Yancey and Rost. In their stead, he would send new ministers plenipotentiary to two different European capitals in the hopes of swaying the European heart and mind. James Mason would travel to London, and John Slidell to Paris, aboard the *Trent*.

In the months that followed the Trent Affair, European diplomatic recognition of the South would become a more realistic possibility. In the summer of 1862, the armies under Gen. Robert E. Lee were victorious from Harper's Ferry to Fredericksburg, and the prospect of a salvaged Union seemed less likely by the week. At that point, no European country seriously believed that the North could win, or that the nation could emerge from the conflict as a strong whole—but extending real recognition could still have meant having to enter the war, and none of the European principals were prepared to take that step.

Moreover, European power politics were at play; and if a nation like Britain, most heavily courted by the Confederates, entered on the side of the South, other nations like Russia certainly would quickly find incentive to enter the war as allies of the Union.

France, under Emperor Napoleon III, also had a soft spot for the Confederacy. In 1862, while Slidell was there, Napoleon talked with him and suggested that France, England, and Russia try to work together to bring about a six-month American armistice. Nothing came of this, and the North, under Seward's lead, rejected any such thought.

Czarist Russia was in fact the only true friend of the North. In 1863, two Russian fleets came to American waters—one in the Atlantic and one in the Pacific: New York and San Francisco, respectively. The ships passed the winter there. Some interpreted this as a means of Russia's warning France and England that if they entered the war, Russia would enter, too. Actually, it was also because Russia wanted to protect their fleets from ice-bound Russian ports, since the nation was conceivably close to war with Britain and France.

Full recognition was foolhardy; and, deep down, Britain knew this. London and Paris thus continued to weigh the idea of offering to mediate between the two sides, but this still would have been another form of recognizing the South and its independence.

★ ★ ★

The Confederacy would continue to work toward gaining recognition directly with the European powers and would take considerable interest in Canada in the hopes of establishing further ties to the Crown. Yet Richmond soon found that Canada's use was not limited to mere diplomacy. The Confederate Army was desperate for intelligence, and the Davis government was in need of locations in which its agents could operate without fear of arrest or execution. As the Federal Army's fortunes slowly turned, and as the Union-occupied territory increased in size, the Confederacy could feel the walls moving in. Canada, at worst indifferent to the Southern cause and at best sympathetic, seemed a perfect choice, a natural back door into enemy lands.

During the period of the Civil War, Canada was actually divided into Upper Canada, or Canada West (today's Ontario), and Lower Canada, or Canada East (today's Quebec). Executive power rested in the hands of Viscount Monck, Canada's first

Governor-General. Monck, forty-five, had lived in Ireland and had served both in the British House of Commons for seven years and in the liberal government of Henry Temple, Viscount Palmerston, as Lord of the Treasury.

Officially, as a jewel in the Crown, Canada under Monck had no choice but to follow Britain's neutrality. Most British and Canadian government officials deftly walked a tightrope. And while some government officials, such as Viscount Monck, might have felt a personal affinity for the Union, as officials they could do little to indulge those feelings.

Moreover, the Canadian people had in fact developed a lenient disposition toward the South over the course of the war. Between 1863 and 1864, thousands of American draft-dodgers, deserters, Southern sympathizers, and escaped Confederate POWs streamed into Canada, rarely bothering to keep their political views in check. The influence of this influx was felt across the country, particularly by French-Canadians, who had become fairly antagonistic toward the Yankees. News of Federal victories became heartfelt losses for the lands north of the Union: "In effect . . . each defeat was an ache in the hearts of the Canadians, each victory was a ray of sunshine," according to David Têtu.

Canada was a logical base of operations for the Confederacy. Firstly, all avenues from the South that led into the heart of the Union were closed off due to the war, and going around would be an efficient way to infiltrate the North for Confederate spies and informants. Secondly, many Canadians, who had descended from those who had fled the American colonies less than a century before, would likely share a commonality with the Rebels at odds with the Union. Thirdly, the British government, while officially neutral, at least turned a blind eye to Southern doings on Canadian soil and at most quietly supported the Southern cause. Fourthly, escaped Confederate prisoners could find safe haven in Canada before being circulated back to the lines. It was decided that Nova Scotia, New Brunswick, Toronto, and Montreal would prove to be ideal grounds for the staging of Confederate operations.

In general, the American Civil War was a boon for British North American business. Canada's agricultural and manufactured goods were much in demand, the largest portion of course going to the Northern side. In addition, because American exports diminished during the war, Canada benefited from great price increases for its exports.

In many ways, living in Montreal, Toronto, or even Halifax during the American Civil War meant living under the specter of American invasion. Because of this, the British kept their garrisons heavily fortified and troops ready.

The threat of annexation hovered over British North America. Finally in 1866, the United States Congress put forward a bill for the admission of the States of Nova Scotia, New Brunswick, Canada East, and Canada West, and for the organization of the Territories of Selkirk, Saskatchewan, and Columbia. While this bill appeared in Congress only after the end of the Civil War, there had long been widespread apprehension in Canada over the likelihood of such a move occurring. When Lincoln had appointed William Seward to be Secretary of State, that would have fed the apprehension; Seward made no secret of his desire to see the United States grow in size.

A popular ditty of the time, sung to the tune of "Yankee Doodle," went like this: "Secession first he would put down, / Wholly and forever; / And afterwards from Britain's Crown / He Canada would sever." After the Americans purchased Alaska in 1867, the worry over annexation only heightened.

In the decades prior to the American Civil War, Quebec saw its population virtually double, despite the exodus of almost two hundred thousand people who left the province for better-paying factory jobs in New England. With the rise in population,

Montreal and Quebec City grew exponentially. In the early 1850s, Montreal had fewer than sixty thousand people living in the city; by 1861, there were an estimated ninety thousand. Quebec City had a population of about fifty thousand by 1861.

At the time the Confederates were establishing a staging ground in Canada, Montreal was the center of British North America. The streets were filled with horse-drawn streetcars; sidewalks and several luxury hotels established the city as a prosperous center. The largest companies and banks of British North America chose Montreal as their headquarters—the Grand Trunk, the Molson Bank, the Merchant's Bank, the Bank of Montreal, and the Bank of British North America. In addition, Montreal's location at the confluence of the St. Lawrence and Ottawa rivers helped establish it as a busy port. It also served as a stopping point for Confederate soldiers who had escaped Federal prisons, for Confederate sympathizers, or for anyone simply seeking to reach the Southern front.

During the war, the Confederates adored the St. Lawrence Hall, whose menu featured mint juleps. They also were known to rent rooms at the Donegana Hotel.

By 1861, Toronto was also one of the largest cities in British North America, with about forty-five thousand calling it home. Like Quebec, Canada West had grown quite a bit between 1840 and 1861. And while Toronto saw an upswing in commercial and industrial growth, its surrounding areas remained mostly agricultural, with more than eighty percent of its inhabitants living in rural areas. Its industry was centered on logging and mills, as well as on canal and railway construction. Much of its manufacturing was centered on farm tools, shoes, and clothing. Toronto's American Hotel lodged many a Confederate spy and politician during the war.

Halifax, originally settled on a small piece of land that juts into Halifax harbor, would play a significant role in the blockades running along the eastern American seaboard. The city was founded in 1749 as part of the province of Nova Scotia; during the first decades of the 1700s, British troops who were posted in the vicinity considered it a hardship posting due to the fact that it was close to the border with the French territory, where conflict could always erupt at a moment's notice. Of course, once Britain defeated France in the Seven Years' War, or French and Indian War, the region discovered a brief period of newfound quiet when it came to military conflict.

Halifax's military role waxed and waned in the nineteenth century. During the War of 1812, the port helped the Crown to launch raids on Baltimore and Washington, D.C., while privateers based in Nova Scotia targeted American shipping. Most of the early settlers of Halifax were discharged soldiers and sailors, and they often left the unsettled and isolated land around Halifax harbor for New York, Boston, or even Virginia and the Carolinas.

Many local banks established themselves in Halifax, such as the Halifax Banking Company, the Union Banks of Halifax, and the Bank of Nova Scotia. The intersection of shipping and finance helped make the city one of the more important, if also more desolate, centers in colonial British North America.

During the American Civil War, Halifax achieved a new kind of role, as Confederate and European ships used the port to circumvent the Union blockade. With the blockade-runners stopping over, Halifax offered refuge and supplies to many a Confederate. This activity saw to it that Halifax and the Maritime Provinces grew fat on the profits made from furnishing supplies and arms.

For some time, the Canadian Government knew of its Southern "problem" and sought to staunch the flow of the so-named

Rebels, if only to keep up appearances. In the summer of 1864, Lord Richard Hickerton Pemell Lyons, the British minister in Washington, whose square face was framed with the mutton-chop sideburns of the era, wrote to Viscount Monck about "an unusual number of persons styled by him disloyal citizens of the United States, through St. John, New Brunswick, en route for Canada."

Some in the Canadian government knew that their situation grew ever more precarious with each Southern partisan who migrated northward into their territory. Viscount Monck cautioned the Duke of Newcastle: "I trust your Grace will approve of the steps I have taken to prevent the infraction of British neutrality by persons enjoying Canadian hospitality."

Despite the position in which the Rebels placed Canada's standing with the United States, popular support north of the border remained on the side of the Southerners. Many Canadians whispered that Union soldiers had been crossing the border to impress men into service, much as the English had done to American colonists several generations before. Lord Lyons repeatedly expressed his concern to U.S. Secretary of State Seward.

Lyons wrote about "Practices resorted to by crimps and other unscrupulous men, in order to obtain recruits from Canada for the United States army . . . Canadians have represented to me that they have been enlisted fraudulently and illegally in the United States army." It mattered not that no cases of forced service were ever substantiated. The continued suspicion over it compounded the distrust directed toward the United States.

"I cannot pretend to say that all or even the greater part of the complaints made to me are well founded," Lyons persisted. "But that there is, in full activity, a system of enticing Her Majesty's subjects to come from Canada to enlist, and even of kidnapping them and carrying them across the frontier, can hardly be doubted, and I am anxious to ask for Your Excellency's advice on the subject."

This is not to say that all Canadians were by any means anti-Union. What Lyons did not mention were the numerous Canadians who in fact waged war on the side of the North. While no precise figures exist, between forty and sixty thousand Canadian men are said to have fought on the side of the Union.

The Canadians who fought for the Union did so for many reasons. Most of them had immigrated to the United States well before the conflict exploded. Like their American brethren, some enlistees took up arms solely for employment and adventure, while ideological reasons motivated those who were devoted to the abolition movement. And, of course, some of the soldiers were actually freed slaves who had traveled the Underground Railroad to its Canadian terminus. Whatever prompted these fighters, a number of them achieved great success in the conflict; four Canadians were promoted to brigadier general, and twenty-nine received the Congressional Medal of Honor.

Nevertheless, the larger geopolitical issue of a growing United States further aroused popular Canadian sentiment for the Confederacy. Whereas Britain viewed the speed with which the United States had gained power since 1812 with guarded concern, Canada viewed it with outright alarm. As far as many Canadians were concerned, the idea of a smaller—and likely weaker—neighbor was a welcome one. Beyond their own national interests, Canadians also found justification in Southern self-determination. Some forcefully argued the idea that the Southern states had as much right to relinquish their ties to the Union as the thirteen original colonies had claimed when they left Great Britain. While the two situations are not really analogous (since the colonies had never promised to remain faithful to Britain in the same way that they did promise to band together to form a new nation), this line of reasoning found support in many places.

That various factions in Canada would find common ground in sympathy for the South confounded the diplomats in Washington. The Federal leadership failed to understand that in 1864, Canada was a simmering stew of French, Irish, Scottish, and British immigrants. The first three groups had trouble with the leadership of Canada, mostly a British–Canadian enterprise in those years. For the majority of the citizens of (mostly French) Montreal, siding with the Confederacy became an avenue for anti-English and anti-establishment sentiments, as their arguments fell beyond the cautious neutrality endorsed by the state.

Many in Canada, in serving their aims, came to look at the Confederacy through a gauzy curtain. They saw only a bastion of chivalry, a romantic and genteel society, merely struggling for its independence.

The Union couldn't help but notice the presence of Confederates across the border, and correspondence frequently spoke of plots and mysterious dealings. "Persons hostile to the United States who have sought asylum in Canada appear to be engaged in a serious and mischievous plot," Lord Lyons himself alerted Secretary of State Seward in a letter.

Not willing to be taken unaware, Governor John Gregory Smith of Vermont requested five thousand rifled muskets, a large supply of ammunition, and the authority to station troops at three cities: Burlington, St. Albans, and Swanton. Rumor and gossip were part and parcel of any war, but this particular concern resonated with the citizens of his state.

On November 25, 1863, Maj. Gen. John A. Dix, the commanding officer at New York, sent a Col. Ludlow to Vermont on a fact-finding mission. Dix wanted to learn just how susceptible the state's northern border was to attack. In short order, Ludlow determined that no Herculean army would be needed to lay siege to Vermont or any other northern state. A small, fleet-footed party could do damage enough.

The governor and the general tried to ensure that their concerns reached the right ears. "I sent a detective into Canada from Buffalo; he returned this morning direct from Montreal, and reports that there is no movement on foot," Gen. Dix wrote to Secretary of War Stanton. "The Governor of Vermont asks for 5,000 rifled muskets, a large quantity of ammunition, horses for a battery, and authority to station troops at Swanton, St. Albans, and Burlington. Should not the Canadian authorities be called on, through the British Minister, to prevent by military force, the organization of marauding expeditions on British soil against the towns on our frontier, as a violation of every principle of international law?"

The Union not only wanted a listening post in Canada, it needed one. Ever aware that Confederate agents such as Bennett Young had been infiltrating their northern neighbor, government officials wanted a way to check on what Confederate agents were doing and to gauge the degree of British North America's sympathies with the South. Former Massachusetts Congressman George Ashmun was appointed special agent to Canada in 1861 for three months, and Mr. Charles S. Ogden was sent to Canada and set up in Quebec, while other agents were dispatched to Halifax and St. Johns, Quebec. The Union also had a special agent in Niagara Falls, New York, to examine anyone coming over the border, instructing him to seize and to hold anyone he found to be sufficiently suspicious.

And yet, despite the precautions urged and the slight measures being taken, warnings continued to flow from the northern border through the early part of 1864. J. T. Howard, U.S. Assistant Secretary of State, who was visiting St. John, New Brunswick, wrote, in a dispatch, "Sir, I beg leave to inform the

Department that an unusually large number of disloyal citizens of the United States have quite recently passed through this city. . . . The greater part of these insurgents have been living for some months in Halifax, others have found their way north from Nassau and Bermuda."

Warm weather in 1864 brought mosquitoes to the Green Mountain State and more small swarms of Confederates to the Canadian provinces. The summer before, Stephen R. Mallory, Secretary of the Navy of the Confederate States of America, had dispatched twenty-seven commissioned and forty noncommissioned officers to Canada "for the purpose of organizing raids into the Union states along the Northern frontier."

"The Confederate officers organized the Provisional Army of the CSA, which included in its ranks several thousand Rebel soldiers who had sought asylum in Canada. The purpose of the Confederate Government was to commit depredations on the Northern frontier by a system of terrorism so as to call back the Union troops to protect the loyal homes of this region," said *The Vermonter*.

★ ★ ★

The rumors continued to simmer. In July, warnings came out about "an attempt by Rebel refugees in Canada, at the destruction of our cities on the Lake." The Rebels were calling for three of the "most prominent of the refugees to Niagara." These three were likely the leaders of the Confederate intelligence network in Canada. Lieutenant Young would report to this trio, first as an instrument of their plans and later as a leader in his own right.

Plenty of government officials were well aware that relations between Canada and the United States, which teetered on the seesaw of amicability, might topple if escaped Rebels increased their use of Canada as a base. Viscount Monck was increasingly alarmed about this growing predicament. As things stood, there was no halting the Confederates from using his country, and he became further concerned with the potential for violence between Canada and the United States.

Monck theorized that a small Royal Navy presence on the Canadian side of Lake Erie would discourage more instigators from traveling north. Such a show of force would serve to underscore Canada's official position of neutrality and let the Union know that they seriously intended to thwart this activity. The governor-general wanted the power to seize vessels and munitions on the Great Lakes, as well as a mandate to expel anyone suspected of violating the Queen's proclamation of neutrality. At the very least, Monck wanted the authority to arrest and jail suspected Rebels.

However, an escalation of naval power had to be avoided on account of the Rush–Bagot Treaty of 1818, which limited the number of warships either country could anchor on the Great Lakes. Monck's idea of increasing firepower on the lakes early in the war attracted high-level attention in Washington, and the governor-general's position prompted some in the War Department to seriously deliberate the advantages of adding U.S. power to the lakes to take care of the insurgent problem. Gen. Dix suggested that the U.S. Navy arm five tugboats and place the vessels at harbor entrances. City leaders in Detroit and Buffalo also agitated Congress for permission to deploy an additional regiment to patrol the border.

Yet Secretary of State Seward reported to Lord Lyons of Canada: "In the present peaceful aspect of affairs we shall not make any such military demonstrations, or preparations on the Vermont line, as General Dix suggests. Nor shall I call on Her Majesty's Government for any special attention in that direction."

Perhaps the powers in Washington did not want to risk offending Canada, or perhaps they simply failed to see the northern landscape for what it was: an attractive plum waiting to be eaten by hungry Confederates.

In the same vein, the legislature of Canada denied Monck's request. The parliamentarians anticipated, correctly, that the Union would answer such a show of force with additional warships flying the Stars and Stripes.

★   ★   ★

In the autumn of 1864, public opinion in Canada was leaning more than ever toward the South in spite of—or perhaps because of—its waning strength. But the European powers had removed any hope that they would recognize or ally with the Confederacy.

"The public opinion grows hourly stronger in our favor, but England and France exhibit the same apathy, if not hostility, in the action of their government, that marked their course when you came out," wrote John Breckinridge Castleman in a letter to Jacob Thompson and also Clement Claiborne Clay, Jr. Castleman, from Lexington, Kentucky, helped plot various schemes to burn supply boats and free Confederate POWs.

While the Crown had refused further involvement, Montreal had grown ever more entwined with the Confederate cause, even playing host to a certain aspiring young actor named John Wilkes Booth, who had taken up residence in the city's most fashionable hotel, the St. Lawrence Hall, where he boasted to companions in the saloon: "Do you know, I have got the sharpest play laid out ever done in America? I can bag the biggest game this side of hell. Just remember my address. Abe's contract is near up and whether re-elected or not, he'll get his goose cooked!"

All the Confederates, even the most extreme, who reported to Canada for special duty in 1864 found themselves working and residing in warm, welcoming surroundings. "The Queen's Hotel where we stopped fronted on Toronto Bay. It may be said we found Confederate headquarters here at this hotel. . . . There was everything in the prospect at Toronto to make a sojourn enjoyable. The leading newspapers of Canada were published here and the South got a friendly comment on the course of events," wrote a twenty-six-year-old captain, John Yates Beall.

Despite the evidence that Vermont, and, for that matter, all the northeastern states sharing a border with Canada, were fast becoming Confederate targets, Washington failed to give them any encouragement or to take any true preventative action. The intelligence was not simply misinterpreted; it was willfully ignored.

Perhaps as importantly, the Union had not appreciated the vigor with which the Confederates had taken to their Canadian initiative. There was no doubt that by 1864, the South was dying. But in dreams of dramatic surprises that would sweep down from the north upon their hated foe, the desperate cause found a remedy for their reality, and more reason to fight yet another day.

5

The Canadian Initiative

★ ★ ★ ★ ★ ★ ★ ★ ★ ★ ★ ★ ★ ★ ★ ★ ★ ★

As the hope for European recognition died south of the Mason–Dixon Line, interest in Canada's territory, as opposed to its influence, grew in Confederate circles. While it appeared that neither Canada nor her European mother would actively support Southern interests, Richmond was hardly willing to turn its back on implicit contributions to its cause. The key, at least at first, would be discretion.

Neither Blue nor Gray could brag about the sophistication of its intelligence organization at the onset of the Civil War. Spying during the conflict was characterized by conditions that should have made it relatively easy. Both sides spoke the same language and were of the same nationality, so years of training to learn foreign manners, eating habits, and rules of etiquette were far from necessary. There were minor differences between the North and South, of course, but nothing like those normally existing between different nations.

The covert technology of the era was manageable and required little expertise, and spies had at their disposal a variety of methods to execute their missions. The media of the craft included photography and the telegraph (which had become an incredibly useful mode for spying during the war, as enemies could listen in on one other by skillfully tapping the lines with a bypass, allowing communications to be read in transit without disturbing the message), and, near the end of the war, even a primitive version of microfilm: Messengers carried information sewn into coat linings and were known to frequently wear metal buttons that, when opened, revealed "dispatches . . . most minutely photographed, not perceptible to the naked eye, but . . . easily read by the aid of a powerful lens," R. J. Kimball, consular officer in Toronto, wrote.

Amateurs could, and did, practice the craft, sometimes to more effect than their professional colleagues. More often than not, problems with the practice of the trade were institutional, as generals and other officers ran their own spy rings, with operatives running to gather information with little oversight or direction.

The South did not take an official concerted interest in its spying operation until 1864, when President Jefferson Davis persuaded the Confederate Congress to pass the Secret Service Act on February 17. Prior to passage of the Secret Service Act, the Confederacy had what was called the General Intelligence Office. Headed by Chaplain William A. Crocker, the department's primary responsibility had been to tally information regarding the sick and wounded. Admittedly, year three of the war was late in the game to launch an organized secret service, and prior to that time the Confederates had boasted a host of agents working loosely affiliated efforts. But looking at an increasingly bleak horizon, the South was grasping at whatever opportunities it could find, and the need for centrally managed and funded covert activity was apparent.

As opposed to many other aspects of the war, the Confederates found a patch of rare equal footing with the Union in starting their intelligence network; for they knew, intimately, the inner workings of the Union government and its own nascent secret service. Just as the current Rebel soldiers had once fought alongside the Yankees, scores of Southerners had served in the Federal government prior to the shots traded at Fort Sumter. Indeed, Jefferson Davis himself had been Secretary of War and Chairman of the Senate Military Affairs Committee earlier in his political career. Once set upon the notion of a Confederate Secret Service, the South knew both how to establish their own organization and how to best counter the North's.

Like the Confederacy, the Union, too, came to the war with a weak intelligence network. Just as Jefferson Davis decided to formalize a secret service, Abraham Lincoln had recognized the need to do the same. Allan Pinkerton, the previous head of the famous Chicago-based Pinkerton's detective agency, had been widely thought of as the premier choice to head a covert organization, and Secretary of State William Seward selected Pinkerton to replace himself as chief of counterintelligence.

Though a popular choice, Pinkerton proved unequal to the task, never appreciating the highly time-sensitive nature of military intelligence. He had been a detective in a field where information was gathered *after* the deed, not before. The general laggardness of his work was evidenced by the work of two of his high-value agents, Timothy Webster and George Curtis, who mined the Confederacy for valuable intelligence but never used couriers to transmit the information, instead bringing the information to Union lines personally, which delayed its arrival and use, and unnecessarily exposed the agents to capture. Pinkerton's detectives rarely turned in accurate information regarding enemy troop strengths, plans, and positions. To be sure, Pinkerton did succeed in corking the flow of classified information from Washington outward, but on the whole he was better suited to the private work that had made him famous.

★   ★   ★

While the Union's efforts stalled under Pinkerton, the Confederates went to work quickly and soon focused their efforts in Canada, the one place where their operators would be out of the Union's grasp. Once the Confederate Congress passed the Secret Service Act, it allocated nearly a million dollars for clandestine operations. Most of that money, derived from the selling of bootleg cotton, was earmarked for Canada. An investigation during the Lincoln assassination conspiracy trial later revealed that at one time, the Confederate commissioners in Canada had about $650,000 at their disposal. To optimize the efficiency of information flow through the base, an elaborate system of secret courier lines and safe houses was established, and most of the operators would successfully maintain their cover throughout the rest of the war.

One of the most successful courier lines was the earliest, the so-named Doctors' Line, worked by both genuine and fake physicians along routes that connected Washington and southern Maryland. Its success stemmed from the natural cover available to doctors of the time, who were frequently summoned in the middle of the night by patients. The doctor's bag, with its concealed compartments, turned out to be the perfect place to secrete information.

In a similar fashion, postmasters of southern Maryland who harbored strong feelings for the South used their positions to found the aptly named Postmasters' Line, which routed information through their respective offices. Legend says that news of what transpired during Lincoln's cabinet meetings was reaching Richmond within twenty-four hours. Other routes and safe houses established along the Potomac River in Washington included the Surratt House and the farm of Thomas Jones, a man who acted as a lookout from his house above the Potomac, warning of Union picket boats that sometimes trolled the river in search of illegal river crossings.

On the Union side, there was Elizabeth Van Lew, who had lived for a long time in Richmond. "Crazy Bett" was what her neighbors called her, and she ran perhaps one of the largest and most successful spy rings in any city during the war. She even had a freed slave working for her, whom she was able to place as a servant in the Confederate White House to eavesdrop on President Jefferson Davis.

All told, the service was comprised of a variety of types, from escaped prisoners, to down-on-their-luck politicians, to society dames; men and women of a conspiracy living and often dying under numerous aliases. The hope was that through their efforts to connect Canada to Richmond, Confederate operatives stationed in Montreal and Toronto could find a little more breathing room to undermine the Union.

With an infrastructure in place to pass information, the Confederacy turned to staffing its Canadian delegation. The first Confederate officer posted to Canada was the same Capt. Thomas H. Hines who had burrowed out of the Ohio State Penitentiary with John Hunt Morgan in 1863. Hines had often served as a clandestine warrior under Morgan, working up to that point in a number of capacities—posing as a doctor, a banker, and a French-Canadian exporter, to name but a few.

Hines arrived in Canada on March 16, 1864. He was not one of the three official Davis-appointed commissioners who would run the Canadian operation; instead, he was there to lay groundwork for the government structure soon to follow. While Hines would prove to be a key player in the Canadian crew, his exploits are not very well known.

Hines had been on the faculty of the Masonic University at La Grange, Kentucky, before enlisting. Working as a spy while under Morgan's command, he liaised with sympathetic groups in Kentucky, as well as others in the Northwest, and quickly took to the clandestine life. After his 1863 turn in prison, he managed to avoid capture time and again. After meeting with Davis and Secretary of War James A. Seddon, Hines met with Secretary of State Gen. Judah P. F. Benjamin.

Davis had first appointed Benjamin his attorney general, before next naming him secretary of war, and then secretary of state. Benjamin had been born in the West Indies in 1811 to observant Jewish parents. They moved to Charleston, South Carolina, and he went to Yale Law School at the young age of fourteen. Benjamin had owned about 140 slaves before selling his plantation in 1850; when he joined the Davis government, he was the only Cabinet member not to own slaves. He was often the target of anti-Semitism and harsh criticism from other members of the Confederate hierarchy.

After his final meeting with Benjamin, Hines worked his way toward Toronto, following Davis's instructions to contact as many Confederate supporters as possible—an easy task for a raider skilled in working new people and new places.

Aside from increasing their political base, the Confederates needed people who would come to their aid when called. Once in Canada, Hines was also charged with organizing the Confederate soldiers already ensconced there into a respectable fighting force that would be on call.

From Canada, Hines further underlined Richmond's belief that the country would provide the ideal staging ground for missions against the North. The cluster of cities along and near the frontier allowed for easy travel between the provinces and the northern United States. Large bodies of water such as the Great Lakes, the St. Lawrence River, and the canals near Niagara Falls meant that the network could easily move equipment, weapons, people, and contraband. Secret agents could ask for no better location than Niagara Falls for meetings and letter drops, and the general geography allowed for spies of the Confederacy to move from bases like Toronto to targets ranging from Detroit to Maine to Vermont.

With Hines finding his footing in Canada, President Davis next recruited Jacob Thompson to head up the official web. Born in North Carolina in 1810, Thompson had graduated from State University in North Carolina in 1831 with his sights set on passing the bar exam, which he did quite easily. Ever ambitious, Thompson soon decided to venture south to Mississippi to explore the development of the Chickasaw Indian lands. After seeing potential in this all-but-uncharted territory, he moved to Pontotoc, a settlement in the heart of Chickasaw country, in 1835. Over time, Thompson amassed considerable wealth through both his legal practice and his marrige to Kate Jones, the daughter of a well-heeled landowner.

The Mississippian Thompson embodied the essence of the era's plantation owner. He possessed scores of slaves, and after election in 1839 he served as a Democrat in Congress for twelve years. Throughout his tenure, rumors of corruption hung like clouds over him, though eventually, as a genuine supporter of President James Buchanan, he ascended to secretary of the interior, a station he filled until he resigned in 1861 because of corruption charges and the subsequent scandal that infiltrated the Department of the Interior.

Still interested in the fate of his beloved North Carolina, the ardent politician moved on to the Confederacy when war came, and served as an aid to Gen. P. G. T. Beauregard until just after the Battle of Shiloh. After the two-day battle, April 6–7, 1862, which claimed nearly twenty-four thousand lives, Thompson became the inspector of troops for Gen. John C. Pemberton, serving in that capacity until July 4, 1863, when Vicksburg, "The Gibraltar of the Confederacy," fell.

With adequate time served on the front now snug in his pocket, Thompson returned home to Oxford, Mississippi, a minor celebrity. The people gamely elected him to public office. But Thompson was barely inside the door of the state legislature when Jefferson Davis asked him to head to Canada to direct the network of spies, a mission that Thompson readily accepted.

Jefferson Davis and Jacob Thompson got along famously. The first meeting between the Confederate president and the hard-line secessionist lasted well into the night hours. Certainly Davis was impressed with the fifty-four-year-old man who spoke fluent French and Italian. Thompson's remaining ties to former business associates in the North were an added dividend, the hope being that the remnants from his legal days would serve him well when he combed the northwest region for possible associates who might consider Confederate employment. Davis concluded the interview with a set of broad instructions. He provided Thompson with an enormous amount of leeway to finance whatever operations he chose, granting Thompson and his group large sums of money to further the cause in whatever manner they saw fit.

In a letter to Thompson, Davis wrote: "Confiding special trust in your zeal, discretion and patriotism I hereby direct you to proceed at once to Canada, there to carry out the instructions you have received from me verbally in such manner as shall seem most likely to come . . . to the furtherance of interests of the Confederates." The first piece of the Confederate–Canadian headquarters was in place.

★ ★ ★

Alabama Attorney Clement Claiborne Clay, Jr. stood next in line for an interview with Davis. An educated man, Clay spoke the language of politics most eloquently. With the help of his wife, Virginia Clopton Clay, he cultivated a very smooth, refined manner that transformed him into a consummate politician and opportunist who mixed among the upper crust of Southern society and became a fixture on the Washington and Richmond party circuit. Though Clay counted Jefferson Davis as one of his friends, the Confederate president thought he would be more suited to the position of second-in-command.

Clay, a slave-holding, states'-rights Democrat, had been elected to the U.S. Senate just like his father, Clement Comer Clay. The younger Clay served there from 1853 to 1861, and, after Alabama seceded, won a seat in the Confederate States Congress, where he served from 1861 to 1863, at which time he lost his bid for re-election.

Throughout his life, asthma and other undefined illnesses—some real, some imagined—plagued Clay, and others held him in low regard on account of it. It was not uncommon, despite his socialite reputation, for Clay to be described by peers as irritable, cranky, impatient, feverish, impulsive, or peevish. "Commissioner Clay's health at the time of his appointment was of itself enough to disqualify him from the important service with which he had been charged," said Hines on one occasion.

Clay had always secretly coveted either a Cabinet post in the Davis administration or a European posting. Although he was never appointed to either, he felt that good performance in Canada would bode well for his future with Davis. But while Davis regarded Clay as merely a good man who was difficult to decipher, many others considered the career politico to be an obvious sycophant.

"Early in the spring of '64, Mr. Clay felt it his duty to accept the high responsibility of a diplomatic mission to Canada, with a view to arousing in the public mind of this near-by British territory a sympathy for our cause and country that should induce a suspension of hostilities," wrote his wife Virginia. "Despite the failure of our representatives in European countries to rouse apathetic kings and dilly-dallying emperors to come to our aid, it was hard for us to believe that our courage would not be rewarded at length by some powerful succour, or yielding."

Before making his way to Canada, Clay complained to his wife: "I am on my way to Canada. It is a very difficult and delicate duty for which I am not suited by my talents, tastes or habits. I cannot enjoy secret service."

Perhaps Clay simply pined for the South—and for his wife, with whom he enjoyed a devoted marriage. His departure for Canada left her heart in threads: "When the parting came, the shadow of impending evil fell so blackly on my soul, I hastened away from disturbed Petersburg, accompanied by my faithful maid, Emily, and her child, determined to act upon Mr. Clay's suggestion and seek my kin in Georgia."

While Clay would work away in relatively favorable Canadian conditions, Virginia would spend 1864 much worse off in their plantation home in South Carolina. As Mrs. Clay detailed in her memoir, the colder months found the Confederacy depleted of everything "edible or wearable." "Delicately bred women were grateful when they were able to secure a pair of rough brogan shoes at one hundred dollars a pair, and coarse cotton cloth from the Macon Mills served to make our gowns. For nearly three years the blockade of our ports and frontier had made the purchase of anything really needful, impracticable. . . . There is a perfect reign of terror in Memphis. Not even a spool of cotton can be purchased without registering your name and address, and 'swearing it is for personal or family use.'"

Furs and silks were now the stuff of dreams for the Belles of the South, so Virginia began to request countless luxuries from her husband headed abroad. "Bring me at least two silk dresses of black and purple. I prefer the purple to be moiré antique, if it is fashionable. If French importations are to be had, bring me a spring bonnet and a walking hat, for the benefit of all my lady friends as well as myself, and do bring some books of fashions."

Comforts were long gone in the south. Pins and needles had been replaced with locust thorns, stationery with wallpaper, and ink with sifted soot scraped from chimney walls mixed with water and vinegar. Even basic sustenance was hard enough to come by, as there was "scarcely a smoke-house in the South having an earthen floor, which had received the drippings from the hams or bacon sides of earlier days, but underwent a scraping and sifting in an effort to secure the precious grains deposited there," she wrote. Although Clement Clay may not have been looking forward to his impending duty in Canada, others such as his wife, trapped in the South, would likely have leaped at the chance for a recess from their daily existence.

The third member of the trio was James Holcombe, a former professor of law at the University of Virginia. More scholar than spy, the spare man preferred black suits and never voyaged without his slim, red-leather-bound book of poetry. Unlike Thompson and Clay, Holcombe would never factor into the Canadian operation to a significant degree. Though he might have been the most intellectual of the three commissioners, he was deficient in experience. He was still an acting professor when Judah Benjamin asked him to travel to Halifax to find ways to wrangle the return of escaped Confederate soldiers to the front lines down South.

With the three commissioners having agreed to their new stations, they set off for Canada, carrying with them their nation's dying hopes.

★ ★ ★

In early May 1864, Thompson and Clay, and another man named William W. Cleary, who had joined the group as the mission's secretary, traveled to Canada aboard the steamship *Thistle*. Holcombe had set off independently and would join the group in Montreal.

The *Thistle* was a 636-ton iron side-wheeler steamship built in Glasgow, Scotland in 1863. (She operated as a blockade-runner until June 4, 1864, when the U.S.S. *Fort Jackson* captured her. Ironically, the *Thistle*, renamed the U.S.S. *Dumbarton* in August 1864, would serve as a blockade *enforcer* on Virginia's James River during February and March 1865.) Like the life of the *Thistle*, the trip of Thompson, Clay, and Cleary had its share of adventure. Constant pursuit by a Union gunboat failed to prevent the completion of their voyage between Wilmington, North Carolina, and St. George, Bermuda; and when the *Thistle* finally arrived at the island, a Union Jack in the port fluttered its greeting. In relieved response, the men hoisted the Confederate flag.

St. George's harbor crawled with Confederate agents and naval officers who used Britain's island ports both for storage and for transport. The blockade business boosted the local economy, transforming the sun-faded ports into vibrant, free-wheeling, free-spending places at which to anchor. Gamblers and speculators alike came in droves, and the people of Bermuda didn't particularly mind, appreciating their Southern guests and the business they brought.

"St. George's [the name of the Bermuda island on which the town of St. George was to be found] became not only a harbor of refuge, but a pleasant resting place after the excitement or fatigue of an outward voyage. Crates marked 'merchandise' jammed W. L. Penno's warehouse. Kegs of 'nails' and cases of 'combustibles' filled J. W. Musson's warehouse."

On the eve of the Civil War, the Federal Navy had primarily been a deep-water fleet. Most crews of the time did not have adequate training, proper boats, and equipment for fighting on the shallow waters of inland rivers. The Confederates fared no better—they had no Navy even to whisper about. Change came fairly quickly, however, when Lincoln, with the guns of Fort Sumter still warm, ordered Navy ships to be stationed outside all Confederate ports.Almost as immediately, Confederate Secretary of the Navy Stephen Mallory applied pressure for the building of Confederate vessels and the acquisition of others from Britain.

Soon, suppliers in England were trying to ship goods directly to Confederate ports; but such unfettered trade wouldn't last long, as the Federal Navy, now positioned off the coast, legally seized the ships and cargoes. Consequently, the Rebel-bound ships attempted to prevent confiscation by calling on Caribbean ports such as Nassau or St. George, but ships were still frequently captured by Federal craft wise to the game. According to established law, the island layover did not constitute a break in a ship's continuity of travel between a neutral port and a belligerent port. All told, about five hundred Federal ships enforced the coastal blockade, which covered about thirty-five hundred miles from Maryland to Mexico, while smaller Union boats patrolled the Mississippi River from Cairo, Illinois, south to the Gulf of Mexico.

The commissioners in Canada and government officials in the South soon found that moving people, documents, and materials was no easy feat and hurriedly developed methods of bypassing the Federal craft strung like triple strands of pearls up and down the East Coast. The structure of the Union blockade positioned smaller ships, known as picket boats, to patrol inshore and fire rocket signals when a potential runner tried either to enter or to exit a harbor. At the sight of a flare, any warships in the immediate area would converge on the renegade boat. Failing that interception, Union ships regularly patrolling a few miles offshore would then give chase.

The principal way to skirt the blockade involved relying on British ships to ferry goods and people to the islands, primarily Nassau, Bermuda, and Havana, which cargo was then relayed to Confederate ports. Once supply boats had anchored in these Caribbean ports, crews transferred the loads onto small, fast blockade-runners, which were better equipped to reach the besieged Confederate ports.

Although there was a fair amount of boredom for officers and sailors assigned to blockade duty, it had its swashbuckling moments. When possible, the blockade-runners slipped out of harbor on moonless nights or under poor weather. Painted gray, with telescoping smokestacks to further cloak their shape, the small, swift boats moved like phantoms on the water.

Many of the blockade-runners sprinted to and from Wilmington, North Carolina, toward the waning days of the war. The city, twenty-eight miles up the Cape Fear River, was a choice site for blockade-runners, and the port was the last one to be closed by the Union. From there, the craft, vital in keeping Gen. Lee's army supplied, only had to make it to and from Bermuda, 674 miles off the coast, which had become the principal island headquarters for boats sailing to sustain the Confederacy.

If a boat carried goods, such as guns, ammunition, or clothing, its route most likely originated in Britain, then led to Halifax, Bermuda, or Nassau, and then to a final destination of Wilmington, Charleston, or Savannah.

If people comprised the cargo—diplomats, soldiers, spies—the blockade-runners followed different routes, from Nassau or Bermuda to Halifax or Great Britain. Or ships crossed the Potomac to the Maryland shore and thence to Baltimore, from where the human cargo could take the train to Buffalo and Niagara Falls, or pass through New York City to Montreal. The Canadian network further disguised the channels of transfer from which they benefited by setting up a shell company, B. Weir and Co., that looked after travelers and ships running people and materials to them.

The blockade never completely stopped Southern trade with foreign countries, but it did curtail—immensely—food and clothing shipments for civilians, and arms and ammunition supplies for the military. The arms and ammunition that Jefferson Davis had purchased on preblockade shopping sprees had long since been depleted. Running the blockade was a frantic dash, and the commissioners of the Canadian operation that would rely so heavily on the runners saw it firsthand as they set foot in St. George.

In making their way to Canada, commissioners Thompson and Clay and secretary Cleary planned the best course of action to combat the Yankees along the asymmetric lines soon to be available to them. Thompson would manage the money for the most part and would accordingly play the decisive role in forming strategy and allocating funds. From the beginning, Thompson decided that he would sanction only operations with a clear political aim. He refused to approve military operations without a political component, and common ideas such as setting fire to villages just for the sake of revenge did not meet his parameters. According to Thompson, they needed "to adopt measures to cripple and embarrass military and naval stores. . . ."

After the brief respite in Bermuda, the group resumed their travel, boarding the British steamer *Alpha* on May 19, hoping to reach Halifax without trouble. On the journey, Thompson and

Clay's brittle relationship started to crack, largely because Clay fell ill and took to bed for ten days. Annoyed, Thompson and Cleary traveled ahead to Quebec without Clay, and finally to Montreal, where they arrived on May 29. The inability of the commission to work together smoothly began with their voyage to Montreal.

Thompson's hand on the purse and Clay's repeated complaints of illness furthered the two men's mutual dislike, and at times they were barely on speaking terms. The passive Holcombe, having arrived independently in Montreal, would never quite figure in the equation. Ill-suited for his role, he seemed more content to leaf through his book of poetry than to formulate strategy with any passion.

Off to a shaky start at best, Thompson and Holcombe held a brief meeting before setting themselves to work. On May 30, Thompson and the already-in-place Thomas Hines, who had met up with the commissioners and Cleary in Montreal, left for Toronto, where they would rent rooms at the Queen's Hotel. Shortly thereafter, Holcombe decided to join Thompson and Hines, leaving the arriving Clay as the lone commissioner in Montreal. To facilitate operations, bank accounts were opened by the commissioners in Montreal and at the Bank of Ontario in Toronto.

With the command structure in place, Rebel agents continued to stream into Canada under new organization. New faces included Beverly Tucker, formerly of the U.S. consulate in Liverpool, who had served as a Confederate agent in Europe at the war's outset and then as an official in Richmond for a time after that. His assignment in Canada was to help ship supplies from Canada to the Southern lines.

Cleary, though technically still the mission's secretary, proved that his specialties were hardly limited to steno and dictation.

Cleary had begun to occupy himself with weapons procurement from Montreal, frequently traveling to New York to purchase guns, ammunition, and the ingredients to manufacture the so-called "Greek Fire."

Greek Fire was a clear liquid chemical mix that resembled water but smelled like rotten eggs. The explosive compound came stored in four-ounce glass vials and was designed to explode in a sheet of flames when thrown against a surface. Once Cleary had procured the necessary supplies, he would mix the goods in Canada and repackage the materials in boxes bearing the words "prayer books," which were stenciled on the outside. Cleary would then send them back across the border to the Midwest for use in attacks behind Union lines.

Aside from Cleary, R. C. Bocking, a chemist from Cincinnati, was another member of the Canadian network who contributed to the development of Greek Fire. He not only produced the explosive brew but actually developed explosive devices with delayed-action fuses.

By the fall of 1864, Greek Fire was being produced in earnest in Windsor, Canada West. Tracking down contraband soon occupied much of the Union intelligence service's time, and dispatches in 1864 would detail a concerted effort on the part of U.S. authorities to piece together the players involved with its manufacture and distribution.

"I have the assurance that 'Greek Fire' is being prepared in Windsor, Buffalo, Cleveland and this city will be the principal cities to be burned, and there will be armed attempts to rob and plunder. Cincinnati and Louisville are also mentioned," reported a Col. R. Hill on December 3, 1864 from Detroit. "I am also informed that by some means a large number of Rebel soldiers have been introduced into Canada, some it is said, have been furloughed, and have made their way through the lines."

Another agent working out of Canada was a smiling devil of a man with Kentucky charm to spare, George N. Sanders. Before setting a leather-clad foot in Canada, Sanders had traveled extensively throughout Europe and consorted with many people who American society considered radicals. Sanders's large personality espoused the overthrow of monarchies and the preservation of slavery. He embraced drama and savored recognition, claiming that Davis had authorized him to negotiate an end to the war in 1862.

Born on February 12, 1812 in Lexington, Fayette County, Kentucky, George Nicholas Sanders was a meddler, a collector of people. In 1843, Sanders had organized a political meeting at Ghent, Kentucky to try to cull a position on the annexation of Texas from potential presidential candidates. Not only did the meeting help shine a spotlight on James K. Polk; it also helped vault Sanders onto the national stage.

Together with his father, Lewis, he imported and bred short-horned cattle and thoroughbred racehorses. Throughout his stormy career, Sanders would be seen cavorting with the likes of Victor Hugo and Giuseppe Garibaldi in Europe while leading the controversial "Young America" movement back home.

The Young America movement had its heyday between the early 1850s and the beginning of the Civil War. President Franklin Pierce supported it, largely to draw attention from the prickly issue of slavery. Sanders's role was to spread the idea of American democracy, not only in the United States but also overseas.

President James Buchanan had appointed Sanders U.S. consul to London in 1851, before which he had been serving as a Navy agent in New York under Pierce. While in London, he made waves for trying to garner support for an armed American takeover of Cuba from Spain. This plan, known as the Ostend Manifesto, found its way into the notice of the public and, for that, Sanders was recalled.

On November 6, 1860, Sanders addressed Republicans in New York on the issue of the looming war. "Few of your party are, I believe, disunionists even in theory; many of you would not continue a line of policy intentionally driving off the Cotton States, if in the abandonment of such policy you surrendered nothing which you possessed, nor compromised your honor. All that the union men of the South ask of you, is to let the South alone. Why then drive her to desperate acts, making her feel her independent power, and then retorting to her just complaints, that this over-shadowing North will not be 'bullied'?"

An air of mystery draped this unofficial member of the commission. Tall, wealthy, and debonair, he possessed many traits that resounded with the bevy of beautiful women often seen in his company. "He [Sanders] sees everybody, talks to everybody, high and low. . . . He is one of the most adept wire-pullers in the United States," said the London *Times*.

The ubiquitous busybody fast became a burr in Thompson's rigid side, although Sanders's flamboyancy did enliven Clay's staid ways. A veritable manipulator of Confederate agents, the spy played many of his associates like marionettes, particularly Clay, who came to demand Sanders's presence at all meetings.

Even so, Clay never completely trusted Sanders, despite falling under his spell. He aired his skepticism in a June 17 letter to Judah P. Benjamin: "George N. Sanders is at Niagara Falls, representing himself as sent by our government to encourage peace. He actually talked to my informant of calling a peace meeting of citizens of the US and CS to devise joint action for that end. I hope he will not do so silly a thing, but wish he were in Europe, Asia or Africa." Nevertheless, while residing in St. Catherines, the two did develop a close working relationship, as Sanders roomed at the Clifton House just a few doors away from where Clay boarded.

A pretty hotel, the Clifton House boasted spacious, well-appointed rooms. Next door stood another hotel, the Table Rock

House, which adjoined the Niagara Falls Museum, Canada's first museum, which had opened in 1827 featuring curator and founder Thomas Barnett's cabinet of curiosities. Barnett had renovated a former brewery to showcase his collection of mostly mounted animals. But the collection slowly grew, spurred by the wonderful addition of three mummies from Egypt procured by Barnett's son Sydney. Each day, the museum opened its doors attracting large crowds of tourists keen on seeing mummies and mastodon remains.

This steady crowd offered the perfect cover for Confederate agents looking to meet unnoticed in rooms where plots could be whispered in darkened corners, with Japanese and Chinese relics, fossilized eggs, and other animal trophies the only witnesses. It was in these surroundings that Sanders meddled in all aspects of Confederate politics, going so far in one instance as to offer Britain and France future rights of free trade with the South in exchange for immediate financial aid.

The man had many ideas, some quite outlandish and most never officially sanctioned by Richmond. Perhaps his most notable scheme was his effort to organize a peace conference, in July 1864, which was ultimately designed to embarrass President Lincoln. For this plan, Sanders managed to obtain the approval of Clay and Holcombe, who helped lay out the details of the proposed conference. Horace Greeley, editor of the *New York Tribune,* involved himself as well, inducing Lincoln to list terms for peace: an end to hostilities, a return to the Union, and an end to slavery.

Upon receiving the invitation, Lincoln made sure to have the talks investigated. General John A. Dix sent Col. Ambrose Stevens, head of the secret service in the New York region, to go to the Clifton House. Stevens donned civilian clothing and circulated undercover among the Confederate agents, the so-called "Copperheads" (Northern citizens who opposed Lincoln's war policy), and other Southern sympathizers. Stevens reported to Dix that many Confederates were in fact talking about trying to murder Lincoln before the November elections, and consideration was promptly withdrawn.

Holcombe, however, wrote to Benjamin on November 16, 1864, regarding his role in the failed peace conference, as well as that of Greeley. Holcombe sought to dispel speculation that the peace conference was a ploy to kidnap Lincoln.

"Sir: I desire to submit to you, as the head of the department to which I am directly responsible, and under whose control they should, if possible have been conducted, the history of certain transactions in which I was engaged whilst in Canada, but which did not fall within the scope of my duties assigned me by the president. . . . Certain editorials which appeared in the *New York Tribune* early in June, connected with intimations from our friends in New York, induced a hope (which with me has ripened into an abiding conviction) that the able editor of that influential journal entertained opinions upon the subject of peace much more reasonable and moderate than those of the Republican party in general. . . . Nothing could be further from the truth than the statement of our ingenious friend, Dr. Mackay, in his letter to the London *Times,* that we laid a trap to catch Mr. Lincoln."

Whether the ultimate aim of the conference was assassination, kidnapping, or something altogether different and innocent, it wasn't the only thing to keep Lincoln from heading to the Niagara Falls region. Thompson, Clay, and Holcombe had no power to negotiate on behalf of the Confederacy as a whole, and as such they were diplomatically impotent in the eyes of Washington. Whatever political designs the men had, they were fast coming to the realization that their direct influence in the arena would be meager at best.

★ ★ ★

The men's efforts were better directed to building their network. Perhaps as one of his more tangible contributions, at some point Sanders recruited an exotic woman named Sarah Slater. Far from just another one of the pretty faces seen with Sanders, Slater was a cunning spy whose mystique still clouds the history of the time.

Sarah Slater, née Gilbert, was born in Connecticut but moved as a small child to New Bern, North Carolina, with her father and two siblings. Known as "Nettie" in the South, Sarah spoke fluent French, a skill bequeathed to her by her Parisian mother. A sylph, she provided a vital link between the Confederates in the South and the Confederate beehive in the North, often working under the assumed name of Kate Thompson.

Slater's fluency in the French language helped her connect Richmond and Montreal, between which Secretary of War James A. Seddon had recruited her to carry messages, papers, and currency.

On her first mission, in which she delivered monies to Canada, a Confederate agent in Maryland escorted her as far as New York City, where she acted, with a veil draped over her face, as if she could speak only French, throwing in some broken English for good measure. From New York, she made her way alone to Canada and successfully completed what would be the first of many assignments to come.

Whatever Slater was carrying, she likely secreted it on her person in the manner that many other female Civil War spies did—either in her hoop skirt, in her corset, in a bun of wound hair, or on the backs of buttons—all knowing that men of the day were loath to search a woman. Messages and military secrets were sewn with silk into the linings of their cloaks and sleeves so as not to rustle or crackle under searching fingers.

Most of the women working as spies belonged to the upper social strata. They were intelligent, many were quite religious in their views, and most of them were not motivated by pay but rather by deep-seated beliefs regarding their cause.

Sanders and Slater ran a host of operations together and separately and were part of a burgeoning infrastructure that was now humming over land and sea between the South and Canada. However, despite the many actors now engaged in the grand Confederate act, the commissioners had yet to pinpoint a satisfactorily significant undertaking that matched their capabilities and capacities.

As the summer of 1864 progressed, Hines and the others arrived at yet another ambitious proposal, though at the very least this idea was grounded in the reality that the Canadian operation was not itself an overt political actor. The plan suggested that an overthrow of the Lincoln government could potentially succeed if the Copperhead movement developed an armed faction. The movement, a semisecret order of Northerners, favored peace on the grounds that the war was illegal, that conquering the South was impossible, and that the loss of lives and money could not be justified.

The group changed its name several times before settling on one. The term "Copperhead" reportedly first appeared in the fall of 1861, when Ohio Republicans began likening anti-war Democrats to the venomous snake that sneaks and strikes without warning. In 1862, Republicans began using the term to describe the entire Democratic Party; but by around 1863 a faction within the anti-war movement began embracing the moniker, rather than hiding from it. Some Peace Democrats even took to sporting badges decorated with the face of the Goddess of Liberty that was originally engraved on the copper penny. Peace Democrats were a rather powerful factor in weakening the

Northern war effort, but not so much in strengthening the anti-war faction in the South.

Largely based in the northwestern part of the Union, the Copperheads adamantly opposed Gen. Grant's strategy of "total war," disgusted by practices that would result in the complete destruction of the South. They wanted the Union restored to its antebellum status, slavery and all, and longed for a status quo that had been defined by peace between the states.

The Confederates couldn't help but smell possibilities. Although the Copperheads' public position was all about saving the Democratic Party, internally many wished to organize non-combatants in the North into a military force. Many Confederate agents believed that they could channel these beliefs and help along such a transformation.

Between 1863 and 1864, the Copperheads grew more radical and began to destroy government warehouses and military installations, while stepping up activities that came to include surveillance, arson, and even murder. Clement L. Vallandigham was the leader of the movement, having become the Grand Commander of the Sons of Liberty in 1864. Vallandigham was born in New Lisbon, Ohio, on July 29, 1820. Before the Civil War, he was a lawyer and editor of the *Dayton Empire* and also served as an Ohio state legislator and U.S. Congressman from Ohio.

From Canada, Thompson offered direct aid in the form of money and arms to help Vallandigham's efforts. Some estimates gave the Sons of Liberty eighty-five thousand members in Illinois, fifty thousand in Indiana, and forty thousand in Ohio. Thompson saw unlimited upside in an association with the Copperheads, and he assumed that Vallandigham would surely find uses for his support.

George Sanders was also pursuing the Copperheads during this time. A low profile just had no place in Sanders's life, so it wasn't long before Thompson learned that Sanders was also talking with Vallandigham. The news didn't make him smile. "George Sanders has come to see Vallandigham. He has come from abroad Europe to do what he says he did not know we were intended to do, and he has gone on to do it. There is such a thing as spoiling the broth by having too many hands in it."

Sanders had a way of meddling that didn't always produce favorable outcomes, and Thompson was territorial when it came to political overtures. Ultimately, whether because of Sanders or because of ineffectiveness on Thompson's part, Vallandigham turned down the Confederates' offers.

Though not in business with the Confederates, and perhaps frustratingly to them, Vallandigham and his work would not go unnoticed. One of his most audacious appearances came at the Democratic National Convention in Chicago on August 29, 1864. The prominent Copperhead wanted to carry out a "revolution in the northern part of the United States," and he quickly found that his kind of speech earned a man jail time for sedition. Lincoln would eventually commute the Ohio native's sentence, but banished him to the South all the same.

Northerners like Vallandigham inspired many Southern soldiers. A Pvt. Sprake, who served in Company A, Eighth Cavalry Regiment of the Kentucky Volunteers, was no exception. The soldier had already been in prison since July 1863, but in his carefully penned diary he wrote in August 1864 about the Chicago convention where Vallandigham made an appearance: "A great crowd gathering at Chicago to be present at convention delegates arriving, the largest crowd it is said ever assembled. Peace is their cry. A great many speeches are being made by different distinguished gentlemen. Vallandigham is the big gun, but McClellan will be the nominee. . . . The platform according to my thinking means anything you want. It protests against the use of arms to restore the Union and argues in favor of state sovereignty."

Yet, for all its bravado, the Canadian network never quite succeeded in pushing the Peace Democrats to action. In all, the Copperhead movement was a snake without venom. They were inherently opposed to war and would not strike their own government wholeheartedly, no matter how much they disagreed with its policies.

★ ★ ★

At the end of the summer of 1864, Holcombe finally left Thompson and Clay, departing from Halifax for Europe. But Holcombe, finding himself aboard the ill-fated *Condor*, would never reach the old country.

The *Condor* had three stacks, and of the seven forerunners to the iron ships, she was the largest. In September, the *Condor* and its forty-five crew members sailed to Halifax to retrieve Holcombe, newly arrived via Niagara Falls. Mrs. Rose O'Neal Greenhow, the "Wild Rose," a famous Confederate spy, joined him on board, having recently returned from Paris where she had been a guest of Emperor Napoleon III and Empress Eugénie.

Rose Greenhow was widely held as a fascinating character and as a legend in her own time. She believed passionately in the Confederate cause and had earned her reputation after successfully sending a secret message, filled with enemy troop information, to Gen. Beauregard during the Battle of First Bull Run. The Confederate triumph in the battle prompted Jefferson Davis to give Greenhow full credit for the victory.

Though the entrance of this widow into covert life soon landed her in jail, nothing could foil her clandestine activities. Even from prison, Greenhow, the mother of an eight-year-old daughter, ensured that pertinent information reached the right eyes and ears, using various methods to conceal her communiqués, sometimes winding them inside a woman's chignon.

After her second stint in jail, Lincoln exiled her to the Confederate states, a punishment about as effective as jail in silencing the unusually outspoken spy.

After her release, the mother-turned-spy-turned-raconteur sailed for London to publish her tell-all memoir, *My Imprisonment and the First Year of Abolition Rule in Washington.* When Greenhow boarded the *Condor* with Holcombe in September of 1864, she was carrying the money she had earned from the book, a reported $2,000 in gold, around her neck in a leather bag.

While the ship departed with Greenhow and Holcombe aboard, Secretary of State Seward received word that the *Condor,* fully loaded with supplies, intended to sail for North Carolina. Seward passed the information to Secretary of the Navy Gideon Welles, who relayed it to Acting Rear Admiral S. P. Lee. In charge of the North Atlantic Blockading Squadron, Lee put the Union fleet on high alert. The *Condor* eventually tried to enter New Inlet, North Carolina, but the U.S.S. *Niphon,* a wooden-and-iron steamer, was there to give chase.

Augustus Charles Hobart-Hampden, a.k.a. Samuel S. Ridge, who commanded the *Condor,* attempted to outrun the *Niphon* and sail under the protection of the Confederate guns at Fort Fisher. But Ridge couldn't do it; and with the *Niphon* closing in, the pilot took a hard starboard turn and slammed into a shoal. The *Condor* nearly crashed into the wrecked hull of a blockade-runner that had been destroyed the night before. Although the guns of Fort Fisher held the *Niphon* at bay, huge waves crashed against the *Condor* and broke it apart as if it were nothing more than a set of loosely bound matchsticks.

Amidst the commotion, the willful Greenhow demanded that she be allowed to go ashore in a small boat. Reluctantly, Ridge granted her permission to take a lifeboat together with Holcombe, the pilot, and two seamen. The lifeboat, tossed by the breaking waves, capsized and sank, and the Wild Rose, weighed down by the purse of gold hanging from her neck, drowned. A Confederate soldier later found her and relieved her body of the gold, but a fit of conscience would compel him to return it to the authorities.

Rose O'Neal Greenhow received full military honors at her funeral. Holcombe, on the other hand, managed to survive the disaster and moved on to advise President Davis in Richmond, unable to make his desired journey to Europe.

As Holcombe settled back in the South, Thompson, Clay, and the remaining leadership in Canada continued to exploit any political opportunity that existed or that could be created in the early fall of 1864. They desperately needed to erode the wills of Yankee civilians who continued to support the war.

The secret agents in Canada had no shortage of money to spend. While some of the funds came from the Davis government, much of the money came from the sale of contraband cotton and the robbing of Northern trains and Federal army-payroll funds. Aside from using the funds to prepare for military action, the Canadian operation also invested in Northern newspapers to buy sympathy and sway public opinion. There were a number of efforts to bribe certain editors. Phineas Wright, editor of the New York *Daily News,* agreed to influence public opinion for a tidy cash sum of $25,000.

Other monies were thrown to political campaigns in the hopes of propelling sympathetic candidates into office. In one case, the commissioners channeled money into the campaign of James C. Robinson, the Peace Democrats' candidate for governor of Illinois; and still another plot involved an attempt to buy actual votes in New York State.

The sub rosa political endeavors of the Canadian operation were worthy undertakings, yet the kind that, by 1864, seemed too little, too late. Even in Toronto and Montreal, Confederates could feel the noose tightening around the South, and pressure was building for more daring and decisive military action. One of the network's newest members, a lieutenant named Bennett H. Young, had much to say on the matter.

6

Young Vigor

★ ★ ★ ★ ★ ★ ★ ★ ★ ★ ★ ★ ★ ★ ★ ★ ★ ★

After his escape from Camp Douglas in 1863, it took Bennett Young several weeks to make his way back to the South. To go south, one had to go north, and traveling the circuitous route of the blockade slowed him. Young traveled to Halifax and soon boarded a blockade-runner that would ultimately deposit him in North Carolina.

As his ship fell under the shadow of the Union-held coast, guns fired at the steamer as it entered the Cape Fear River. As the bullets found their mark, the lookout refused to stay in position; Young took his place without hesitation and "gave the signal to the Captain and remained in the position of peril until the steamer was safely under the guns of Fort Fisher."

The tumult of the journey endured, Young finally arrived in Richmond with the hope of rejoining his old unit to resume his role in the fight against the Yankees. But this wasn't to happen. Young hadn't been in the Confederate capital for long when Secretary of State James Seddon tapped the soldier for duty in the Confederate Secret Service, promoting him to the rank of first lieutenant.

Seddon favored a long moustache with a goatee-type beard. He was born in 1815 in Falmouth, Virginia, and went to law school at the University of Virginia at Charlottesville. He passed the bar exam in 1836 and then served as a representative from Virginia. Though of a different stock than Young, he recognized the soldier's capacity for courage and daring, and he encouraged the government to find other plans for the energetic, resourceful young man.

Seddon ordered Young "to proceed without delay by the route already indicated by you and report to C. C. Clay for orders. You will collect together such Confederate soldiers who have escaped from the enemy, not exceeding twenty in number that you may deem suitable for the purpose and execute such enterprises as may be indicated to you."

When word reached the Southern contingent that Bennett Young was coming their way, they likely sighed in relief. After all, Young had served with John Hunt Morgan and had been schooled in the dual arts of subterfuge and swift incursions. The commissioners were desperately seeking a victory, and Young's arrival proclaimed possibility in a time when defeat seemed to cling to the Confederate Army like mud from a swamp.

For the Canadian contingent, there were few intelligence coups worth mentioning. The plan to burn Chicago had fallen apart; although some saboteurs had seen to it that individual Federal transports had gone up in flames, they were never able to completely cripple supply lines; Capt. Beall's plan to take the U.S.S. *Michigan* and to free prisoners on Johnson's Island had come to a less-than-stellar ending, with the ship damaged but operable and Beall sentenced to death; and Copperhead leaders had been arrested, exiled, or even executed and were effectively prevented from further agitating against the Union.

This spate of bad news meant that it was high time to try a new strategy. The commissioners needed a plan to replace flagging enthusiasm for the war with hope, and to relieve pressure on the men in gray by turning Union attention elsewhere. After

Young called on Clement Clay in St. Catherines, he went to Montreal to meet the rest of the commissioners.

Clay and Young hit it off straightaway, and Young's determination impressed the commissioner. During these first meetings with Clay, Young suggested ways and means to harness the skills of escaped prisoners of war and sought to devise plans that would alter the course of the war.

On August 20, 1864, Seddon sent Young a cipher dispatch with instructions to scout towns along the Canadian–U.S. frontier that would be most exposed to attack. "It is right that the people of New England and Vermont especially, some of whose officers and troops have been foremost in excesses and whose people have approved of their course, should have brought home to them some of the horrors of such warfare." (U.S. Congress, House Judicial Committee Report, 39th Congress, 1st Session, Vol. 1, No. 104 has instructions in cipher dispatch.) The Yankees would eat from the same dish of suffering on which the Southerners had dined for years.

Southern anger over Sheridan's orders to burn the Shenandoah Valley and Sherman's destructive march across their lands infuriated Southerners, to say the least. It shouldn't have come as a surprise to those in the North that their enemies would want them to be similarly victimized.

The largely open border between Canada and the United States seemed to simply beg the Rebels to launch an attack. The terrain promised easy access to Union territory—so easy, in fact, that in winter one could walk across the St. Clair River to Detroit; and in summer one could sail a boat across Lake Erie or Lake Ontario. Furthermore, when the Confederates did venture across the border into northern towns, they could easily pass themselves off as Canadians. After combing through the countryside of northern New York and Vermont, Lt. Young settled on St. Albans. It was in a perfect location; furthermore, most of St. Albans's men were down South fighting the war.

The raiders would be able to easily infiltrate St. Albans in small groups by road, train, and boat. Locals never paid much heed to the comings and goings of strangers, because St. Albans was a trade town located near the border. They would blend in seamlessly, and Young knew that he and his men would not arouse suspicion. As a juicy bonus, the town's three banks were situated within a block and a half of each other around the town green. The town's proximity to the Canadian border would allow for a quick escape after the deed was done; and in the unlikely event that anyone from the town did give chase, Young assumed that Canada would most definitely offer legal protection.

"St. Albans will merely be the starting point, the inauguration of a system of warfare which will carry desolation all along the frontier," George Sanders said. "There will be war to the knife and to the hilt. They will be made to think 20,000 men wait in Canada, across the border, eager and prepared. The towns will burn and be pillaged."

The very thought of this military operation excited Sanders and Clay most of all. "Burn the town and sack the banks," Clay said in an early meeting about the raid. The suggestion for a lightning attack on Yankee ground had always resonated with Sanders, and Young found himself an immediate ally and sympathetic ear. Earlier that summer, while at the Clifton House, Sanders had tried to persuade Thomas Hines to stage bank heists in Niagara and Buffalo, New York, but Hines had scratched the suggestion, thinking that such a mission would endanger the ability of the commissioners to operate in neutral Canada.

But once Sanders latched on to the idea, he wouldn't let go, and he was soon channeling his efforts through Young. The two agreed that the idea of robbing banks and delivering terror to the North was most appetizing, and both saw the strategic possibility of forcing the Federals to reposition their troops as particularly appealing.

However, Commissioner Jacob Thompson, acting like the group's governess, instantly stifled any enthusiasm for a raid into Vermont. He favored instead a proposal to free prisoners in Camp Chase near Columbus, Ohio, and he selected Young to lead the mission.

Like a good soldier, Young immersed himself in this new plan, putting the idea for the Vermont raid to the side for the time being. The dashing officer told Thompson and Clement Clay that he required at least thirty men to successfully break out the thousands of prisoners corralled behind the Ohio walls. At midnight, according to the plan, Young and his men would ambush the Camp Chase arsenal, which stood roughly four miles from the barracks. Once arms were secured, the men would then head for the prison grounds. Any guards would be killed, and all of the prisoners would be liberated. Afterward, the group would gallop to the Confederate lines on horses stolen from stables in neighboring Columbus.

This audacious plan never came to fruition. Many of the recruits were not only poorly qualified, but they never even showed up for the mission. In addition, the Federals had discovered the plot before Young's horse even started trotting toward Ohio.

Bennett Young quickly grew tired of failure. He was also growing weary of carrying out someone else's plans. After two unsuccessful bids to free prisoners, the Kentuckian pursued his own plan with renewed vigor. Desperate to make a mark on the war, he persuaded the commissioners to let him not only execute the raid on St. Albans but to plan it as well.

As disastrous as the Camp Chase liberation scheme had been, Young learned some valuable lessons. The idea of collecting horses and arms and ammunition from the very towns targeted for attack was valid. Young had also deplored the quality of the men assigned to work with him on the Camp Chase mission, and this time he would cherry-pick his men, just as his mentor, John Hunt Morgan, had done.

Motivations for joining with Young included the deeply entrenched hatred of the Union held by most young Confederates. But the hatred was not even so much a question of protecting a station in life, even that of the lowest farmer above an African–American, or of preserving the states' rights with respect to slavery; no, much of the hatred stemmed from the fact that Southerners deeply felt that their way of life was superior to that provided in the North—that their society was distinct, much more refined and elegant than the brutal North. They often described Yankee opponents as tricky, deceitful, and slick. The propaganda spread stories of atrocities, of a heartless and soulless army. Stories fluttered throughout Rebel camps of Union snipers who would pick off Confederate soldiers in the act of caring for wounded Federal troops. Other stories reached Southern lines of Union soldiers who would perfunctorily slit the throats of prisoners rather than take them to camp. All these tales helped fuel the desire of Young's recruits to strike.

Now settled on the plan for an attack on the town of St. Albans, Vermont, on September 20, Young wrote to Clay from Hamilton, Canada West: "I will see you probably no more ere the attempt is made. I hope ere long to gratify you with a report of success. All told, I have about twenty-seven men. I hope to make it thirty. . . . I will never return, Mr. Clay, until I have done something. If nothing else, may I destroy the northern border of Vermont and New Hampshire for 150 miles?"

Now with the supposed backing of commissioners, Young looked in earnest for recruits. He sneaked across the border into Chicago during the Democratic convention, where Southern soldiers were already mingling in the crowds, trying to stir up anti-Lincoln sentiment. It was among these men that Young found a crew ready to risk everything in the name of the Confederate States of America.

"I owe no allegiance to the so-called United States but am a foreigner and a public enemy to the Yankee Government," justified Thomas Bronsdon Collins. "The Yankees dragged my father from his peaceful fireside and family circle, and imprisoned him in Camp Chase, where his sufferings impaired his health and mind." Collins, twenty-nine, a commissioned officer in the Confederate Army, had actually served with Young under Gen. John Morgan. His father was a Baptist minister; like his father, Thomas Collins also held strong religious convictions. With his strong military bearing, imposing height, and dark eyes, Collins epitomized the ideal recruit.

Another motivation for men to join Young was a common one of the time, perhaps best expressed by one Robert C. Kennedy, who would be hanged in March 1865 for his role in an attempted firebombing of New York City, to which Kennedy confessed shortly before his execution. His confession, read by Col. Martin Burke during the Lincoln Assassination Conspiracy trials on May 29, 1865, expressed a sentiment shared by many a St. Albans raider: "I wish to say that killing women and children was the last thing thought of. We wanted to let the North understand that there were two sides to this war, and that they can't be rolling in wealth and comfort, while we at the South are bearing all the hardships and privations. In retaliation for Sheridan's atrocities in the Shenandoah Valley, we desired to destroy property, not the lives of women and children, although that would of course, have followed in its train."

For the most part, Young's raiders came from "excellent" rich Kentucky families, and their good looks and charisma impressed almost everyone. George Scott was a picture of an elegant ladies' man, svelte and loyal to the South; Caleb McDowell Wallace of Kentucky had quite the political connections—his uncle was

John J. Crittenden, a U.S. senator, attorney general under Presidents William Henry Harrison and Millard Fillmore, and governor of Kentucky; Alamanda Pope Bruce had a distinguished air and manner of speech; James Alexander Doty enlisted as a private on September 15, 1862 in Company A of the Sixth Kentucky Cavalry at Perryville, Kentucky; Marcus Spurr rode with the Kentucky 8th Cavalry Regiment and came from Jessamine County in Kentucky; Samuel Eugene Lackey had roots in Lincoln County, Kentucky, and had served under Gen. Morgan before being captured in Ohio and escaping from Camp Douglas; and, while short, James Doty exhibited great physical force, even if he was a tad impetuous. Young selected elite men with whom he shared similar attributes and a common upbringing.

His team coalescing, Young had begun to test the vulnerabilities of the buzzing St. Albans. During one of Young's reconnaissance forays while he was still based in Montreal, he had the occasion to visit the home of Governor John Gregory Smith himself. Young told Smith and his wife Anna that he was a theology student from Montreal. The young man had always enjoyed a reputation with the ladies, and this was certainly no time to turn off the charm. Quite taken with Young, Anna Eliza Brainerd Smith graciously escorted him about the mansion and its beautifully kept grounds, taking care to point out the stables. She found him to be "a nice mannered man."

"Their manners were peaceable, and under pretence of a desire to hunt in the wooded parts of the country, they borrowed or bought fire-arms and ammunition," wrote Anna Smith, recalling their encounter. "For a week these advance scouts . . . were studying the habits of the people, the situation of the banks, noting the livery stables and other places where horses were kept, also examining the more prominent residences."

After culling the necessary information, Young didn't linger. He departed for Canada, eager to share his findings with Clay, hearing the screams of terrorized Vermonters in his head. When Young returned to Montreal, he reported to the commissioners, all of whom had gathered together to hear the findings. The elegant lieutenant drew the assembled men a detailed picture of a town practically devoid of fighting-age men.

Outlining his plan, Young explained that rather than riding into St. Albans as one group on the day of the raid, he and the men would journey in small groups over the last few days preceding the actual attack. Young had already mapped the distances between the key targets: the Fuller Livery stable was near the American House, which would make stealing horses on-site as easy as pinching apples from an orchard; and of course the three banks, now the principal targets of the raid, as mentioned earlier, were situated within a block and a half of each other around the town green.

George Sanders was pleased with the information, and he thereafter considered St. Albans a marked town. "They know how defenseless the town is. They know there are no firearms of any account in town and what there are [will be] little account against a sudden attack of men thoroughly armed with the best of revolvers."

Inspired, Young continued to select men for the mission. Most of the would-be marauders were between twenty and twenty-six years old, with only two members of the band being older: Joseph McGrorty, known as "Grandpappy," and Charles Higbie. Higbie often boasted of his escapades with William Clarke Quantrill, the notorious, nearly psychopathic Southern soldier who had slaughtered nearly two hundred unresisting men and boys in Lawrence, Kansas, in 1863 (among Quantrill's vicious riders were Frank and Jesse James). Raiders like Higbie wanted to give the Yankees "a taste of what Sheridan gave us!"

This kind of specious reasoning pervaded the thoughts of all the raiders. If Sheridan was guilty of what the Southerners claimed, military crimes against civilians, then the proper course of action would have been to first win the war, and then prosecute Sheridan as a war criminal. Instead, they had decided to simply replicate his crimes for simple revenge, thus making themselves war criminals.

On October 6, Clay issued Young a check for $1,400 to cover the cost of the attack. Clay also told Young that if anything went wrong and they were arrested in Canada after their escape, he'd be sure to spring them from jail within twenty-four hours. He never proposed, however, a course of action that he would take if they were apprehended on the U.S. side of the border. Meanwhile, Young made it a point to tell Clay that whatever money he took from Vermont banks would not line his, or any of the raiders', pockets, but would be turned over to the government, or at least to its representatives in foreign lands.

"This, I approved . . . my instructions to him, oft repeated, were to destroy whatever was valuable, not to stop to rob; but after firing a town he could seize and carry off money or treasury or bank notes, he might do so on condition that they were delivered to the proper authorities of the Confederate States," Clay later wrote to Benjamin.

Before descending into Vermont, Young and William Huntley Hutchinson, accompanied by two other raiders, registered under assumed names at Leonard Hogle's hotel in St. Johns, Canada East for a few days. While there, they received newspapers from St. Albans that helped to provide a sense of the town and its populace, and they inquired as to the relative distances of Frelighsburg and Philipsburg, two Canadian border towns, from St. Albans. When the time came to depart for St. Albans, the men split up and traveled under assumed names.

Over the course of several days, the twenty-one men of the Southern raiding party slipped across the frontier and checked in to the town's three inns. Each day, two or three more men arrived until the whole gang was on the scene. Young had been among the first to arrive in town, by way of the Montreal Express, and he checked in at the American House. Hutchinson, who had registered under the name of J. A. Jones, left on the five o'clock train at Rousse's Point, a spit of land jutting into Lake Champlain.

The men told townspeople they were horse traders, vacationers, fishermen, English tourists seeking peace and quiet, invalids in search of health, or members of a Canadian sportsmen's club on the hunt. Friendly and engaging, the men joshed with the locals. When registering at the American House Hotel, Thomas B. Collins told the desk clerk, George W. Roberts, "I'm Jefferson Davis." The clerk and those in the lobby laughed at the preposterous joke. Had they only known the truth, they likely wouldn't have been so hospitable. Young later chastised Collins for this attempt at humor, quite properly concerned that the slightest misstep could cost them their cover.

Bennett Young moved from American House and, with Squire Turner Teavis and William Hutchinson, took up lodging at the Tremont House, which had been built in 1820 on North Main Street. The five-story building had just been purchased by its proprietor, S. W. Skinner.

James Alexander Doty, Joseph McGrorty, Marcus Spurr, and Caleb M. Wallace took rooms over at the St. Albans House on Champlain Street, built in 1840, telling its owner Willard Pierce that they had come to town to partake in outdoor sports. Thomas Collins, Charles Moore Swager, and Samuel Simpson Gregg registered down the way at the American House, which had been constructed in 1815.

While Young rehashed and refined the plan from inside his quarters at the Tremont House, he left ample time to cultivate a friendship that would help his cover and make his sojourn in St.

Albans all the more pleasant. A certain young lady, also lodging at the Tremont House, had caught the eye of the young Southerner. Like many single New England women at the time, Sarah Clark and her friend Margaret Smith, who shared a room with her, had left their family farms to find jobs in the better-paying mills. Each morning, Bennett Young greeted both women on his way to breakfast, and the three would cross each other's paths with frequency in their comings and goings.

Early one evening, Sarah came upon Young reading aloud in his room and, pausing in the narrow hallway outside the door, heard Bible scripture passing from his lips. Her interest in the well-mannered, polite, clean-shaven man quickened. Chatting with the house clerk, Sarah Clark learned that the impeccable gentleman named Bennett H. Young was a divinity student from St. Johns, Canada. His friend, the gruff-looking older man, was William Hutchinson, also from St. Johns.

It wasn't until the third day that Young summoned the nerve to actually speak with the two young ladies. He invited Sarah, whom he had described as "pretty, with a sweet smile," to dine with him the following evening at the American Hotel, considered the finest restaurant in town. During dinner and the days that followed, the pair spent many hours together sharing meals, discussing the Bible, and walking about the village. Miss Clark would point out places of interest in St. Albans, and together the couple would sit in Taylor Park and enjoy the fleeting autumn. The color had begun fading from the elm trees that bordered the green and, unless the snows came first, the grasses would soon turn pale brown.

★ ★ ★

The Union had an inkling of Young's plan, thanks to an earnest young man named Richard Montgomery. Montgomery worked as a clerk in Washington, D.C., during the summer of 1864, where he volunteered for secret service; he was soon sent to Richmond under the alias James Thompson. "Thompson" convinced the Confederate Secret Service that he was the most capable man to carry messages between Richmond and St. Catherines, Canada; and throughout the rest of the war, Montgomery/Thompson worked this route, always stopping in Washington on his way north to brief his handlers. The Union was receiving intelligence chatter that the Confederates were planning to raid Vermont, as well as vulnerable towns in New York; yet, because officials in Washington never learned precisely which town lay in the Confederate sights, they took only half-measures.

Meanwhile, the Southern invaders continued to comport themselves with immaculate manners and neat dress. They did not openly associate with one another. They carefully masked their Southern accents. They aroused not one whit of suspicion as they gathered further intelligence, trying to ascertain what resistance, if any, they might face.

The hurdle of blending into town now cleared, Young and his crew needed to know what kinds of weapons the St. Albans residents had and in what conditions those weapons might be. Each raider had for himself a Navy six and plenty of ammunition.

The "Navy six" was the Colt Navy revolver. Samuel Colt of Hartford, Connecticut, manufactured this handgun and others. He had made about a hundred and fifty thousand .44-caliber six-shot revolvers. The Navy model was a .36-caliber introduced in 1851; it was a favorite of cavalrymen like Bennett Young. Most of Colt's guns went to the Union; but many made their way south, even after Colt stopped selling to the region a few days after Fort Sumter.

After posing as hunters in search of additional firearms, Thomas Collins and Joseph McGrorty concluded that few weapons of quality were to be had in town. Duly noted, however, were the strong and capable men working in the railroad shops and in the St. Albans foundry, just a few hundred feet to the west of the green on Champlain Street. They could pose a resistance and the raiders wouldn't have enough men to watch them; but if the attack were executed quickly enough, the workers could be kept at bay. As far as having enough horses for escape, there would be no problem; raider James Alexander Doty reported "a goodly number of horses."

While keeping their distance from one another during the day, the band of twenty-one managed to trade intelligence by night, dining together inconspicuously or in seclusion.

The "Vairmont Yankee Scare Party," as some in Young's band called their mission, would be a coordinated operation, intended to hit the town's three major banks. Thirteen of the twenty-one would loot the banks: five at the American, four each at the Franklin and the First National. That would leave four raiders to filch horses, one to help whichever group might come up short-handed, one to oversee the prisoners on the green, and two to throw Greek Fire. Young allotted fifteen minutes for the entire operation, intent on riding out of town no more than twenty minutes after they had begun. On the night of October 17, as six of the party dined at the Tremont, all the raiders prepared themselves for the next day—the day they would shake the foundations of the Union home front.

★ ★ ★

Clouds and drizzle masked the sunrise on Tuesday, October 18. The weather was hardly a problem for the young but seasoned soldiers, but the unexpected throngs of people in the streets were. It was Market Day—or, as the locals called it, Butter Day.

Area farmers selling produce and peddlers hawking all kinds of wares crowded the green. They came from as far away as

Canada and from as close as the next town over. Young and Hutchinson, caught unaware, walked the streets of the town, moving from store to store and passing through the crowds with any number of window-shoppers. Now and again they paused to converse with other men who had just arrived in town on the train. With the sudden inflation of the male population of St. Albans, prospects for the day quickly faded.

Young had no choice but to call off the attack. He would wait one more day, until October 19, when the streets would be calm, the visitors gone, and the banks filled with cash.

7

The Vairmont Yankee Scare Party

★ ★ ★ ★ ★ ★ ★ ★ ★ ★ ★ ★ ★ ★ ★ ★ ★ ★

The rain sluiced down on October 19, 1864, drenching the entire swath of land from the north end of Lake Champlain to southeast of the Green Mountains and beyond. The muddy roads sucked in wagon wheels; in houses all across town, woodstoves burned to ward off the damp, aching chill.

"We have had a month of rainy weather. Our expectations were excited this morning that we were about to be blessed with fair weather. The sun appeared this forenoon, and shone bright for some time. It was generally supposed that the equinoctial rains were over. But this afternoon it is as cloudy and dark as ever," wrote Judge James Davis in his diary.

Anna Smith had sent a manservant gathering wood on the morning of the raid. "Wood from the surrounding forests was superabundant. It was hauled sled length into the back yards, chopped or sawn into proper proportions, split and stored in ample sheds," she recollected thirty years later.

An empty quiet had descended on Main Street; the last peddler had packed up and gone with the previous day's nightfall. The trees, now nearly bare, stood as sentinels along the streets. Governor Smith and County Sheriff Renesselaer R. Sherman, along with most of the town's remaining men, had left to attend either the legislative session in Montpelier or the court opening in Burlington.

All morning, the raiders waited in their respective hotels. Finally noon announced itself and the Southern gentlemen passed the time over a final St. Albans meal. Around 2:30 P.M., when the last napkin was laid on the table and the last chair pushed in, the twenty men reported to their assigned positions. Several of them gathered outside Bennett Young's door at the Tremont Hotel. As they then entered the room, they happened upon Young kneeling in prayer. He quickly rose, keen on reviewing the plans one last time. Then, one by one, the men from the hills of Kentucky walked out of the room and down the stairs.

Although some in the group acted as if they were about to embark on an exciting adventure, Young remained preternaturally focused on the task at hand. Any traces of the flirtatious theological student had long since evaporated.

Shortly before three o'clock, Young stood on the wet steps of the American Hotel. Flanking the hazel-eyed horseman stood some of the other raiders, each of whom wore a pair of Navy sixes belted on the outside of their clothes. Young turned toward his fellow soldiers as if to receive their silent benediction for what they were about to do.

He then faced the civilians who happened to be on the street, and, without mincing words, told them he was an officer of the Confederate Service come to take the town.

Upon hearing those words, the few passersby—farmers and other local residents—stopped midstep. Surely the man in the long gray coat had a strange sense of humor. Some probably even laughed. After all, the nearest battlefield lay about six hundred miles to the south.

But with Young's words, and with guns now drawn upon them, all the citizens were ordered to move to Taylor Park, the town green, and they were to remain there until further notice.

During one of Bennett Young's outwardly innocent strolls with Sarah Clark, he had realized that the grassy parcel of land would serve nicely as a holding pen. One or two of his cavalrymen could easily guard it—and his assessment was borne out as the townspeople huddled together, offering little if any resistance once on the green.

When some of the townspeople hesitated, Young pulled the trigger on his Navy Colt. There is nothing like a few pistol shots in the air to sober a crowd.

"The citizens now realized that the exhibition was not a joke," recalled resident John Headley many years later.

Until this moment, war had always been a distant scourge. Battles were names printed in the *St. Albans Daily Messenger* or described in letters home. No one in St. Albans had ever seen a Confederate soldier—save for those who had served. Really, the only uniforms they had seen were those worn by their own boys and men.

"I never saw a mob in St. Albans armed the way they were, with one of their members proclaiming himself an officer in the Confederate service. I have never seen any of the Confederate troops. I have never seen Confederate troops in active service," said George Roberts, a clerk in the American House.

Roberts had been standing on the steps of the American House when he watched Young take over the town. He followed his neighbors to the green, where Alamanda Pope Bruce guarded everyone for about ten minutes.

Four raiders who had been waiting in a line charged forward, the Rebel yell on their lips. James Doty rode in on horseback from the yard of the American House. About twelve others, on horseback, also approached from the yard of the American House, armed with at least two revolvers each. As they went for the banks, they began taking any horses they saw in the streets.

As the clock struck three times, Sarah Clark walked out of the Kingman Store, just a few doors down from the Tremont House. She saw Bennett Young, clad in a plum-colored shirt, a coonskin hat, and a coat, charging his horse down Main Street with three other riders just behind. He brandished a gun in his right hand, bellowing to all: "We are Confederate soldiers!" Sarah ran inside the Tremont House, never again to lay eyes on her Southern sweetheart.

St. Albans Bank

Now the war barged through the door of the St. Albans Bank on the corner of North Main and Bank Streets. It came in the person of four men: Thomas Collins, Marcus Spurr, Louis Sutton Price, and Squire Turner Teavis.

Cyrus Newton Bishop, the bank's chief teller, was standing behind the counter, sorting money, when the armed men barreled through. At first, he believed the rough-looking men were customers, but their drawn pistols immediately changed his mind. Bishop hurried into the back office to warn Martin A. Seymour, who was poring over the ledgers. Suddenly, one of the robbers threw open the door, striking Bishop smack in the middle of his forehead. "If you stir or make any resistance, we will blow your brains out."

Meanwhile Samuel Breck, a merchant in the enterprise of Weatherbee and Breck, walked over to the bank to make a deposit. He noticed that the doors to the St. Albans Bank were locked. He knocked on the door. There was no answer. He knocked again. This time Teavis opened the door and pushed his gun into Breck's face.

"I take deposits," he said. Then Squire Teavis grabbed Breck by the shoulder, pulled him inside, and said: "Give me money or I'll shoot you. I am a Confederate soldier." He took four hundred dollars from Breck's pocket. Bishop, tied up in the back, heard this and called out "Breck, we are caught; you had better give it for." Breck needed no further convincing.

"Not a word," the menacing soldier breathed. "We're Confederate soldiers detailed from General Early's army to come north, and to rob and plunder as your soldiers are doing in the Shenandoah Valley."

Another knock sounded on the heavy wooden door. One of the raiders opened the door to find a young telegraph operator, holding a package of money in his hands, standing before him. Staring at the guns now pointed at him, the young man decided he'd rather leave. Unfortunately for him, the raiders couldn't have disagreed more. They ordered the shaking operator to stay put and told him that if they found him working in the telegraph office later, they'd shoot him on the spot.

"They compelled him to sit on the bed that was in the room, giving him to understand that if he did not, they would shoot him; and he, in consequence, remained," said Benjamin.

The Rebels prodded, harassed, and threatened the bankers some more. They fancied gold. Martin Seymour refused to reveal where on the premises the gold was stored. Spurr said he'd "put a bullet through his head" if Seymour continued to keep his silence. But Collins, acting with a somewhat cooler head, said: "Forget the gold." Instead he ordered Cyrus Bishop to open a small vault. Inside lay several sacks of the bank's silver and stacks of money wrapped with paper bands that were marked with the signature of Abner Forbes, the Vermont Central Railroad cashier.

The robbers lustfully stuffed their pockets and satchels. Barely sated, the Rebels took off with more than $80,000. Fortunately,

Seymour's pleas had distracted the robbers long enough that they overlooked about $50,000 in cash and $50,000 in new St. Albans Bank notes. They actually left more money in the bank than they took. The robbery lasted all of about twelve minutes, and Hiram B. Sowles, the bank president, set to work on posting a $10,000 reward for the capture of both fiends and funds.

"There was a rank atmosphere of alcoholic fumes about the robbers," Martin Seymour would later tell the local newspapermen for the evening edition of the *St. Albans Daily Messenger.*

Before leaving the St. Albans Bank, the four Confederates bullied their victims one last time, forcing them to stand against the wall, to raise their hands and solemnly swear to obey and respect the Constitution of the Confederate States of America. They told the men not to fire on them or anyone of "that government [the Confederacy] and not report the robbery until two hours after they had left." The three trembling men stayed put— for a moment.

Once the bank seemed all clear, chief teller Bishop stepped outside. From the sidewalk in front of the bank, he saw several men on horseback, riding in a northerly direction. Bishop saw what he estimated as between twenty-five and thirty men shooting at the citizens, many of whom were women and children.

"This party to which I referred was dressed in civilian's dress, and so also were the five persons who committed the robbery in the said St. Albans bank. They presented nothing in their appearance or dress to lead to the belief that they were soldiers, unless it was their possession of revolvers," Bishop said.

Around a quarter past three, Charles Alexander Marvin, a clerk in town, was standing across the street from the bank, on the step of his brother's store. He happened to see Doty astride an ebony horse. "The armed party all rode off together on horseback about twenty minutes after I first saw them; they seemed to be in great haste, and appeared all to act in concert together, and as one party."

Franklin County Bank
Though working quickly, the Rebel raiders made certain nonetheless to sow the seeds of terror in the minds of the citizens. They proclaimed that hundreds, if not thousands, of likeminded villains waited at the border, ready to swoop into town. As mentioned, some raiders said they were part of Gen. Jubal Early's army, whose sole mission in St. Albans was supposedly to avenge Sherman's march through the South and Sheridan's destruction of the Shenandoah.

"We are Confederate soldiers, Sir. There are one hundred of us in town. We have come to rob the banks and burn your town! We are going to do it!" roared William Huntley Hutchinson. That morning, Hutchinson, clad in a dark, amply cut coat, had topped his head with a narrow-brimmed small black hat. Now he purposefully entered the Franklin County Bank. Daniel Butterworth, Dudley Moore, and John Moss followed in his wake.

Inside, blissfully unaware for just a moment more of the mounting pandemonium outside, James Saxe and Jackson Clark, a wood sawyer, conversed before the glow of the woodstove. The cashier, Marcus W. Beardsley, was attending to James Russell Armington, a twenty-seven-year-old merchant. Acting like a patient customer, Hutchinson waited until Armington completed his transaction before he approached Beardsley. He actually had the temerity to inquire about the price of gold. Armington and Saxe left the bank. Now the robbers drew their weapons and said that they were but four of hundreds of Confederates who had come to raid the North.

Beardsley and Clark tried twice to escape. Pistols pushed against their heads changed their minds.

"I will blow your brains out if you stir another inch," Hutchinson said. The raiders locked them inside the walk-in vault. Already full of fear, Beardsley and Clark complained of being imprisoned with no air. Beardsley started whimpering, fearful that he would either suffocate or be burned alive if the raiders set fire to the bank. Huntington had no tolerance for sniveling of any kind: "You are treating the people in the South in the same manner."

The shouts penetrated the thick walls of the vault. Fortunately, Armington and Dana R. Bailey heard the ruckus and reentered the bank. They worked in vain to open the door, though their nerves were obviously frayed—the key was right there, rattling in the lock. The Rebels were gone, off with around $75,000 worth of greenbacks, St. Albans notes, and other currencies.

The First National Bank

Meanwhile, over at The First National Bank of St. Albans, Albert E. Sowles, the cashier, busied himself while eighty-two-year-old Gen. John Nason rested in the corner, newspaper in hand.

General Nason had come to St. Albans as a mere slip of a lad in 1796 with his father William, his mother, and four sisters. They had come from Epsom, New Hampshire, carrying all their belongings on four sleighs and one ox team. Nason liked to tell the story of how it took them seven days to make the journey. At the time, people still lived in log houses, similar to the one Jesse Welden had built in the southern part of the town. John Nason would grow up and serve his state and country in the War of 1812. These days, when the rain came, the octogenarian often liked to keep company with the clerks in some of the banks, warming himself before the hot stoves and reading the *St. Albans Daily Messenger*.

Perhaps Nason daydreamed about the time in 1838 when he had been stationed with the local militia along the border to help prevent hostilities from breaking out between Canada and the United States. In January 1838, the United States voiced its commitment to neutrality regarding the struggle for independence taking place in Canada, and in February a force of about six hundred French Canadians crossed Lake Champlain into Vermont and then up into Lower Canada. They declared their independence from Britain but were soon forced back from the United States, and their leaders were promptly arrested. Nason likely assumed now that he'd meet death before seeing another day of military conflict.

The doors flew open. "You are my prisoners," boomed Joseph McGrorty upon entering the bank. "If you offer any resistance, I will shoot you dead. We represent the Confederate States of America, and we come here to retaliate for acts committed against our people by General Sherman. It will be of no use to offer any resistance, as there are a hundred soldiers belonging to our party in your village. You have got a very nice village here, and if there is the least resistance to us, or any of our men are shot, we shall burn the village. These are our orders, and each man is sworn to carry them out."

James Doty, Alamanda Pope Bruce, and Caleb McDowell Wallace stood behind him like a wall. Quite deaf, Nason spent the entire time of the robbery sitting in the bank's reception area reading his newspaper. For some reason, that annoyed one of the raiders, who wanted to "Shoot the old cuss." Showing some restraint, the others forbade him.

At that very moment, William Blaisdell entered the bank, interrupted the robbery, and without a word violently attacked one of the raiders. The other three quickly overpowered Blaisdell and ordered him taken to Taylor Park. It wasn't until the Southern soldiers prepared to leave with Blaisdell that Gen. Nason looked up and muttered: "Two against one isn't fair," before turning to resume his reading.

Ignoring the old man, the raiders ordered Sowles to unbolt the vault. Sacks and sacks of coins filled the space like the treasury of King Midas.

"What is in here?" demanded one of the raiders.

"Cents," answered clerk Sowles.

McGrorty leaped over the counter and furiously began emptying the small chamber. He managed to stop for a moment and slash open a few of the cloth sacks; sure enough, pennies tumbled out and clattered across the floor. The raiders absconded with about $55,000—in their haste leaving behind the one and only sack containing gold pieces.

Quiet filled the room as soon as the robbery ended. Nason looked up for the third time that morning and said: "What gentlemen were those? It seems to me they were rather rude in their behavior."

Outside on the street, raider Caleb Wallace met William Blaisdell and his rather gruff escort and promptly put a gun to Blaisdell's head. Blaisdell thrust the pistol away, grabbed Wallace around the neck, and threw him hard to the ground. The two wrestled in the rain-slick street. Two other raiders, who had been in the First National Bank, came to rescue Wallace. They shouted at Wallace to shoot Blaisdell. The Confederates cocked their weapons and threatened to kill Blaisdell unless he released their friend. Blaisdell did, though reluctantly.

End of the Raid

Standing across the street, watching the raid unfold, stood Capt. George S. Conger. The brief bit of impunity that Young and company had enjoyed so far was just about to expire. Conger saw before him the townspeople, forced onto the green, some with revolvers pointed at their heads. A flurry of commotion swirled as raiders scrambled to snatch horses, while any townspeople not on the green ran for cover and safety as firearms discharged around them.

Conger, only nineteen, had served with the Vermont First Cavalry in 1861 and 1862. He came from a house divided, with his brother fighting on the side of the Confederacy after having moved to Tennessee prior to the war. Conger had returned to his parents' home on the outskirts of St. Albans after resigning his commission.

Just as the raid began, Conger happened to enter the northern part of the village from the east, driving a wagon pulled by two horses. He watched a group of men and horses in the road near the southern end of Main Street. His attention was quickly drawn to another man approaching on a fast-moving horse. Conger got down off his wagon.

The rider called: "What is going on? There are men with pistols taking horses from the stable!"

Conger, armed with a breech-loading carbine, walked quickly in that direction. On the way, he met Bennett Young. The leader of the raid asked Conger if he was a soldier. The captain denied his service to buy more time.

"Get with the other civilians on the green," Young ordered, waving a raider forward to shepherd him. Conger broke away and sprinted through one of the hotels, out the back door, down the steps, and down Lake Street, shouting "Raid! Raid! We have a lot of raiders upon us. Let us catch them!"

Loren Downing raced toward Conger, carrying a rifle in one hand. He passed it off to the captain in one fluid motion, as Conger turned up Main Street in pursuit of Bennett Young. He saw the brown-coated Rebel, stopped in his tracks, and took aim. The rifle jammed. Young and Charles Higbie fired three times at Conger but missed with each attempt as Conger darted for cover.

Meanwhile, Collins Hickox Huntington left his jewelry store determined to pick his children up from school to whisk them away from the madness. Huntington had just passed the Franklin

Bank when he arrived at the crosswalk in front of American House. He ran into Young, who ordered him to Taylor Park. Huntington walked past him in silence.

"If you don't go, I'll shoot ye," Young said.

"No! You won't shoot me," challenged Huntington, taking a few steps.

A shot rang out. The ball pierced Huntington near his spine and burrowed some six inches through his back and side. By grace, it was a minor flesh wound. Somehow, Huntington managed to cross the road to the town green, where the townspeople-turned-prisoners bandaged his torso.

All over town, citizens scrambled to react to the attack unfolding before them. The plain brick façade of the new St. Albans Academy stood opposite the town green. Inside, Dorsey Taylor, the principal, presided over the third-floor assembly. Suddenly the sound of shouts and gunshots pierced the walls. Principal Taylor hurried the children to their home rooms, trying his best to reassure his charges: "Little dears, wicked men have done very bad things here. Now do as you are told. Go down the stairs quietly to your rooms." Curious and excited, the students watched the raid with noses pressed against the windows. Some even tried to sneak outside and watch the events from the schoolhouse steps.

Leonard Leandre Cross, the town photographer, also heard the ruckus and ventured out of his house. He watched as the party of armed men moved through the village streets on horseback, with their revolvers waving in the air. They were strangers, with the exception of Young, whom Cross later testified he had seen in town once before this day.

"What are you trying to celebrate here?" called Cross.

"I'll let you know," Young said, firing his revolver. "Come out; let every one of you walk out into the street." Cross looked on as Young then ordered a raider to throw Greek Fire into store owner Victor Atwood's building. The raider threw a bottle, or something made of glass, against the sign over the door of the building. Young said then: "Boys, march up the street, there is too great a crowd gathering round here." He started off and fired again at Cross. The bullet sailed over Cross's head as he dove back indoors.

★ ★ ★

The day's events were particularly jarring to the people of St. Albans since the assailants had freely lived and moved among them while pursuing their nefarious ends. Most of them had used their own names, merely fabricating their personal background just enough so that no one questioned the influx of twenty-one young men of fighting age into town. The men had been so subtle that even Anna Smith, the governor's wife, had not yet connected the engaging student who had arrived on her doorstep just a few weeks before to the events of the day.

In the years of war, Anna busied herself with household chores, caring for an infant, and finding housing in Massachusetts for her son who would soon be attending Phillips Andover Academy.

During the summer of 1864, she had actually accompanied her husband to Washington, D.C., where she had had the chance to meet Secretary of War Edwin M. Stanton. Years later, she wrote an article for *The Vermonter* about the occasion: "His piercing black eyes, unusually large, and his grand, stern mien somewhat awed me, but his words were courteous and his manner reassuring."

That evening in D.C., Stanton had invited the Smiths to dine. During the meal, Stanton had asked Anna how the war affected those in Vermont. As she recalled it for the paper, "Not very seriously. Things go on much as usual. Of course, we are intensely anxious, but it is only as we hear of the wounding or death of some acquaintance, that the reality is forced upon us."

"Ah," said Mr. Stanton, "I fear it is so, the people don't pray enough." He added with emphasis, "They eat and drink, they marry and are given in marriage, forgetting the mortal throes in which the nation is struggling, the horrors of war and its tearful uncertainty."

She would later offer an account of the raid's tumultuous events in a letter she penned to her husband. "We have had, to use cousin Joe's forcible expression, a 'raid from hell.' For about a half an hour yesterday afternoon I thought that we should be burnt up and robbed . . . but I hope you don't imagine I was one moment frightened, though the noise of guns, the agitated looks of the rushing men, and our powerless condition were startling enough."

At the time of the raid, their eldest son, George, was boarding in a home near Phillips Andover. The Smiths' coachman was in Burlington for the day on business; and the gardener had left for the cider mill, bearing a load of apples, accompanied by ten-year-old Edward. Some distance away, the farmhands were harvesting potatoes.

Anna worked around the house, performing chores with one hand while balancing her baby on her hip. All of a sudden, a servant girl rushed in from a neighbor's house. "The Rebels are in town, robbing banks, burning the houses, and killing the people. They are on their way up the hill, intending to burn your house," she cried.

Anna Smith knew that Union troops had recently burned the homes of the governors of Virginia and Georgia. She had every reason to believe that the Confederates intended to torch her house.

Though poor in quality, this rare photo shows a youthful Bennett H. Young, the twenty-one-year-old Confederate soldier who would lead twenty-one men on a daring raid of St. Albans, Vermont. *Courtesy of the St. Albans Historical Society, St. Albans, Vermont.*

After serving honorably in the Vermont First Cavalry, nineteen-year-old Captain George Conger led the posse that captured Bennett H.Young just over the Canadian border. However, Young didn't remain Conger's prisoner for long. After a confrontation with a British soldier, Conger had to release Young into British-Canadian custody. *Courtesy of the St. Albans Historical Society, St. Albans, Vermont.*

While this photo has faded over time, it provides a rare glimpse of the raiders and their co-conspirators, Rev. Stephen Cameron, who helped secure evidence of James Seddon's orders to raid St. Albans, and George N. Sanders, who helped devise the plot. Back row, left to right: Rev. Stephen Cameron, George Scott, Squire Turner Teavis. Front row: William H. Hutchinson, George N. Sanders, Bennett H. Young. *Courtesy of the St. Albans Historical Society, St. Albans, Vermont.*

After the Civil War, Thomas B. Collins lived in Belgium and France. He had served with Company F of the 11th Kentucky Cavalry before joining Bennett H. Young. *Courtesy of the St. Albans Historical Society, St. Albans, Vermont.*

Raider Marcus A. Spurr escaped from Camp Douglas before joining Bennett H. Young on the infamous raid. *Courtesy of the St. Albans Historical Society, St. Albans, Vermont.*

Raider James A. Doty
was twenty-four years
old when he raided St.
Albans. *Courtesy of the
St. Albans Historical
Society, St. Albans,
Vermont.*

A native of Kentucky, twenty-one-
year-old Squire Turner Teavis
served with Company B, 11th
Kentucky Calvary. Like many of
the raiders, Teavis rode with
General John H. Morgan. *Courtesy
of the St. Albans Historical Society,
St. Albans, Vermont.*

At the age of thirty-seven William Hutchinson was the "grandpa" of the raiders. He had previously served with Company H, 4th Georgia Infantry. *Courtesy of the St. Albans Historical Society, St. Albans, Vermont.*

President Jefferson Davis & Clement C. Clay, Jr., one of three Confederate commissioners, were incarcerated in Fortress Monroe after the Civil War. After their imprisonment the two returned south. *Belle of the Fifties: Memoirs of Mrs. Clay of Alabama—Virginia Clay-Clopton.*

Montreal Police Chief Guillaume Jean-Baptiste LaMothe helped arrest the raiders. Yet when Judge Charles-Joseph Coursol dismissed the charges during the first trial, both he and LaMothe were investigated for their rather close relationship with the Rebels. *Courtesy of the St. Albans Historical Society, St. Albans, Vermont.*

In 1903 Bennett H. Young had established himself as a sort of keeper of the facts regarding Civil War history. *Courtesy of the St. Albans Historical Society, St. Albans, Vermont.*

Bennett H. Young was once asked to visit St. Albans to mark the anniversary of the raid, but after many townspeople protested the idea he quietly declined the invitation. *Courtesy of the St. Albans Historical Society, St. Albans, Vermont.*

Until his death in 1919, Bennett H. Young resided in Louisville, Kentucky, where he practiced law and became a renowned orator. Here he is seen at the unveiling of a Confederate monument in Arlington, Virginia, 1914. *Courtesy of the Library of Congress.*

Lord Lyons worked closely with Secretary of State William Seward to ensure that tensions among Canada, Britain, and the United States would not erupt during the aftermath of the St. Albans raid. *Belle of the Fifties: Memoirs of Mrs. Clay of Alabama— Virginia Clay-Clopton.*

"Our great danger was only too apparent," Smith recalled later. "There were no men on the premises, my daughters were too young for aid or counsel, perceiving something dreadful had happened they began to cry."

The peril of the situation actually steadied her nerves. Together with another servant, Emma Inglis, a Scottish girl, Anna Smith kept her house calm. They bolted the doors and drew the curtains and blinds. Inglis wondered if they should flee the house, but Anna said no, figuring that the Rebels might notice and then set fire to the house.

"My first impulse was to run up the flag [so] that if we went down it might be with flying colors, but realizing the rashness of such an act I desisted," Anna wrote.

She hunted for weapons upstairs and downstairs. Her search yielded one rifle and a single pistol, but no ammunition. She stepped out onto the front porch with the unloaded pistol, just hoping that the mere sight of her with a pistol would intimidate any raider inclined to approach.

Standing guard in front of her house, she glimpsed a horseman galloping up the hill. Anna thought he was part of the raiding party; but, in fact, the rider was none other than her brother-in-law, F. Stewart Stranahan, who was home on sick leave. He served on Gen. George A. Custer's staff in the Army of the Potomac; had he not been home, he surely would have been fighting his way through the woods of Cedar Creek, Virginia, that very day. Stranahan told her that the raiders were soon to be heading north and that he needed arms to assist the posse that would be assembled to chase them. She gave him the pistol. "If you come up with them, kill them! Kill them!" she called, as he flew away.

Once Stranahan left, Smith walked over to the stable. She found a cluster of residents hiding in the stalls. They told her that while the raiders had stolen many horses from other stables, those belonging to the Smith family hadn't yet been touched. This led Anna to give Stranahan's growing posse her horse, Major, and three others for the purpose of tracking down the raiders.

Continuing to do what little she could, Anna scoured her house and discovered another rifle, which she took with the intention of heading into town. On the way, however, she chanced upon a townsman and pressed the rifle into his hands. According to the Smith family papers, "Our little Ed's [Edward Curtis Smith] spirit was superb, while Julia [Julia Burnett Smith Stevens] and some of the rest were crying terrible. He was awful mad. 'What did you let that rifle go for?' says he to me. 'It is the only thing in the house that I can use.' Cousin William [William Smith] was in Burlington and was extremely worried about the horses and ran to the depot and boarded a freight train to return to St. Albans."

Back in the heart of town, the mêlée worsened. Edward Nettleton, from Newport, New Hampshire, and George Edward Fairchild, a clerk, warmed themselves beside a stove in the William N. Smith store. They happened to glance outside just as a horse threw one of the raiders, likely Hutchinson, off his back and dumped him in the black mud. His hat landed beside him in the muck. Wanting a new hat, the raider strode into the store and demanded Nettleton's hat. Nettleton sat mute. The raider drew his gun and Nettleton said "No!"

Hutchinson cocked his pistol and threatened to blow off Nettleton's head. Nettleton slipped his hand inside his overcoat as if he had a pistol. Hutchinson drew another pistol, cocked, and aimed it at Nettleton too.

"Open your coat, I'll kill you if ye don't obey."

"You don't have to stand for this insult. You don't have to obey," Fairchild told Nettleton.

"Shoot the damned cuss!" cajoled another raider who had also lost his hat.

Young's voice boomed from behind. "Fall in line!"

And just like that, the men backed off.

★ ★ ★

Chaos walked the streets. Townsfolk huddled on the green, unable to reconcile the violence that had so swiftly entered their community. The raiders had begun stealing horses in earnest, compelled by Young to make a quick escape. James McGrorty stole the first horse from Dennis Gilmore's stable on Champlain Street, located right near the Vermont District Court Building. With great ceremony, he led the animal to Bennett Young. "Here's your hobby-horse, Cap'n," McGrorty pronounced.

Charles Higbie walked into the Field Livery Stable near the top of Champlain Street. A man resisted the raider and Higbie fired a shot. The ball passed through the air, wounding only the stovepipe hat of one Sylvester K. Field.

Meanwhile, other raiders were harassing Mrs. Emma Danforth, from North Fairfax, who had come to St. Albans that day to deliver eggs. Throwing their Southern charm aside, the raiders slashed the reins of the horses from her wagon and made off with a pair of horses.

George Shepard, a farmer from Highgate who had come to St. Albans on an errand, found a similar welcome to town when he parked his carriage across the street from the Franklin County Bank, ready to deposit his proceeds from Market Day. Shepard never made it inside. Two raiders cut Shepard's carriage loose, stole his horses, and ordered him into Taylor Park with everyone else.

Unlike many of the others paralyzed by shock, townsman Lorenzo Bingham wasn't about to let thieves, Confederate or otherwise, run off with his animal. As he strode past the Franklin County Bank, he saw a raider stealing his horse out in front of Webster and Farley's store. Bingham shot into a sprint toward the raider, intending to knock him off the horse. But the raider saw him first and fired. Bingham, hit, dropped to the ground with a thud, but rose again.

Stunned, Bingham ran into Mary Wheeler's store and lifted both his vest and shirt to reveal a blazing red spot on his abdomen. Amazingly, the bullet had struck only a heavy silver watch in his vest pocket.

As confusion continued to reign, in front of Joseph Jacques's grocery store on North Main Street, a French Canadian named Euclide Boivin watched in a daze as one of Young's men stole his horse. Snapping to attention, Boivin pulled the raider off and attacked him until he felt the pistol of another Southern brute pressed against his head. Ordered onto the green, Boivin kept muttering: "He's got a good horse."

At this time, Elinus J. Morrison of New Hampshire watched the scene from his perch on a scaffolding that hugged the side of the Welden House. E. J. Morrison was not a resident of St. Albans; he had merely come looking for good wages. Morrison lived in Manchester, New Hampshire, but worked as a contractor in erecting the brickwork of the Welden House. According to the diary of Judge James Davis, Morrison had taken several heavy jobs as a mason contractor, the latest to build the large hotel. He was also involved in construction of the Academy and Union School and the Second Congregational Church.

As the raid unfolded before him, so far Morrison had quite successfully managed to escape notice. But when he saw the raiders about to make off with yet another horse, he yelled out.

"What do you want to take that man's horse for? Let him alone!" shouted Morrison from up on high.

Nearby down below, M. F. Wilson warned Erasmus Fuller from the steps of the *St. Albans Daily Messenger:* "Look out; that fellow is aiming at you!" Fuller ducked behind an elm tree as Young fired three shots at him. No longer invisible to the interlopers, Morrison had scrambled down from his roost in search of cover and followed Fuller.

A bullet struck Morrison the instant he opened the door of Miss Bettie's millinery shop. The ball passed through his left hand, which was in his pocket. It then pierced his body, punctured his intestines, and screeched to a halt near his spine.

"They've shot me through the body," he exhaled, stumbling down the steps and collapsing on the sidewalk.

Fuller and Wilson carried the gravely wounded man to Luther L. Dutcher's pharmacy, where they laid him down in the back room. Dr. Seth R. Day examined Morrison and asked the gentlemen to take Morrison to his room at American House. Little could be done, other than to make the dying man comfortable.

Elsewhere in town, just north of Bank Street, two raiders, George Scott and Daniel Butterworth, entered William and Erasmus Fuller's livery stable on the west side of North Main Street behind the old Bellevue Theater. Like many people, the Fullers had not been immediately aware of the raid taking place on this gray afternoon. Their stables were far enough away that the commotion didn't immediately reach them.

Scott and Butterworth looked to steal seven horses from the livery stable, a father-and-son business. However, just as the two thieves were about to make off with the horses, the Reverend Francis Wyman Smith came riding in from Fairfield, Vermont. Smith had planned to return the horse and go to his father's store, but the sight of the men at the stable stopped him.

"Upon this the man called upon rode up in front of Fuller's livery stables, and demanded Mr. Fuller's saddler to lead down a horse that had just been rode into town by a Mr. Smith, and then standing in front of the livery stables. The man hesitated at first; and the man who rode up, and demanded the horse, told him that if he did not comply he would shoot him."

The raider in question, either Scott or Butterworth, then aimed his revolver at Smith and instructed him to give him the horse. He kept the revolver pointed at him until they had reached the stable. Scott and Butterworth now took the reins of the horses and rode off with the rest of the men.

Around the same time, Erasmus Fuller arrived on the scene. Already incensed about the mortal wound inflicted upon Morrison, Fuller hurled invectives at the two raiders, demanding that they surrender the horses.

"God damn it! We will shoot you," he shouted.

Fuller drew his six-shooter, a poor one at that, and tried to shoot. Click. Click. Click. Young laughed in his face and shouted at him to run over to the harness shop at Bedards saddlery and fetch him some spurs.

The raiders gathered at the foot of Bank Street, ordering anyone and everyone off the streets. They continued to fire wildly as windows shattered around town like the clicks of a metronome. The situation had fast deteriorated.

Young barked commands: He needed to rein in the unruly bunch, and he needed to do it now. He ordered the raiders to hurl their vials of Greek Fire at the buildings, including the American House and the hardware store. The bottles smashed against the buildings, and the volatile contents ignited but sputtered as soon as they had sparked. Except for a single woodshed that burned, the rain-soaked buildings simply wouldn't allow the fire to feed.

As the glass fell to the ground like thousands of spun-sugar snowflakes, the mood in the town began to shift. Anger soon replaced fear, and armed and irate citizens rapidly filled the streets. With their work done and a growing sense of the town's changing temperament, the Southern invaders rode off on their stolen horses, some of them bareback. With the last sack of money tied to a horse and everyone accounted for, the raiders bolted out of town, continuing to exchange shots with the townspeople who had not been herded onto the green, who had begun firing at the aggressors, but to little end. Their weapons were old and ineffective, and the shots were poorly aimed. In any event, the raiders understood that they had lost control.

"Keep cool boys, keep cool," Bennett Young said through the flurry of bullets.

"We're coming back and we'll burn every damned town in Vermont," he shouted to his fleeing band of ruffians.

Just then, Conger and fifty-four-year-old Wilder Gilson stood and fired at the last group of raiders as they rounded the corner of Main and Bank streets. One of the raiders, Charles Higbie, slumped in his saddle.

8

Flight and Pursuit

★ ★ ★ ★ ★ ★ ★ ★ ★ ★ ★ ★ ★ ★ ★ ★ ★

"We have a lot of Rebel raiders here! Let's catch them! Get your guns!" yelled Capt. Conger. Conger rallied the town's citizens, imploring them to join him on his quest to track the raiders and drag them back to town to face justice.

It took time for the Vermonters to answer Conger's call. They had to round up horses—no easy feat, given that the raiders had stolen so many—and they had to scrounge for ammunition and quality weapons, since both were scarce. By the time a fifty-man posse had been formed, the Southerners had a substantial lead. The game of catch-up had begun.

Young and his men were moving north in a quasi-military formation. The lieutenant directed his men to assemble in groups of four. For Charles Higbie, this was near impossible. He desperately needed help; leaking blood from where the bullet had blasted through his shoulders, he had weakened tremendously. Barely able to hold the reins, two other raiders rode on each side of him, trying as best as they could to buttress his slumping body. Two other Confederates had been wounded in firefights that afternoon, though neither had sustained life-threatening injuries.

The Southerners followed an east-northeast route. It might not have been the most direct route to Canada, but it avoided the spongy marshes along the railroad tracks. Here and there, a house interrupted the rolling farmland, and to the east the Green Mountains rose alongside them.

The group continued its frenetic dash toward the next town, Sheldon, and the toll road, a plank road fashioned from rough-hewn boards laid side by side that creaked under the weight of horses, carts, and wagons. Tollhouses stood at Green's Corners and at St. Albans on the old Sheldon Road, and Young knew that the waystations could prove to be their undoing—not that he considered paying the fare; but should someone inside want to fight, it was possible that the raiding party would be slowed enough to give Conger and his posse a chance to overtake them.

About five miles northeast of St. Albans, they turned onto the Fairfield Pond Road and followed it to Sheldon, to which visitors often traveled to benefit from the healing properties of the town's natural springs. The fugitives rode ever more eastward as the road wound next to the narrow Missisquoi River, which was swollen with rushing water. They needed to find a bridge to cross the river.

Before long, the raiders came upon Horatio P. Seymour's farm, where several young boys played outside in the yard. As the raiders thundered past, Seymour, the toll keeper, shouted for them to pay. "Go to hell," yelled back a raider. Seymour shrank back; he didn't dare provoke the menacing group, and the raiders pressed on.

The raiders knew they were being followed, and they attempted by means of sheer determination to increase the distance between themselves and their pursuers. How much longer they'd be able to sustain their momentum, however, was not clear. The raiders desperately needed fresh horses, as the ones they'd stolen from St. Albans, already in poor condition, were quickly foundering.

In pursuit, Conger and his fifty men galloped furiously, closing the distance, now about twenty minutes behind the fugitives. Accustomed to leading men, Lt. F. Stewart Stranahan, Anna Smith's brother-in-law, led a second party of about forty men. Some of the posse rode on horses, some drove buggies, and all were armed with anything and everything they could lay their hands on, from pitchforks to shotguns.

By the time the raiding party had put some distance between themselves and St. Albans, Higbie suddenly crumpled to the side of the road. His compatriots rode on—having no choice but to leave their man behind.

Summoning his very last drops of strength, Higbie crawled through the dirt and grass to a nearby house. One can only imagine the surprise of the lady who opened her door to find a Confederate raider lying in a heap before her. Out of charity, she gave him refuge and eventually nursed him back to health so he could cross the border.

Around seven o'clock in the evening, after crossing the Missisquoi, Young and his men tried to burn Black Creek Bridge, but alert villagers and wet wood saved it from ruin. At the time, this suspension bridge was the only such span in Vermont. The raiders abandoned their plans to dip into the local bank, feeling their lead shrink with every minute.

At this point, Conger's men had no trouble following the raiders' path. Thanks to their hasty departure, some of the Rebels hadn't checked to see that all the satchels had been properly secured. Bank notes fluttered to the ground behind them and left a trail like Hansel and Gretel's crumbs.

Young and his men continued at a mad pace, now toward Shelburne, whereupon they reached another bridge. The group paused to let a wagon full of hay cross. Out of frustration or belligerence, Young fired at the horse-drawn wagon before pushing forward.

Evening arrived, and news of the raid had finally reached the Union capital. General Dix telegraphed Lt. Col. Reuben C. Benton, who had been dispatched to St. Albans and put in temporary charge of troops there, with instructions to apprehend the raiders.

"Put a discreet officer in command and, if they cannot be found this side of the line, pursue them into Canada if necessary and destroy them."

★ ★ ★

Somewhere between Sheldon and Enosburg Falls, a village just a few miles shy of the Canadian border, Bennett Young, James Doty, Alamanda Pope Bruce, and the others began to straggle. They gave one last push and crossed over the line. The marathon had ended. The men were in Canada.

Bennett Young directed his men to break into smaller groups to elude capture. They agreed to meet in Montreal.

Captain Conger's party faltered right before Enosburg Falls. Had he received the telegram from Gen. Dix ordering an international chase, he likely would have wasted no time. Now, however, they dealt with exhausted horses and the heavy darkness that had swallowed the unfamiliar road. Reservations mounted as to whether they could chase and apprehend an armed party of equal size. By this time, only twenty-one men remained in the posse, the others having turned back.

Looking down, Conger's men found more bank notes, scattered like leaves along the road, and a bloodstained holster and pistol. But the posse didn't find the party. From the beginning of the impudent operation, the Confederate marauders seemed to remain just out of the grasp of Yankee justice.

Just after seven o'clock, Conger and his party crossed the dark water of the Missisquoi at Enosburg Falls. They and their horses were just on the other side of the dark water at exactly the moment the raiders crossed into British North America.

The gang didn't arrive in Frelighsburg, the first town over the border, until nearly midnight. He directed his men to form a line in front of the hotel and entered alone; but inside, Conger learned that the raiders had already been there and left.

During the hours before midnight, a nearby town, Stanbridge, Canada, a small place of a few shops and even fewer cafes, slumbered. Snug in their beds, not one resident was yet aware of the raid when at midnight Messrs. Smith and Holmes, Canadian police, awoke Henry Nelson Whitman Esquire, Justice of the Peace. The pair informed Whitman that a group of men who had just shot down men in the streets of St. Albans and robbed banks were on their way, at this very moment, loaded down with sacks of money and silver. Worse yet, an irate band of Yankees was close behind.

An immediate twinge of irritation pinched Whitman. Surely the raiders and their pursuers had somehow breached Canadian sovereignty and neutrality. Perhaps mindful of the greater implications of this unfolding drama, the Canadians scrambled to position a militia force along the frontier, both to prevent any other raiding parties from re-entering Canada and to stop mobs of angry Americans from crossing the border and seizing the raiders. Despite a broader affinity with the South's cause, the Canadian police tracked the raiders with determination. There was a sense that if they didn't round up the marauders, the people of St. Albans would, and that that could trigger hostilities between Canada and the Union.

★ ★ ★

Once over the border, the raiders didn't try to hide. They felt completely safe from Uncle Sam's grip. But in their newfound confidence, they underestimated the situation. Thanks to the vigilance of one Col. Edward Ermatinger, fourteen of them would be in jail by the third day following the raid.

Bennett Young, William Hutchinson, and Caleb Wallace continued to travel together on the road toward Montreal. Somehow news reached them that seven of their men had already been taken prisoner near Stanbridge. Against Hutchinson's advice, Young decided to surrender himself, believing it to be a gesture that would slow the pursuit of the others, or end it altogether.

Wheeling his horse about, he set forth back toward the U.S. border. Maybe it was the darkness, maybe it was the fatigue, maybe it was the solitude, but amazingly the experienced horseman got quite lost on the dark wet roads. Flustered, and a bit fickle in his dramatic decision to surrender, Young changed his mind and once again decided to flee further into Canada.

In the darkness, Young divined the silhouette of a house. The owners of the abode welcomed the ringleader in from the cold and installed him before a freshly stoked fire. Young relaxed before the kitchen hearth, even leaving his revolvers in the adjacent room.

So it was that Conger and his party happened upon the Southern gentleman. Without announcing themselves for who they were, Conger and company burst in, training their pistols on the heart and soul of the raid. At this point, Young offered no resistance, only words of explanation.

"I am their leader. Their cause is my cause. I alone had the authority and command of the raid," Young claimed.

In so many ways, Young was speaking not just on behalf of the twenty other raiders; he spoke on behalf of the entire South and its persistent need to defend itself against those who viewed them as inferior on the moral and military fronts.

Captain George Conger, however, cared not one iota for Young and his majestic declarations. Without ceremony, Conger tossed Young into a wagon escorted by armed horsemen, and the group rode hard toward Vermont.

Somewhere during the wagon ride, the thought of standing before Federal authority once again lost its luster. Perhaps he changed his mind because of the thought of being forced to stand trial before a Yankee judge and jury—they would certainly condemn him before he had a chance to utter a single word in his defense. So Young leaped out of the cart; but Conger's quick-footed men wrestled him down into the muddy road. Suddenly, a voice sliced through the noisy scuffle. A British major stepped out of the blackness and asserted his right, as Her Majesty Queen Victoria's representative, to gain custody of this Southern soldier.

Young's heart perked up at the voice; he knew he would be safer in the hands of the British. Quite obviously schooled in the finer points of international law, he told the officer how the Americans were trying to take him in violation of British neutrality.

The officer handled the volatile situation with finesse, not only promising the Americans that he would shepherd Young to prison, where it turned out the rest of the Confederate bandits were being held, but, come morning, he assured, he would return the entire crew to the authorities in St. Albans. This promise would prove as empty as the holding cell waiting for the raiders back in Vermont.

Nevertheless, Her Majesty's officer did make good on the first part of his promise. He did send Young and five men about twenty miles away to St. Johns, where he locked them behind bars. St. Johns hosted a garrison of British regulars, who by all accounts treated the prisoners most cordially.

★ ★ ★

Back in St. Albans, the day's first light crept across the sky and helped clear the heads of those who hadn't ridden with Conger and Stranahan. Unaware that most of the raiders had been apprehended, some townspeople began to leave for Montreal to push the Canadian authorities to take action.

Albert Sowles, an attorney who worked at The First National Bank in St. Albans, was one of the first to catch a train north. Sowles was sent to help apprehend the raiders. Judge Charles-Joseph Coursol had already informed Montreal Chief of Water Police John McLoughlin and Detective John O'Leary of Sowles's imminent arrival. McLoughlin and O'Leary boarded the 6:00 A.M. train to St. Johns. From there, they traveled on to nearby Farnham so they could welcome their American visitor.

While at the St. Johns station, the three men scanned the crowd for anyone who looked or acted the least bit dubious. O'Leary approached a sinister-looking person and motioned him to step outside. The man claimed his name was George Williams and that he resided in Montreal. Given the situation, O'Leary wasn't so easily swayed, and he arrested him. Upon a search, O'Leary found maps of Canada and a few thousand dollars stuffed in his pockets. Finally, the man admitted his real name, George Scott, and his real occupation, Confederate soldier. The detectives ushered Scott directly to jail.

James Alexander Doty and Joseph McGrorty were arrested at two A.M. on October 21 in Dunham, where they had spent a restless night in a barn. Police found their loaded Colts strewn about the hay along with their pungent overcoats and outer clothes.

Sometime around six o'clock in the morning, Roswell Albert Ellis, the Justice of the Peace of Waterloo, arrested Dudley Moore. Ellis found Moore holed up in Hull's Hotel adjacent to the train station. He nabbed him just before the train left. Moore carried $95 U.S., a knife, and a $5 gold piece.

McLoughlin apprehended Samuel Simpson Gregg at seven A.M. at the railroad depot in Farnham. Gregg spun a fantastic yarn about his innocent intent to visit a group of friends in Quebec City, but the tale could not withstand scrutiny. First of all, he was hobbling because of an injured leg; second, he had only about $30 in his pocket, not nearly enough for the trip. But the crowning touch lay in his pocketful of photographs of the other raiders and of his Southern belle.

Thomas Bronsdon Collins, meanwhile, had come face to face with Henry Whitman, Justice of the Peace in Stanbridge, between one and two o'clock in the morning. Whitman arrested the raider, who was covered in mud-caked clothes that were thoroughly soaked, and confiscated more than two thousand dollars from him.

Spurr and Bruce were arrested between one and three in the morning. Thoroughly exhausted from the raid and the flight to Canada, the two had taken a room at William Elder's tavern in Stanbridge. Whitman, together with Edmund Conant Knight, a policeman, kicked down the door of the room. Several other law officers rushed in and tackled the men in their bed before they had even a second to plant a foot on the floor. The arresting officers discovered four six-chamber Colt revolvers and about $35,000 stuffed between the mattresses.

A bit slow to comprehend the situation, Spurr and Alamanda Bruce actually asked if they were going to be arrested. Bruce babbled on about how the raid was executed solely to retaliate for Gen. Sheridan's ferocious campaign through the Shenandoah Valley. As their confession droned on, more Canadian police were marching to take up position at the border.

The manhunt progressed. During the next few days, many more arrests were made, and the remaining raiders were rounded up like errant sheep. William H. Hutchinson was the last of the band to be captured—he had made it all the way to Montreal.

Chief of Police Guillaume Lamothe snared the hat-wearing raider at dusk on October 24.

One member of the group, however, who avoided arrest altogether was Higbie, the raider shot while fleeing St. Albans and shortly after left behind. Still weak and somewhat disoriented, Higbie eventually arrived in Montreal. He wasn't sure where his comrades were or even how to link up with them again, so he found shelter on the land of the St. Jean Baptiste Society. The Quebecois society, founded in 1834, worked to promote and preserve the French language—it was a patriotic organization whose sympathies lay with the South.

Higbie rested comfortably in this safe haven, enjoying the lavish attention. After a few days, his tranquility was cut short when society president Charles-Joseph Coursol discovered Higbie on the premises and ordered him to leave. The command went unheeded, and the society allowed Dr. Montrose A. Pallen, a Confederate living in Canada, to continue to care for Higbie in secret. The Rebel remained under the watchful eyes and healing hands of the St. Jean Baptiste Society, until February 1865, when he left for Toronto.

Always the politician and often the coward, Commissioner Clement Clay sought immediate deniability over everything that had so far transpired, as news reached the Confederate Canadian operation that the raiders were being rounded up. He backpedaled and blustered his way through an explanation about the less-than-positive results of the raid.

"I am no less surprised, shocked and disturbed than you can be," he told Jacob Thompson. "I will explain when we meet. I have full proof that I discountenanced it. I did not know that anything would be attempted."

But, Clay added, even though he believed the Kentucky gentlemen had descended upon St. Albans to benefit their own wallets, he would find it in himself to help their defense. He made a grand show of sending $6,000 to George Sanders in Montreal to help pay for counsel.

Inside the Union, officials from Vermont to Washington, D.C., were learning of the news. Minutes after 10:30 P.M. on October 20, Secretary of State Seward had received news from the Provost-Marshal of New York, Rollo Gleason.

"My order to the officer who went in pursuit of the marauders at Saint Albans was to follow them, if necessary, into Canada, and destroy them. My direction was, further, that the pursuit must be instant and continuous if carried across the line," Gleason informed Seward in a telegram. "Your order was perfectly understood. The pursuing parties were close upon the raiders when they crossed the lines, and continued the pursuit, and at last accounts had captured eight, who are held by Canadian authorities awaiting requisitions."

In New York, Gen. Dix promised that any raider caught would face a swift court-martial and a quick walk to the gallows. He informed Secretary of War Stanton of his intention: "I have been advised that a party of Rebels from Canada have robbed the banks at Saint Albans, Vt., and killed several citizens. I have ordered the provost marshal at Burlington to send his whole efficient force there, and have also ordered 100 men from Boston. I have directed a discreet officer to be put in command, with orders, in case the marauders are found on our side of the line, to pursue them, if necessary, into Canada, and destroy them."

But as quickly as Conger and Stranahan had been ordered to pursue Bennett Young and his merry band of marauders, they were called back.

"Countermand the order sent last night directing troops to go to Saint Albans, Vt. If already started telegraph them to come back," read the telegram from Headquarters, Department of the East on October 20.

One can only imagine the irritation Dix, Smith, and the others felt upon learning of these orders. They were well aware that President Jefferson Davis lay at the end of this mad raid, and they knew that Davis supported the idea of hitting Northern towns and cities all along the border, not just in Vermont. Nabbing the raiders would have gone a long way in chastening what the North perceived to be Southern arrogance.

With the Kentucky men seeming to escape Federal hands, Confederate plots continued. In November 1864, one month after the raid, Confederate agents would travel to New York City and start fires in ten hotels. Jacob Thompson approved the plan, hoping that the anti-war Democrats would then seize control of the city. Like the St. Albans raid, the Confederates were also motivated by revenge for Sheridan's actions.

"In realization for Sheridan's atrocities in the Shenandoah Valley, we desired to destroy property, not the lives of women and children, although that would have followed in its train," Capt. Robert C. Kennedy said. Despite the conviction of their desire for revenge, however, the Confederates would be left to their own devices; the New York sympathizers wouldn't follow through.

In the November 27, 1864, *New York Times* appeared a lengthy account of the plot. "The diabolical plot to burn the City of New York. . . . It has already been proved to the entire satisfaction of the authorities, that the affair was planned by the Rebels and has been in preparation for a long time past, the men selected to perform the work were sent to this City at various times and under various pretexts. . . . The plan was excellently well conceived, and evidently prepared with great care, and had it been executed with one-half the ability with which it was drawn up, no human power could have saved this city from utter destruction. . . . But fortunately, thanks to the Police, Fire Department, and the bungling manner in which the plan was executed by the conspirators, it proved a complete and miserable failure."

A military commission soon investigated the failed plot and found "sufficient evidence before them to show that the conspiracy which broke out here this day is merely an extension of the Rebel burglary operations on the Canadian frontier," said the *New York Times*. "It is feared that some of the more vicious of the gang have been able to make good their escape across the border. It is of the utmost importance that, *pari passu* [Latin for at an equal pace or rate] with the proceedings before the Military Commission, general registration of the Southern refugees should be enforced, without any nervous scruples as to its effect on the sensibilities of the parties concerned. The prime question is not what will inconvenience the skulking Rebel population in our midst, but what will insure protection, effectual and permanent, against even the faintest attempt to repeat the dastardly plot of last week."

As fear continued to race throughout the Northeast, with plots like the one for New York City afoot, St. Albans had been pushed from a tranquil town filled with a sense of honor for their men in uniform, to a fearful one filled with dread for what the morning might bring. Governor Gregory Smith, hoping to keep Vermont calm, declared a state of emergency, and summoned the state militia to St. Albans.

9

Rumors of Terror

★ ★ ★ ★ ★ ★ ★ ★ ★ ★ ★ ★ ★ ★ ★ ★ ★ ★

"I worried very much about you, thought you would suffer great anxiety on our account—but my dear, never after this think that I shall be frightened or that I cannot do all that my best judgment dictates. . . . How foolish and frantic our people have been not to heed your warning—I hope this affair will settle matters at once. Good bye—God give you grace to act wisely in these trying times," Anna Smith wrote to her husband on October 20.

Mrs. Smith may have shown exemplary composure just one day after the raid; after all, she and her husband had seen this coming. Citizens in the rest of the town and in the rest of the northern border states would not be so calm. In the days following the raid, disquiet thrummed throughout the region.

Two days after the raid kindled the town, Mr. E. J. Morrison succumbed to his wounds. "The remains of Mr. Morrison, who died of the wounds he received by the robbers on Wednesday, have been taken to Manchester, N.H. where he resided. Previous to leaving in the car yesterday morning, funeral services were held at the American Hotel. Mr. Bliss, the rector of St. Luke's Church, officiated. Many of our citizens attended the funeral solemnities out of respect they had for the deceased. His contract respecting the new hotel, I believe, will be completed by Mr. Newcomb, the architect of the building," wrote Judge Davis.

Judge James Davis was born in North Kingston, Rhode Island, on August 8, 1783. His father, Joshua Davis, was a farmer and the owner of a gristmill. James Davis worked the land until he was about seventeen years old, and then he worked the mill for about three years. This last job gave him ample time to read, and he thirsted for more education, so he enrolled at Washington Academy in Wickford. In November 1795 he entered Union College in Schenectady, New York. He became a judge in St. Albans later.

In February 1859, he had attended the funeral of a Mrs. Cynthia Penniman. He was one of the pallbearers and was severely injured when the carriage in which he was riding overturned. Then he fell again a year later, an accident that left him confined to his home, where he passed the time reading, writing, and studying. He was something of a local wise man to the people of St. Albans, and his accounts of the raid and the subsequent days bear witness to his thoughtfulness and sincerity.

The townsfolk of St. Albans, and those of towns and cities all along the northern border, slowly began to believe that war could visit them at any time and that there was little they could do to stop it. Shock had indeed given way to anger and fear.

"I am feeling tonight as I never felt before in my life. This day seems to be the beginning of trouble in St. Albans and the Lord knows when it will end, their [sic] was a band of men appeared on the streets all at once. . . . They were armed. . . . They walked into the banks and demanded all the money and they presented revolvers and of course they got it," St. Albans resident Ann Pierce wrote to her son Marshall Pierce that very same night. "They shot Mr. Morrison just at the door. He had hold of the latch as he fell. He is not dead and the last I heard they also shot C. H. Huntington, they think he will die. They also shot Mr. Bingham slitly hurt and other slightly injured. . . . They tried to take some men prisoners but did not make much at it after they took the money out of one of the Banks they put Mr. Beardsly into the safe and locked him in took the keys and Left They called themselves Confederate officers, Devil officers I should think, our men were running in great confusion to collect what arms they could. The first I knew of it was Mr. Eliott came running and asked for Tell's gun I went & got it saw he was excited. I asked if he was agoing to shoot a dog, he told me there were raiders in town that were robbing and shooting people, Just think of it all in broad daylight. Our men rallied all the arms and horses they could and started after them. Our poor men with nothing but old guns. What will become of this dark dark night we know not. . . . Your Father started for Boston tuesday morning. I hope he arrived safe. We are well as usual here at home but wee *do not know what will be next* . . . the raiders say that general Early sent them here knowing wee were without Arms or Ammunition so I think some of our copperheads have let them know about it. From Mother Pierce, now write quick."

Word of the raid had sped along the telegraph wires linking St. Albans to Montpelier, where Governor Smith and the state legislature remained in session. The young telegraph operator who had been held hostage inside the St. Albans Bank during the raid relayed a message to Governor Smith after the raid: "Southern raiders are in town, robbing banks, shooting citizens and burning houses." After relaying the message, the operator then locked his office and joined the enraged crowd in the streets.

The legislative session came to an abrupt close. Of course, the Governor's immediate impulse was to return home right away, but his duty to the state overrode his personal concern for his family. He had yet to get a very accurate picture of what had happened, and just in case there really was a conspiracy afoot to attack the entire northern frontier, he needed to stay in Montpelier.

It was time to arm and organize. Thirsty for news, Smith tried in vain to snatch more details from the telegraph wires. No more news came forth, and Smith and the legislators worried that the raiders had cut the telegraph wires, unaware that the young man manning the station back in St. Albans had fled immediately after sending the one message about the raid.

As president of the Central Vermont Railway, Smith ordered that every train on the Vermont line be stopped. Even the one northbound train that had departed Montpelier Junction moments before the raid began had been called back once it became apparent that an attack was taking place. Smith didn't want to take any chances that additional insurgents might be headed to Vermont via the railway, and, being the president of the railroad, there was of course no bureaucratic delay.

A Burlington newspaper published a letter in the days that followed: "The excitement in the borough has by no means sub-sided. Revolvers are the most saleable articles of hardware, and rumors of all sorts of coming horrors keep prudent people on the alert and nervous persons in a state of chronic perspiration. The rumors of to-day are that Plattsburg was invaded yesterday and the banks robbed by a party of raiders, and that authentic advices have been received by Governor Smith that two thousand armed and organized Rebels in Canada are about to invade St. Albans and complete the devastation which the Rebels left unfinished."

Stores and doors had closed in St. Albans. Immediately after the raid, Smith sent word for two cannons and four companies of volunteer militia to deploy in town and along the border. Cadets from Norwich University at Northfield mustered on the border. In addition, a train full of recovering soldiers from the veteran invalid corps currently recovering in the U.S. hospital in Mont-pelier chugged toward St. Albans.

Disease, accidents, and of course war itself had disabled thousands upon thousands of Civil War soldiers. At first, permanently disabled soldiers got medical discharges from the Army. As the war and the need for live bodies continued, many of these soldiers remained in the service and fulfilled noncombatant duties, relieving able-bodied soldiers to fight. In 1862, the chief medical officers in the Union were allowed to organize "convalescent wounded and feeble men" into detachments and have them work as nurses, cooks, and hospital attendants.

By April 1863, the U.S. War Department established the more official Invalid Corps of disabled officers and soldiers who were still, or recently had been, in the Army. This corps was divided into two sorts of battalions—one for those who could bear arms and perform garrison duty, and the second for those too severely handicapped to do anything more than hospital service. In March 1864, the corps was renamed the Veteran Reserve Corps. An estimated sixty thousand soldiers served in the corps from 1863 until it was disbanded in the summer of 1866.

For the purposes of St. Albans and other border towns, the Union scraped the barrel clean. About a hundred convalescents and thirty of the Veteran Reserve Corps, with two officers, were collected from the General Hospital in New York City, and they too were sent to St. Albans.

"A large party of raiders from the Province of Canada have invaded this state, robbed all the banks at St. Albans, killed several citizens and are plundering and destroying property," read the telegram Governor Gregory Smith sent to Lord Monck, Governor-General of the North-American Provinces.

Once informed of the attack, Smith had sent a message off to Gen. Dix. "Two of our citizens badly wounded at Saint Albans by the Rebels, all three of the banks robbed, one hotel fired, and about $150,000 taken, and about twenty-five horses. A company of volunteers was organized to pursue the Rebels in their flight to Canada. Telegram this morning says that eight of the raiders captured by the pursuing party in Canada, nine horses, and a portion of the money recovered. Not able to say how much. Party still pursuing the raiders. It was a most daring adventure."

It was at this point that Dix, not the type to sit back and wait for instructions, had ordered the commanding officer at Burlington to send troops to St. Albans, find the raiders, pursue them into Canada, and, if need be, destroy them.

"What news from Saint Albans? I trust the officer understood my order in regard to pursuing the Rebel raiders into Canada. It is only in case they are found on our side of the line, and the pursuit then must be instant and continuous. Advise him so," Dix telegraphed to the provost marshal in Burlington on October 20.

General Dix had been born in Boscawen, New Hampshire, on July 24, 1798. After completing a year at Phillips Exeter Academy, his parents enrolled him in the College of Montreal, a Catholic school. They wanted him to discover another culture and learn another language.

During the War of 1812, his parents sent him to live with relatives in Boston, but the fourteen-year-old decided he would rather join the military. His father, an infantry major, helped his son land a commission. Dix served as an ensign at the Battle of Niagara.

In 1813, Dix's father was killed in battle, leaving behind a widowed mother of nine. The future general helped support his mother and siblings and served on the Canadian frontier, attaining the rank of captain—the first on a long list of promotions.

The general's forthright, take-no-prisoners attitude characterized his lengthy career. In one incident during his tenure as secretary of the treasury under President Buchanan, Dix stared down the populace of New Orleans, which had been growing steadily opposed to the Federal government, with his characteristic cold calm. The strife in New Orleans peaked on January 29, 1861, just months before the Civil War began, when citizens threatened to storm the building that housed the New Orleans Treasury. Dix telegraphed the office with orders to resist any effort to take over the building. "If anyone attempts to haul down the American flag, shoot him on the spot." Lincoln soon commissioned Dix a major general and placed him in command of the Northeast.

Familiar terrain for the general; with the border under threat of further attack, he wasted no time in moving additional men and munitions into place to guard against what he believed to be an ongoing threat from Canada. Dix recommended that the selectmen of all border towns organize every able-bodied man, under a suitable chief. He also suggested that each man receive a musket and ammunition and, with a nod to the Revolutionary-era Minutemen, Dix further advised that the men be ready to assemble on short notice at a predetermined signal.

Within a day after the raid, nearly a thousand armed men protected the border.

"All military commanders on the frontier, are therefore instructed in case further acts of depredation and murder are attempted, whether by marauders or persons acting under commissions from the Rebel authorities at Richmond, to shoot down the depredators if possible while in the commission of their crimes . . . and if captured, they are under no circumstances to be surrendered, but are to be sent to these headquarters for trial and punishment by martial law."

Under the command of a Lt. Murphy, seventy-five more men were deployed to St. Albans. Major William Austine, provost general of the state, ordered two more companies of invalid veterans from Brattleboro to go to St. Albans to assist in the town's defense. They arrived on October 20. Twenty of them were detailed to guard the length of the railroad bridge at Alburg.

Town leaders organized a home guard of infantry and cavalry. Colonel R. C. Benton, who had served with the Eleventh Vermont, patrolled the mostly-deserted streets. Benton ordered the state to raise an additional company to take command of the local militia. Louis M. Smith was appointed captain of the Home Guard Infantry. Resident John W. Newton was named captain of the local cavalry company.

Down in Montpelier, guards were placed around the State House and patrolled the streets. Colonel Redfield Proctor was put in charge of the Burlington militia.

Three days after the raid, Governor Smith requested that Secretary of War Stanton make available hundreds of bridles, saddles, sabers, pistols, and carbines. "The excitement still continues, though somewhat abated. Threats are still made of a return to burn this and other villages. . . . I have encouraged the organization of cavalry forces at several points on the frontier, to be kept in readiness for any emergency."

Stanton agreed to furnish the equipment. Some years later, he recounted these horrifying days for *The Vermonter,* a newspaper to which Anna Smith contributed frequently. "The hours of the night dragged slowly on, the suspense was intolerable. Stanton went out for a walk in the middle of the night when a cavalryman came dashing up. 'There has been a great battle at Cedar Creek, the enemy became entangled in the streets of Winchester. Tremendous victory, thousands of prisoners and forty-five cannon captured!' Throwing up my hands toward heaven, I exclaimed, 'Thank God, I will now go home and sleep.' Immediately after came word from St. Albans that the raiders had fled into Canada, and the town was strongly guarded."

A frontier cavalry composed of seven companies from New York state, three from Massachusetts, and two from Vermont assembled to guard their respective states. The Vermont companies trained in Burlington until midwinter, when they moved into new barracks in St. Albans. They drilled daily and performed picket duty between St. Albans and the Canadian border. They would stand guard along the jittery frontier through the end of 1865.

On November 22, 1864, Dix notified Secretary of War Stanton about a group of forty Rebels in Marysburgh, Prince Edward's County, Canada, on the north side of Lake Ontario and northwest of Oswego. In the dispatch, he said the men drilled thrice weekly and were armed with revolvers.

"They board with the farmers in the neighborhood; seem to have plenty of money and say they belong to John Morgan's corps. These organizations for hostile purposes on Canadian soil are so plainly in violation of all the obligations of neutrality that I cannot doubt the willingness of the Canadian authorities to put an end to them on proper notice."

Naturally, a diplomatic response followed the rapid deployment of support troops. Slamming shut the door of the once-open border was perhaps the most significant act. From the White House, President Lincoln decreed that henceforth no traveler would be allowed to enter the United States from a foreign country without a passport. If an American citizen desired to travel outside of the United States, then a passport had to be obtained from the State Department. The regulation was expressly intended to single out those hoping to travel to the United States from the neighboring British Provinces. Lincoln made sure that all officers, be they civil or military, strictly enforced the orders.

★ ★ ★

Though they had been swift, the arrests of the raiders did nothing to quell the fear in St. Albans and elsewhere, or to quiet the mounting anger in Washington. Secretary of State Seward took Lord Lyons to task for allowing Canada to offer itself as a refuge. Seward wrote that the "unprovoked aggressions from Canada no longer allow our border citizens to navigate the intervening waters with safety, or to rest at home with confidence of security for their property and lives. . . . It is not the Government nor is it the people of the United States that are delinquent in the fulfillment of fraternal national obligations."

Nerves remained strung out along the northern states, and Secretary Stanton was forced to finally recognize the degree to which the border lay exposed. Although Governor John Smith and other northeastern officials had long warned Washington about of the lack of security along the border, it never got adequate protection or attention until after the raid.

"Information having been received at these headquarters that the Rebel marauders who were guilty of murder and robbery at St. Albans, have been discharged from arrest, and that other enterprises are actually in preparation in Canada, the Commanding-General deems it due to the people of the frontier towns to adopt the most prompt and efficient measures for the security of their lives and property," ordered Gen. Dix on December 14, 1864.

Whatever lack of attention Secretary of War Stanton had previously shown regarding the vulnerability of the Union's northern states, he quickly corrected his course. To his credit, Stanton responded quickly when news of the raid reached him in Washington, as seen in his October 23 dispatch to Gen. Ulysses S. Grant. Stanton demanded increased security for the forts and harbors of New York, as well as defense of the Great Lakes from invasion. Visible force would go a long way in preserving public peace, wrote Stanton soon after consulting with

Gen. Dix, who had reported a most disconcerting fact: The forts in New York Harbor were nowhere near secure. Moreover, Stanton reminded Grant that there were not enough troops to be spared in Washington or elsewhere to meet the need for heightened protection.

"Allow me to suggest whether, in view of their accession to your army, you cannot spare 2,000 or 3,000 men, temporarily to be sent to New York and placed under his command."

Up in St. Albans, far from the corridors of the White House or the strategy sessions of the military commanders, townspeople were struggling to pull themselves together.

The afternoon after the raid, a tall man in U.S. military uniform knocked upon the door of Governor Smith's home, enquiring for the lady of the house. When Anna Smith opened the door, the soldier saluted: "Madame, I am the officer of the guard. I come to you for orders." Astonished, she said: "My God, is this a military situation? War in northern Vermont. Terrible." Having had no orders to give, Anna implored the soldiers to make themselves as comfortable as possible in the outbuildings and to do what they were trained to do if trouble were to reappear.

Two more companies arrived in the ensuing days to guard the town. They joined a recently organized Home Guard of infantry and cavalry. Soldiers regularly patrolled the eerily subdued streets and were under orders to arrest any suspicious-looking person.

Apprehension clung to the town. During the night of the twentieth, only one day after the raid, a fire lit up a barn just west of the village. Not knowing whether Confederate soldiers had once again laid siege to the town, Anna Smith invited the officer and his men to investigate what turned out to be an accidental blaze. While the rain quickly extinguished the potential threat, it did nothing to soothe the town's nerves.

"I shall never forget the cries of my little children wakened from sleep by the confusion," Anna Smith wrote.

For nine months after the last raider galloped out of town, a patrol of Union soldiers camped on the gently sloping grounds outside the Smith house. They were there so long that the governor oversaw construction of a sentinel house for the soldiers. Alarms in St. Albans and the surrounding environs kept the troops occupied. While there would be no other attacks, that knowledge remained beyond the ken of the citizens and their leaders.

"During all that time there was a Henry seventeen shooter on hooks over my bed and a sheathed Bowie knife within reach of my hand," said Anna Smith.

Smith later reflected on the reputation of Young and his circle for being Southern gentlemen: "Southern soldiers, Southern gentlemen they called themselves. Soldiers? They wore no uniform, they carried no colors, and they belonged to no military organization. Southern gentlemen? Such men do not pass for gentlemen in the South or North. Their manners and methods were those of marauders in the dark ages."

Terror reigned throughout the frontier. "It was the prevailing opinion that these marauders were but an advanced guards of an army from Canada, which had, by surprise or collusion, temporarily overpowered their local government, and were marching through our State carrying all the horrors of war to our homes and firesides," recalled the Hon. Edward Albert Sowles some years later.

Fear swirled like heavy rain clouds over not only St. Albans but also many other towns along the border with Canada. In cities across upstate New York—Ogdensburg, Rochester, and Buffalo—and even in Cleveland, Ohio, word of the raid spread, and with that a feeling of alarm gripped the region from Maine to Michigan. Every available soldier was called out, doors were locked, and bells tolled. The border was to remain in an uproar.

A large volunteer police force was raised to supplement the military presence in the hopes of offering some greater measure of protection for cities stretching from Detroit to New York City. The whole length of America's northern border lay exposed, and in one of just many instances of pleas for protection, it was "respectfully asked that the Government take such measures as will effectually prevent robbers and raiders from visiting the border along the St. Clair River."

Anxious citizens of all ages were instructed to arm and be ready to fight. In Plattsburgh, New York, the townspeople ripped up a section of railroad track because they had heard that hordes of Rebels were coming their way. Hysteria reigned in Burlington and Brattleboro, where people were convinced that a Confederate party planned to come ashore via a steamer on Lake Champlain. "The citizens were utterly paralyzed by the boldness and suddenness of the attack," according to Col. Van Buren of Brattleboro.

Mrs. Henry Seymour wrote: "We begin to realize the war! For we have had a veritable Rebel raid. All the neighbors were out and I flew over to Miranda [Mrs. F. S. Stranahan, wife of Lt. Stranahan] who looked the most war-like as she was giving some directions to a man with a gun! She said they had fired and killed Mr. Morrison, the master builder of the hotel. That they had shot Collins Huntington while peaceably riding his wagon. At Mrs. Beattie's I found Julius and Neo [Edmund Seymour] examining the blood spots where Mr. Morrison was shot, poor man!"

Even those in the military not directly linked to the region felt duty-bound to act. Major-General Joseph Hooker wrote to

Senator Zachariah Chandler of Michigan on December 19, pledging his aid. "I assure you, Senator, in case a raid should be attempted from Canada, I intend that somebody shall be hurt, if I have to go to Canada to do it. Then if exception is taken, it can be adjusted by negotiation afterward. I want full swing at the devils once, and I think they will never attempt to disturb our quiet a second time. Cost what it may, the property and persons of our citizens shall be fully protected while I am in the exercise of the command of this department."

Hooker's overly eager attitude came in part from his desire to vindicate his defeat at the Battle of Chancellorsville in May 1863, while he was in command of the Army of the Potomac. But in truth he sincerely wanted to strike back at these raiders, as did many people in the North. No one could believe that a town so far north had been so viciously assaulted.

No matter his motivation, Hooker's words must have pleased Zachariah Chandler, who was enraged: "Vermont might submit to have her towns burned and her citizens murdered, but the Northwest will not." Chandler said he expected that retaliatory raids upon Canada might soon be expected if raids like that on St. Albans continued.

Lord Viscount Monck let Edward Cardwell, a noted theologian and British statesman, know in an October 27, 1864 dispatch that the authorities had successfully apprehended the suspected raiders. Indeed, thirteen of the twenty-one were in Canadian custody.

"I am happy to be able to say that there is no reason to believe that any British subject has been in any way a participant in the affair. . . . I also enclose a letter copied from the *Evening Telegraph*, of Montreal, and addressed to the editor of that paper by a Mr. Bennett H. Young, one of the persons in custody, in which you will observe that he asserts that the enterprise was engaged in with the assent and under the authority of the President of the so-called Confederate States of America and that the perpetrators are commanding officers of those States."

In Canada, British army units stationed in Canada were now at the disposal of legal authorities to halt the prisoners from escaping, and to prevent vengeful American civilians from crossing the border. Monck had called a special meeting with Judge Charles-Joseph Coursol, the police magistrate of Montreal, and decided to send a force to the border to arrest any raiders found trying to cross, in either direction.

The militia had been summoned to the border "not for the purpose of warfare, but with the object of aiding a Civil power in its efforts to prevent aggression on the territories of a friendly state . . . and to maintain, as regards Canada, that complete neutrality with respect to the war now existing in the U.S., which Her Majesty has enjoined all her subjects."

Yet rumors continued to abound in the weeks following the lightning raid. The Confederacy launched an active psychological warfare campaign after the nineteenth. Reports reached many U.S. consuls that Rebel raids were imminent. The Halifax consul heard tell of a group of three to four hundred Confederate men on boats just offshore, getting ready to attack. Other reports named Oswego, New York as a possible target of further Rebel hostility.

It was whispered that as many as twenty thousand Confederate troops were busy sneaking along the border, preparing a large-scale invasion. Word spread that other towns had been hit, or were about to be set upon, by bloodthirsty Rebels. Hysteria had taken hold, for surely clear-thinking men and women would have realized if the South had troops to spare they would have used them to fight against Sherman and Sheridan.

On December 10, 1864, Dix reported to Stanton that there

was a "strong indication that Rebels in Canada want to further burn and pillage frontier towns. . . . I ask authority to raise five companies of mounted men, to be distributed along the frontiers of New York and Vermont. It is very desirable that they be mounted in order to make the pursuit of the raiders effectual."

While these all proved to be false alarms, they succeeded in sowing fear not only among the people of St. Albans but also among their loved ones fighting on the front.

A letter from William White of Sheldon, Vermont, to his friend Jacob Wead shows how, for the first time, Union soldiers on the front worried over the well-being of those living so far from the battlefields. White served with Co. I of the 10th Vermont and was in a camp near Cedar Creek, Virginia, when he penned this November 5 letter.

Dear Jacob, My dear friend,

I was really surprised when I heard of the raid in St. Albans and Sheldon, and yet not entirely so for I have been expecting something of that kind for the last five to six weeks. It was no doubt a bold, daring and well-planned scheme, and had it not been for the interference of the Strong Arm of Divine Providence, it might have terminated in the destruction of a great deal of life or property. . . . The great wonder to me is, when they halted to burn the bridge why was it that they did not go into your Father's store and plunder that? Oh! I only wish that our little regiment was there then I think we would make them dance to as lively a music as they every [sic] heard. They certainly would have to pay dear for their fun. . . . I am glad you are making preparations for them fellows should they or any other visit you again but I do not think they will, they know you are fully prepared for them and they know it as well as you do so they will not come there while your men keep on alert. But you may be sure they will strike at some other weak point. They will not give up so, or if they find that your men thinking [*sic*] themselves safe and free from further trouble they may pay you another visit. . . . I should like to be there with you now."

Ben H. Dewey wrote to Col. William Wells, who was with the First Vermont Cavalry. Wells, from Waterbury, Vermont, had fought at Cedar Creek: "Presume you have heard of the raid on St. Albans. It was a rough affair—and undoubtedly it is not the last of its kind. The towns in the northern part of the state are armed, and in fact, generally the towns are taking measures to protect themselves. Our town has started a company and we are daily expecting our arms. Revolvers have been in good demand, and a great many are carried here. The state is full of strangers prowling around with no apparent business.

Fraternally, Ben H. Dewey

Naturally, the raid filled the pages of local, regional, and international newspapers—not just Canadian papers, but British, too. The story had it all: suspense, violence, and a soupçon of romance. The press influenced the stand that both the U.S. and British North American governments took.

In Vermont, newsboys hawked a special evening edition of the *St. Albans Daily Messenger:* "St. Albans Has Been Surprised and Excited Today," ran the banner headline. It announced that Governor Smith had declared a state of emergency and had summoned more troops.

Still, citizens were decidedly on edge, and it didn't help that the news was still so unclear. Telegraph lines, messengers on horses, and letters were the only means of communication. As is so often the case, misinformation dominated the first wave of news after the attack. Many newspapers carried reports of a little girl shot to death a mile north of the besieged town. Other articles insinuated that Vermont deserters had ridden among the raiding party.

For all the anxiety that the news of the raid spread in New England, it was matched by pride and joy in the South. The reports had traveled so quickly that the news even reached soldiers in Union-run prison camps. Private Sprake, the Confederate soldier who had languished for more than a year in a Union camp, felt his spirits rise just a bit at the news. "In the cold and no fire, hungry and cold," he wrote in his October 20, 1864 diary entry. "Campaign in Georgia very active. Sherman retreating. [Gen. John Bell] Hood thinking their movements a mystery, some sharp fighting . . . the Rebels from Canada made a raid on St. Albans, headed by Bennett H. Young, committed considerable depredation, robbed some banks, in all $25,000; this was grapevine!"

Across the border, Canadian public opinion came down largely on the side of Dixie. Many Canadians were not happy to learn that the Union posse and troops had crossed into their country, or at least had been authorized to do so, intent on rounding up the Confederate soldiers. On the other hand, when put into terms of a neighboring town having been robbed and possibly burned, Canadian citizens understood the dismay to their immediate south. They were unhappy about the prospect of the dismay turning to vengeance.

It was highly questionable whether the Confederates truly could have created a two-front situation for the Union. Given the state of the war in 1864 and the distances Southern troops would have had to travel, it hardly seems feasible. Yet, the men in gray were more than capable of destabilizing Union confidence and were able to force them to keep more men on active duty in the North than had been necessary otherwise—but the raid's larger impact was mitigated by the near-inevitable momentum of the Union.

However, the raid did soon give rise to a slew of investigations. It was time-consuming to find out whether plots were grounded in truth or were just wisps of wishful thinking, and every rumor had to be indulged.

A letter from County Carleton, West Canada, dated March 13, 1865, to The Honorable Secretary of War, Washington conveys the frustrating ambiguity of the day: "Sir, I have the honor to inform you that a plot is about being entered into by a number of Rebel refugees which has for its object pillage and destruction. The principal rendezvous of the Rebels is Arnprior, which is situated about forty-five miles, or perhaps fifty miles, from Brockville, with which it is connected by railroad. I have ever felt a deep sympathy for the Northern States in their noble efforts to stop and put down this unnatural Rebellion, and eventually to liberate the slave; and therefore I give this information to your Government."

In this case, the writer was a con man, D. Campbell McNab, who took singular advantage of the unease that had extended across the North. He asked the Union, in exchange for information, to honor a few requests. "All I ask is that my expenses be paid to Morristown; and when I shall have given the proper details, with the names of the parties, I shall request of the Government to procure for me the degree of M.A. from Yale College as it is the most renowned university on this side of the Atlantic."

Another story emerged in January 1865. The U.S. consul in Halifax said he had a letter from a Pittsburgh resident who knew a Confederate officer living there who wanted a pardon from the Federal government in exchange for information about Confederate plans for operations along the Canadian border. Supposedly six hundred men were planning a raid and were reconfiguring blockade-runners into armed raiding vessels to attack the coast of the United States. Again, although this rumor also proved to be false, it had to be investigated.

Rumors like this were gifts to the Southern men still working to hatch real plots. While the raiders waited in jail, Jacob Thompson refused to give up the cause. In fact, he exhibited a complete shift in emphasis; no longer only willing to participate in politically oriented missions, he devised his plan to firebomb New York City. Like Young, he relied on veterans of Morgan's Cavalry, Lt. John Headley and Col. Robert Martin.

★   ★   ★

Clement Clay continued to seek distance from the act in the days after the raid. Clay, who supposedly detested his time in Canada, shuddered at the possibility of either arrest or expulsion from the territory. He actually had the nerve to deny any involvement at all in the whole affair. In a letter partially quoted above, he said: "I am no less surprised, shocked and disturbed at the St. Albans affair than you can be. I will explain to you when we meet. I have full proof that I discountenanced it in advance. If the town had been burned, I would not have been surprised or condemned the act, although I did not know that anything would be attempted. You will be advised in person in due time of all I know about the matter. I think, however, it is my duty to those who are arrested to try to save them from death or imprisonment, and I will do so. I believe that they were trying to serve their country; notwithstanding it looks like mere selfish plunder.

"I am sure that the Secretary of War authorized Young to do anything in the way of injury to the enemy that had been done by them to us. If the town had been burned, I should have felt no distress about the affair, but so it is only retaliation in fact, although it may not be so appearing in law."

Clay laid responsibility for the raid straight at Seddon's feet when he said "I am sure that the Secretary of War authorized

Young to do anything in the way of injury to the enemy that had been done by them against us."

In addition, Clay resolved to inform Secretary of State Benjamin about the likelihood of an impending trial. By the first of November, counsel had already been retained.

Clay, fearful of implication, was recalled to Richmond through a "personal" advertisement placed in the *New York News*. During the war, Confederate officials relayed messages to one another via coded personal ads published in certain sympathetic newspapers.

Thompson received an alert that he too should leave the Dominion without even bothering to wait for his replacement, who happened to be a cousin of Gen. Robert E. Lee. Brigadier General Edwin Gray Lee, who had retired from active duty because of ill health, was supposed to organize future clandestine operations from Canadian soil.

Secretary of State Benjamin wrote Thompson again on the thirtieth, saying: "From reports which reach us from trustworthy sources, we are satisfied that so close an espionage is kept upon you that your services have been deprived of the value which is attached to your residence in Canada. The President thinks therefore that as soon as the gentleman arrives, it will be better that you transfer to him, as quietly as possible, all the information that you have obtained and the release of funds in your hands, and then return to the Confederacy."

Thompson had little intention of obeying the recall. He went underground, so to speak, and founded the Order of the Star, a secret organization that was purely military in nature. Thompson would channel his stubbornness to achieve more tangible goals. He wanted to sabotage railroads and burn property in the North—yet a further departure from his earlier insistence that all missions required a concrete political objective. His actions only reflected the growing desperation many Southerners were feeling.

J. J. C. Abbott, the leading counsel for the defense, never seemed overly concerned about extradition. Sir John Joseph Caldwell Abbott had played many roles in his life: lawyer, businessman, educator, politician, militia officer, and gentleman farmer. But nothing in his career won him more recognition, both good and bad, than his defense, together with Toussaint-Antoine-Rodolphe Laflamme and William Warren Hastings Kerr, of the St. Albans raiders.

Abbott was admitted to the bar in 1847 and became a dean at McGill University, a title he would keep until 1880, long after he stopped teaching. Among his students had been Laflamme, now a member of the defense team.

"We conceive the strength of our position to consist in the documents we hold establishing the authority of the raiders from the Confederate States Government," Abbott wrote to Clay. Still, Abbott laid the groundwork early for the need for the Confederate government to officially recognize the acts of Lt. Young and his party; to "find means to convey such recognition to the prisoners here in such a form as can be proven before our Courts."

Abbott said Richmond must not hesitate to fully admit responsibility for Young's mission. Otherwise, Abbott said the lieutenant and his men would be given up to the United States authorities and if that were the case they "would be placed before a Court and jury personally hostile to them; composed of enemies inflamed against them to an unprecedented degree by the virulence of the struggle between the two sections [North and South]."

The raid now over, it was not long before many high-placed people in the South realized that twilight had fallen on the heady days of its secret service in Canada. The commissioners were being watched more carefully than ever before, and Union detectives, informers, and military officers prowled the streets of Montreal and Toronto, looking for any clues to new action afoot.

10

Cause Célèbre

★ ★ ★ ★ ★ ★ ★ ★ ★ ★ ★ ★ ★ ★ ★ ★ ★ ★ ★

"It may be termed an outrage, a violation of the
modern usages of war; but history will look upon it
as a bold and daring feat."

After spending a few days in an unremarkable jail in Philipsburg, Canadian authorities escorted the raiders to Montreal.
Cheers burst through the air as the party entered the city limits.
An artillery company escorted Young and his band to the jail, a
converted parlor in the home of Guillaume Lamothe, Montreal's
Chief of Police. Once they were properly installed, Lamothe took
custody of the stolen money and securities.

The citizens of Montreal couldn't have been more enthralled
with these Southern men: They doted on the prisoners as though
they were stars of the stage. History will not say that these prisoners languished there. Rather, they entertained a constant
gaggle of folk all vying for a glimpse of the handsome bunch.
Not one visitor cared about the violence and mayhem the men
had caused. Even Mary Coursol, the judge's daughter, visited
Young bearing fruit, flowers, and perhaps more than a bit of
infatuation. In an interview long after the war had ended and

Young had returned to the United States, he related how he had charmed and seduced the lovely Miss Coursol.

While in jail, the Kentuckians ate exquisitely prepared meals off of china dinnerware placed upon fine linens. They sipped wine and ale. They had tobacco, newspapers, and stationery. U.S. Attorney Edward A. Sowles wrote that their apartments "were furnished with all the improvements of the European plan. Their dinners were served with bills of fare, not mentioning the wines, et cetera, such as would grace the table of a prince."

One afternoon, while enjoying their newfound celebrity, Bennett Young had the audacity to send an open letter from his gilded confines to the people of St. Albans. On November 20, Wilber P. Davis, an editor at the *Daily Messenger*, received a letter together with three dollars neatly tucked inside the envelope. The bills had of course been stolen from the Franklin County Bank.

"To the editor of the *St. Albans Messenger*: will you please send me two copies of your daily, during the present investigation. Your editorials are quite interesting and will furnish considerable amusement, to myself, and comrades. You are somewhat abusive but I have sufficient magnanimity to overlook your ire, feeling that in after years you will do me the justice to repair the wrong. I am extremely sorry that I cannot visit your town and subscribe to your valuable journal in person. My business engagements in Montreal prevent my coming at present. Address me, care of 'Montreal Jail.' Should you not send me the papers I hope you will remit enclosed bill by return mail. Should you visit Montreal in the next few weeks I will be found at Payette's Hotel (Louis Payette is jailer) and will be gratified to see you. Yours respectfully, Bennett H. Young, 1st Lieut. Provisional Army Confederate States."

S. W. Skinner, the proprietor of the Tremont Hotel, also received a letter from Young apologizing for his sudden departure.

This one contained a five-dollar St. Albans Bank note to settle the raider's outstanding hotel bill.

Not ignored, the manager of the American House also received a letter from Young: "You will probably remember I was a guest at your house. I regret I neglected to settle my hotel bill. Nevertheless, I am enclosing five dollars drawn on the Bank of St. Albans. Please tender my regards to Mr. Bishop; in hopes he still bears faith and allegiance to the Confederate States of America, which he so solemnly swore to do. We have heard nothing of the old gent, president of the institution at the time we suspended him and began running his bank, I presume he is still faithful to the pledge and is fixed to that armchair. If so, tell the old 'boozer' his term of sentence has now expired." And lastly, a parting word for Sarah Clark, "Please remember me to the lady next door whose good opinion I had the fortune to win, on account of our theological proclivities. Make to her your best bow. . . ."

These letters display the teasing, taunting, and, yes, quite charming manner of Bennett Young that the people of Montreal came to adore.

In no time, the raid and its players achieved international notoriety. At first, the United States had boldly offered a $10,000 reward for each raider captured alive. But President Abraham Lincoln soon rescinded his order permitting Capt. George Conger, or anyone else, to cross the border to haul the raiders back to stand trial before a Federal judge. The administration plainly wanted to defuse any threat of conflict, diplomatic or otherwise, with Great Britain.

Lincoln, together with others in the administration, then set off on a course of determined diplomacy to get the raiders back. At first, this wasn't merely fantasy: The Canadians had promised to turn the Confederate crew over to the Americans. However, the Canadian government, from the Montreal Police

Superintendent to the defense counsel, was quite besotted with the Southern cause. They did little to mask their sympathy for the raiders.

Although Clement Clay visited the raiders in jail, he continued to publicly distance himself from them, going so far as to deny that he had ever authorized their plan.

He publicly described them as a band of thieves and wished "the whole party, with the exception of Young, in a warmer climate than that in which they were born." Furthermore, Clay demanded that the raiders turn the loot over to him, since he designated himself the sole representative of the Confederate government.

J. D. McGinnis, one of the few raiders to escape arrest, thought Clay's behavior bizarre, to say the least. Everyone in the group knew that Clay had been a key organizer and wholehearted supporter of the attack.

Clay's abrupt about-face hurt no one more than Young. "I have ever done my duty to you and my country. I ask that you make me right with the War Department. That the raid has done good no one can deny and I trust that you will give a fair and just statement of all that I did," was the content of a passionate letter Young wrote to Clay on November 21, 1864.

As for the money, Young, in the same letter, said that the raiders had been ready to hand it over; but the "language you used in regards to them, they all expressed a determination to be extradited rather than yield. I have ever loved you Mr. Clay more so as a father rather than a superior and come what will . . . my heart will ever be open to you with a warm and gushing spring of love. I love my country and I love you and there's nothing I won't do to serve them."

Finding Clay unresponsive, Young turned to Thompson. "I feel it to be my duty Col. Thompson in this affair to lay aside all personal feelings and animosities. . . . It is your duty as Confederate agent to take charge of this matter and every one of the party feel that you will do them justice. . . ."

None of the men wanted to give Clay any uncaptured loot; rather, they wanted to turn it over to Commissioner Thompson. However, Thompson didn't want the plunder, despite Clay's missives.

"He [McGinnis] offered me the money and I told him I would at once turn it over to you and therefore he had better pay it to you at once. To this, he agreed to do," Clay wrote in a November 22 letter to Thompson.

When the trial opened on November 5, 1864, seats were hard to come by and everyone clamored for a view of the proceedings, which promised to be rich with excitement. A host of characters, from the raiders themselves to a number of St. Albans residents, were slated to take the stand. The courtroom was so mobbed that spectators spilled into the hallway.

Young and his men faced seven separate charges. The first was the robbery of Samuel Breck, from whom they had stolen nearly four hundred dollars upon entering the Bank of St. Albans. The heart of the court case revolved around one question: whether the raid was an officially approved military operation, or a criminal felony of robbery, arson, and murder. If the judge found the latter to be true, then the prisoners would be extradited to face a tribunal in the United States according to the tenth article of the Webster–Ashburton Treaty, which said extradition would take place for murder, assault with intent to commit murder, piracy, arson, robbery, or forgery.

But if Coursol found for the defense, and determined that the raiders were carrying out orders of the Confederate government, then the United States would have no jurisdiction. Only the "principles of international law as they relate to belligerents engaged in acts of war" would apply.

Great Britain and the United States had signed the Webster–Ashburton Treaty in 1842. It was an agreement designed to settle the Northeast Boundary Dispute, which had caused many border conflicts, including the so-called Aroostook War, a tense but bloodless conflict. The Treaty also settled the contested international border in the Great Lakes region, as well as establishing cooperation for suppression of the slave trade and mutual extradition of criminals. Both countries had signed the treaty with much optimism; it was a first step toward ending the friction between the two nations. The St. Albans raid threatened to reignite the tension, however, and any misstep, perceived or real, could cause it to rise to the surface once more.

While the opposing attorneys prepared, George Sanders began his own sort of defense. He took charge of the prisoners' comfort, taking care to make sure that their every desire was met. Each night, while holding court at a local pub, he ordered an array of foods delivered to the jailed men. He also made daily statements to the press regarding the defense progress and strategy.

Moreover, Sanders attempted to pin the entire responsibility for the raid on Clay's shoulders. This was in case the defense never got the required proof from Richmond. To drive home his case, Sanders furnished a letter, reportedly from Clay, saying that Sanders's suggestion for a raid on towns in Vermont, starting with St. Albans, had been approved. The letter, according to Sanders, authorized the raid.

Yet his most brilliant move had to be the day he decided to retain nearly every attorney in the vicinity of Montreal and assembled an imposing and talented defense team. As chief attorney, Abbott's sole aim was to persuade Justice Charles-Joseph Coursol that he lacked jurisdiction over the case. Abbott wrote to Clay on October 25, 1864: "We all think it quite clear that the facts will not justify a commitment under the law as it now stands and we conceive the strength of our position to consist in the documents we now hold, establishing the authority of the raiders from the Confederate States government."

No one on the defense, not even the raiders themselves, denied that the raid had taken place. But to be acquitted, they had to prove that they had acted on orders from the Confederate government. John Abbott knew that the defense absolutely needed copies of the orders for the raid from the authorities in Richmond. Such proof would snuff out all talk of extradition. Abbott sought and received a postponement from the judge, thus allowing more time to prepare and gather evidence. The attorney immediately sent someone to Richmond to find the confirmation they needed.

At the prosecution table, Bernard Devlin, attorney for the United States, took issue with the defense's repeated claims that the raiders would be summarily executed if extradited to the United States. Devlin insisted that the group would receive a fair trial.

Bennett Young couldn't have disagreed more. He was "convinced that if extradited I would have been put to death as were other men, like Captains Beall and Davis engaged in similar enterprises."

This was no trial for the accused to sit as unemotional mutes. This was a spicy stew of international relations, Southern honor, and daring adventure. Two days after opening statements, on November 7, the raiders began to testify.

Naturally, as the group leader, Lt. Bennett H. Young took the stand first. He declared himself a commissioned officer of the Confederate army operating with the unqualified approval of the Confederate government. He brandished his commission as first lieutenant in the Army and proceeded to address the crowd, which sat rapt with attention.

"I am a native of Kentucky, and a citizen of the Confederate States, to which I owe allegiance. I am a commissioned officer in the Army of the Confederate States, with which the United States are now at war. I owe no allegiance to the United States," Young said. "The course I intended to pursue in Vermont, and which I was able to carry out but partially, was to retaliate in some measure for the barbarous atrocities of Grant, Butler, Sherman, Hunter, Milroy, Sheridan, Grierson, and other Yankee officers, except that I would scorn to harm women and children under any provocation, or unarmed, defenseless, and unresisting citizens, even Yankees, or to plunder for my own benefit."

Young insisted that the "expedition," as he referred to the raid, was neither planned in Canada nor an infringement of Canadian neutrality. He boasted about how Seddon had authorized him to organize a company not to exceed twenty. Young told the court that he and his party were "entitled to their pay, rations, clothing, and transportation, but no other compensation for any service which they may be called upon to render."

The defense knew that pushing the idea that Young and his men were only following orders would become the center of their case. John Abbott explained with the utmost confidence that, once in the open, the facts would not justify extradition. "The strength of our position to consist in the documents we hold establishing the authority of the raiders from the C.S. Government." Abbot wanted the court to "consider it to be their duty to recognize officially the acts of Lieutenant Young and his party." He assured the judge that such proof was coming.

Abbott had already written to Clay, telling him in so many words that he had better step up and deliver the evidence. He further explained to Clay that even if President Jefferson Davis were to assume responsibility for Young's actions, it wouldn't be enough. "You [Clay] will signify it in such form as will entitle it to admission as evidence in the pending trial."

Why, then, did Clement Clay try so hard to deny the raiders? He was, by all accounts, a man seemingly swayed by George Sanders, seemingly totally under the influence of Bennett Young, and seemingly quite supportive of the Confederate cause. But Clay feared that the trial would tarnish any chance of political fortune that might, one day, yet shine on him.

The frustration of the defense was compounded by the fact that nearly everyone in the Confederate circle agreed that Clay had, at the very least, given the raiders his verbal blessing. What's more, Clay's actions seemed at odds with themselves—he sent a check for $6,074 "to be put in the hands of George N. Sanders for the defense of the raiders." Despite his apparently conflicted conscience, Clay refused to stop distancing himself from the event, as letters addressed to Thompson indicate.

Without the papers, Abbott resorted to showcasing Young's character. Abbott talked about how he had met Lt. Young in Halifax back in May 1864. Abbott made much of Young's moral fiber, promoting him as someone who "was not prompted by selfish or mercenary motives, and that he did not intend to convert the funds taken to his own use, but to that of the Confederate States." Abbott introduced letters from "men whom I knew by reputation to be true friends of States' rights, and therefore of Southern independence, vouching for his integrity as a man, his piety as a Christian, and his loyalty as a soldier of the South."

Cyrus Newton Bishop, the teller at the St. Albans bank, testified first for the prosecution. All eyes were riveted on Bishop as he took the stand. He recounted how he had quaked in bodily fear as Thomas Bronsdon Collins and Marcus Spurr "immediately advanced towards the counter behind which I was, and each of them pointed a revolver of a large size to my breast, I being then about three feet distant from them."

The teller described how Collins grabbed his coat collar and pressed the pistol to his head. "If I made any further resistance or gave any further alarm they would blow my brains out," Bishop told the courtroom.

Next the prosecution called George Roberts, clerk at the American House in St. Albans, to testify. Roberts had worked at the boarding house for more than a year before the fateful day.

"I recognize two of the prisoners, namely Young and Doty, having seen them in St. Albans prior to the nineteenth day of October last past. I saw Young there, I think twice before that day; but I am not sure if it was more than once. I saw him certainly once in the American House during the month prior to the nineteenth of October last."

Roberts slowly wore a chink in the raiders' defense as soldiers, as he described how they were "dressed in ordinary civilian's clothes. I saw nothing either in demeanor or dress to indicate that they had or claimed any military character whatever. On the afternoon of the nineteenth of October last past, the occurrences I have spoken of did not look like a military expedition. I thought the armed persons were a mob."

Much has been made over the raiders' dress on that rain-soaked afternoon. Were they robbers? If so, they didn't take the pains to mask their faces; rather, they brazenly invoked the name of the Confederacy. But if they were indeed soldiers, why didn't any of them wear a uniform?

To answer this, the defense called Thomas Stone, who had lived in Richmond, Kentucky, before leaving to fight for the Confederacy. Stone too had served under Morgan in the Seventh Kentucky Cavalry, Second Brigade.

"I knew that Mr. Young had the authority to raise the Company in question. I saw his authority in writing, in August of last year—being shown the paper filed by Mr. Young at his voluntary statement. . . . It would be impossible to describe the dress of Morgan's command, it was so varied; the articles of war provided for a uniform for the command, but the Quarter

Master's department never issued them; each man dressed according to his own taste or according to his means of providing them; some would have some part of the Confederate uniform, remainder plain, some in colors. I have seen a whole regiment dressed in Yankee uniform; this of course was after a raid. The principal source from which clothing was obtained was from captures from the enemy."

The defense highlighted the absence of uniforms to underscore their principal argument that the raiders were soldiers, not common criminals—or at least as no proof that they were not Confederate soldiers. Furthermore, civilian clothing was their key to stealth, as in any special-operations mission.

William L. T. Price, who hailed from the same Kentucky county as Young, testified. Having also served under Gen. Morgan, Price explained the view on uniforms. "The advanced guards were dressed in citizens' clothing, and so were Morgan's command always dressed, except some Yankee garments and overcoats. I have not seen Bennett Young for twenty months, until I saw him here. I then saw him engaged in a raid under Col. Cluke, in the uniform used by Morgan's command. Morgan's command generally wears the clothes of citizens."

As expected, the prosecution continued to spin the lack of military threads most differently: The raiders "dressed as citizens, entered a town where there was not an armed soldier, and, in broad daylight, committed what was known as common robbery."

Next, the testimony of Henry Nelson Whitman, Esquire, who helped arrest Alamanda Pope Bruce at William Elder's tavern, told of the pride with which the raiders admitted their involvement in the events of October 19: "When I arrested the said Bruce and Spurr. . . . They then asked me to telegraph to C. C. Clay, at Montreal, to inform him that they were captured, and to do his best for them. . . . I informed them that there was no telegraphic communication from that place, that they would as soon get an answer by letters, and the next day they wrote a letter, addressed, as I believe, to C. C. Clay. They told me that the said Clay was a Confederate agent at Montreal."

★ ★ ★

If the courtroom found Young spellbinding, then they must have found the next string of testimony equally transfixing.

"I owe no allegiance to the so-called United States, but to the Confederate States of America," stated Marcus Spurr, a Kentucky native, from the stand. "I was held prisoner of war in a Yankee Bastille, and by bribing a 'Yankee pay-triot' and by daring, escaped. . . . Last summer at Chicago, I placed myself under the command of Lt. Young. What I may have done at St. Albans, I did as a soldier of the Confederate States Army, and in accordance with orders from Lt. Young of said Army. In doing this, I have violated no law of Canada or Great Britain. I have lost kindred, and have had kindred plundered."

Alamanda Bruce's testimony described a cousin who had been brutally murdered in Camp Douglas as one reason he joined the Young party: "Yankee plundering and cruel atrocities without parallel provoked the attack on St. Albans as a mild retaliation."

Raider Joseph McGrorty, a native Irishman turned Texan, vowed that neither he nor his comrades were criminals. But had they been captured by the Federals on U.S. territory, "we would have been tried, not by civil law, but by a military commission or drumhead court-martial. But they found us on neutral territory, and now seek by Yankee ingenuity and the boasted influence of their government to get us into their power."

All this merely warmed the room for Thomas Bronsdon Collins, another Kentucky son who had ridden with John Hunt Morgan.

Collins passionately talked about his reasons for joining the raiding party: "The Yankees dragged my father from his peaceful fireside and family circle, and imprisoned him in Camp Chase, where his sufferings impaired his health and mind. They have stolen Negroes and forced them into their armies, leaving their women and children to die. They have pillaged and burned private dwellings, banks, villages and depopulated whole districts, boasting of their inhuman acts as deeds of heroism and exhibiting their plunder in northern cities as trophies of Federal victories."

Collins's testimony further pushed the case that extradition applies only to robbers, murderers, and thieves—a group to which, he said, neither he nor the other men belonged. He said that he was but a foot soldier serving his country in "a war commenced and waged against us by a barbarous foe in violation of their own constitution, in disregard of all the rules of warfare as interpreted by civilized nations . . . who whilst prating of neutrality seduce your own people along the border to violate the proclamation of your august Sovereign by joining their armies, and leave them when captured by us to languish as prisoners in a climate unwholesome to them."

As the trial unfolded and as his name kept appearing in testimony, Clement Clay was making no secret of his desire to return home to begin a job he had been offered in San Antonio, Texas. A Boston man had selected the commissioner to look after his interests on a large, landed estate.

On November 1, Clay dashed off a letter to Thompson: "I do not see that I can achieve anything by remaining longer in the province; and, unless instructed to stay, shall leave here by the 20th for Halifax and take my chances at running the blockade." He tried to blame his decision on his health. All the while, there was no word about Clay's supposed request to Secretary of State Benjamin asking Richmond to assume responsibility for the raid.

In the meantime, Virginia Clay desperately wanted to rejoin her husband. She could only reach him through personal ads published in the *Richmond Enquirer*, which had an arrangement with the New York *Daily News* for these kinds of messages. In November, he posted an ad "To Honorable H. L. Clay, Richmond, Virginia. I am well. Have written every week, but received no answer later than the 30th of June. Can I return at once? If not, send my wife to me by flag of truce, via Washington, but not by sea. Do write by flag of truce care John Potts Brown, No. 93 Beaver Street, New York. Answer by personal through *Richmond Enquirer* and New York *News*."

And with that, Clay left Montreal on December 10. So afraid was he that the raiders and Thompson's complaints would land him in trouble with Richmond, Clay asked Beverly Tucker, his associate and housemate in St. Catherines, to write a letter on his behalf. "Lest misunderstanding be imparted to their friends at home and place you in a false position, I write you this note before your departure for the South which you are at liberty to use as you may find necessary."

The letter Clay carried explained how all the stolen money, minus the amount needed required for the defense, should have been turned over to him, the representative of the Confederacy. Tucker used the letter to describe the fair-mindedness of Clay and the idea that the raiders were most wrong to think he had turned his back on them.

A British boat carried Clay to Bermuda, where he boarded the blockade-runner *Rattlesnake*. He arrived in Nassau on January 30, 1865. On February 3, his ship ran aground in the Charleston harbor and promptly burst into flames. The passengers scrambled into lifeboats, but they too ran aground. Clay abandoned his luggage in the hold and waded ashore, carrying only what he could, along with the letter tied in an oilskin sack about his neck. Two months later, he reached Richmond and told them his version of what had happened.

★ ★ ★

In Montreal, the extradition trial ground on. William Kerr, counsel for the defense, challenged Judge Coursol's right to hear the case. He used every tool imaginable, even persistently arguing a technical point—namely, that the raiders never should have been arrested in the first place because the Governor-General, not the local magistrate, should have issued the warrant.

Bernard Devlin, attorney for the United States, voiced his objections, but to little effect. Surprisingly, it appeared that Coursol found merit in Kerr's questions and decided to adjourn the court until the afternoon so he could more properly consider the question. He walked out of the courthouse, leaving the spectators buzzing with anticipation.

The crowd didn't have long to wait, as the judge returned an hour later to announce that a dismissal of the trial was the only course possible. Coursol based his decision on the fact that he had no warrant from Monck and so he had no jurisdiction. "Consequently, I am bound in law, justice and fairness to order the immediate release of the prisoners upon all charges brought before me. Let the prisoners be discharged."

And thus the police superintendent unconditionally freed the prisoners, to thunderous applause that echoed throughout the courtroom. A bailiff escorted the prisoners out a back door.

The cold air rejuvenated the Southern men. For three days, the raiders rested. Then they went on the run. Although they didn't have much of a head start, they made for New Brunswick, which lay outside Coursol's jurisdiction. The raiders knew that this dismissal was a mere postponement of another trial. Meanwhile, two new constables, Edward Ermatinger and Adolph Bissonnette, eager to retry the case, figured that the raiders would react as they did and took off in pursuit. Over the next few weeks, the raiders would be rounded up once more and taken back to "Payette's Hotel." In the meantime, tension and anger burned through diplomatic circles.

★ ★ ★

As for the Union attorneys, they greeted the dismissal with smoldering fury. They had had little faith in the Montreal justice system, and Coursol's decision simply validated their view. For starters, the prisoners had been charged on seven counts, but Coursol had heard only one. Furious, Bernard Devlin questioned the judge as to why of the seven charges, only those pertaining to Cyrus Newton Bishop were heard.

Devlin tried to challenge Judge Coursol's findings. At the same time, attorney Edward Sowles and Thomas Ritchie, two other lawyers on the case, wasted no time in preparing a fresh warrant. Together with George Edmonds, the attorney representing the State of Vermont, Sowles and Ritchie approached two superior court judges, hopeful that they would agree to rein in the raiders.

Some months later, Devlin delivered a speech before the Montreal City Council saying the prisoners and their friends had apparently known in advance of the decision that they'd be freed on a technicality. According to Devlin, Police Chief Guillaume Lamothe had deposited the purloined money in a bank where it could easily be accessed. Then, minutes before Judge Coursol finished reading his decision, a Confederate agent, George Porterfield, had abruptly left the room.

Porterfield had been the financial agent of the commissioners and would later be implicated in the trial of Lincoln's assassins for relaying messages between Richmond and Canada. He met

Lamothe in the hall and agreed to remove the money. Outside, a sleigh waited, and the driver whisked Porterfield to the bank, where he withdrew the money. (This is a theory published in the Louisville *Courier-Journal* on March 12, 1899 by Bennett Young, based on a letter he had received from F. L. McChesney of Paris, Kentucky, on January 5, 1899. McChesney was reportedly in contact with the raiders during their sojourn in the Montreal jail.)

★ ★ ★

In the meantime, the Coursol ruling arrived in Washington like a tempest. It certainly wasn't what the Lincoln government had wished for as a Christmas present. Tensions flickered between the United States and Canada, with even more heat than during the Trent Affair of 1861.

"And thus richly furnished with the spoils of our citizens they were conveyed, amid popular acclamation, in sleighs which had been prepared for their escape, from the court room, beyond the reach of fresh pursuit; when new warrants were issued the police were dilatory and treacherous in their execution. It is impossible to consider those proceedings as either legal, just or friendly towards the United States," Secretary of State William Seward wrote to Hon. Charles Francis Adams, United States Minister to Great Britain, on December 24, 1864.

This time, Gen. John Dix, in command of the Department of the East, took it upon himself to alert the public of the raiders' flight. Dix viewed the possibility of other attacks as extremely likely, given the raiders' discharge. He urged the people of the frontier towns to use any means necessary to protect their lives and property: "All military commanders on the frontier are therefore instructed in case further acts of depredation and murder are attempted, whether by marauders or persons acting under commissions from the Rebel authorities at Richmond, to shoot down the depredators, if possible while in the commission of their crimes, or if it be necessary with a view to their capture, to cross the boundary between the United States and Canada, said commanders are directed to pursue them wherever they may take refuge, and if captured, they are under no circumstances to be surrendered, but are to be sent to these headquarters for trial and punishment by martial law."

Dix also conveyed his displeasure to Secretary of State Seward about the hearing's outcome, making sure to "inform him that I will do everything that I can do to remedy the effect of Judge Coursol's proceedings."

On December 14, the U.S. Senate passed two resolutions condemning the Canadian ruling. Seeking some kind of retribution, Congress demanded an accounting of vessels destroyed on the border lakes by Confederate soldiers acting from Canada and charges with interest for loss presented to the British government for restitution.

Viscount Monck was himself quite steamed about the prisoners' release. In a December 14 dispatch, Monck said that the St. Albans men had been discharged on absurd grounds. Monck finally ordered that the men be re-arrested. He also ordered that a unit of special secret police be created and that they be sent to patrol the border, already on high alert.

Additionally, Monck called for an investigation into the existence or extent of Coursol and Lamothe's involvement with the raiders. The inquiry found that a day prior to the prisoners' release, Lamothe and George Sanders had met and planned to hide money in the Ontario Bank. The investigations concluded rather quickly and deemed that while the two officials had not been prudent, they hadn't broken the law. Nevertheless, Lamothe resigned and Coursol was suspended.

As diplomats continued to fire off dispatches, the U.S. attorneys continued their search for the one judge who would agree

to convene a new trial. Police Chief Lamothe would have nothing to do with this. So the trio of lawyers went to Montreal's high constable, Adolph Bissonnette, who agreed to execute the warrant. With agreements in hand that Canada would re-arrest the fugitives, animosity between the United States and Canada slowly abated.

Nevertheless, Washington followed through on actions inspired by its displeasure over the ruling. The Lincoln White House decided to retaliate by tightening passport controls between the two countries. On December 17, the State Department issued the directive, mentioned above, requiring full application of passport regulation to all visitors from Canada. It slowed commerce, dealing a heavy blow to the Canadian provinces that depended on open access with their neighbor to the south. Beneath the surface, Secretary of State Seward and others in the White House hoped the strict passport controls would induce Canada to pass an official Neutrality Act, which would make it more difficult for Confederates to mount attacks from Canada.

"It would be difficult indeed to believe that they would have attempted to elevate a daring act of robbery to the dignity of a manly deed of warfare, or claimed for its guilty perpetrators the consideration due to the honest warrior who uses his arms for the legitimate objects of war, and not as the prisoners did at St. Albans, for the ignoble and savage purpose of robbing and murdering unarmed and defenseless citizens . . . it has become a cause célèbre," said attorney Devlin for the prosecution on March 21, 1865. Though he spoke those words during the second trial for extradition, which began on December 27, 1864, it speaks to the intense coverage given at the time.

A cause célèbre indeed. Newspapers from Montreal to England weighed in about the affair and its aftermath. Until the trial of the Lincoln assassins, this could be considered the most sensational bit of politics in a long time. It wasn't every day that a band of Southern soldiers invaded a Northern town, fled on horseback, and threatened the neutrality of an entire nation.

The Canadian press, like the Canadian people, mostly sided with the Confederate cause, their sympathies resting comfortably with Young and his twenty men. A majority of the newspapers justified or excused the raiders' act as merely retaliatory and advocated a desire for the authority of the Confederate government to assert itself and to refuse their extradition.

In addition, Lincoln's passport controls did little to win him friends. An editorial in the *Toronto Leader* called the directive "vindictive." Even border cities such as Detroit had little cause for celebration. The *Detroit Free Press* ran an editorial chastising the Lincoln government for the law, saying that it hurt people in Windsor, Canada, who needed to travel to Detroit every day for work.

Yet for all the griping about the travel restrictions, and for all the support for the raiders, there were some editorials in Canada and Great Britain that wanted to see the Confederates sent across the border. In the December 29, 1864 edition of the *London Post,* an article said it had no doubt that the raiders should be extradited. "War is only war when it is waged either from the open sea, or from territory belonging to the attacking belligerents. If, in the course of the recent Danish war, Prussians had secreted themselves on the shores of Norfolk with the view of making an attack . . . we should certainly have arrested them without any special treaty of extradition."

From the *London News,* December 29, 1864: "We should expect France to do thus much for us if were unhappily at war with America, and Americans plotted and directed from Calais expeditions to sack Brighton or burn Hastings. And it is clear that what we should regard as the duty of France in such a case would be still more her duty if the war were made upon our seaboard, not by a foreign nation, but by our own subjects in revolt. This is the American case at present, and there must be no hesitation in our doing to them the justice which we should look for from every friendly power if the case were our own."

Other opinions saw an imminent danger of war if Canada didn't enact laws to guarantee and enforce neutrality. There was a worry that if the Confederates continued to disrespect Canadian neutrality, then it wouldn't be long before the Union ignored it too.

In its October 20, 1864 edition, the Montreal *Gazette* reported: "We must, we repeat, preserve our neutrality, and their right of asylum which British soil affords inviolate, and punish with the sternest severity any breach which can be discovered. If we do not we shall find ourselves dragged into the war for needless cause; our eastern frontier lit up with the fires of now peaceful homes, and the country on both sides of the line made red with murders. . . . To surprise a peaceful town and shoot down people in the streets, committing at the same time robbery, is not civilized war; it is that of savages."

Finally, a new trial date was set, with Justice James Smith of the Superior Court presiding. A sequel to the first trial, this one would again revolve around whether Richmond had officially sanctioned the raid and whether the raiders were acting as soldiers or civilian criminals.

Smith had issued a warrant for the re-arrest of the raiders, and five of the thirteen were apprehended near Quebec. Once again, Young, Hutchinson, Teavis, Swager, and Spurr found themselves the forced guests of Canadian justice. The trial opened in Montreal on December 27. Attorney John Abbott once again addressed the dicey matter of how to justify the raiders' plotting of what he defined as a legitimate act of war on neutral soil.

One witness for the defense was William W. Cleary, who, in addition to his Canadian service, had also worked in Richmond in the Treasury Department. Cleary attested to the authenticity of the signatures of James Seddon and Clement Clay on documents, having seen them on numerous occasions while performing administrative duties in the Confederate capital. He pointed to documents and confirmed that they were "in the handwriting of said Clement C. Clay. I have no doubt of it at all. His handwriting is peculiar and very characteristic, and I could not very well mistake it. . . . I became aware a short time after the raid occurred that he had authorized it. I know this from himself."

Of course, no trial would be complete without an appearance by George N. Sanders. Once more, he stepped up to the witness box with all the flare appropriate to the Canadians' view of a Southern gentleman. Sanders regaled the court with his version of events, describing several conversations he and Clay had shared about the St. Albans raid. Not only did Clay order the raid and instruct Young to execute the mission, but "about the eighth day of December last, a few days before he left, that he would leave such a letter as the paper writing. . . . The letter which he said he would write on that occasion was a letter assuming all the responsibility of the St. Albans raid, for which he was responsible."

For the second trial, William Kerr carefully laid out the reasons, in a written paper to Judge Smith, why the raiders deserved protection in Canada.

Kerr's points were, as outlined in the trial transcripts, that (1) Young was a commissioned officer in the Confederate service in command of a party of Confederate States troops; (2) Young was ordered and directed by a superior officer for the raid; (3) The tenth article of the Webster–Ashburton Treaty was limited in operation to crimes recognized by the common law of both countries; (4) Acts of hostility on both sides were not recognized by the treaty; (5) The United States no longer existed. Since ratification of Ashburton in 1842, five or six states had been admitted into, and nine or ten states had seceded from, the Union. (Kerr argued that the treaty was not retroactive); (6) That both the Federal states and the Confederate States are entitled to all belligerent rights given by war to sovereign governments; and (7) Under the law of nations, members of one belligerent nation may lawfully kill members of the other belligerent nation, or seize or capture their property wherever found, except in neutral territory.

Kerr stipulated that extraditing to a foreign power a "man who has committed no crime against our law, but who seeks solely in a British colony an asylum from the enemies of his country would be wrong!"

Kerr also played upon the insecurity suffered by the South, and tried to cast the prosecution as nothing more than bullies acting on the behest of the Union: "They appear to have imbibed the prejudices of their client, the United States Government, and to be unwilling to admit that our clients have any claim to be belligerents. The people of the State of Vermont are, it is said, frightfully excited at the idea of one of their towns having been captured and held for three hours by a band of twenty-one pretended Confederate soldiers. The booty taken from the banks, no doubt, has also tended to exacerbate their feelings, and they still continue to brand the St. Albans raid as unsoldierly, dastardly, in violation of the rules of war, and perfectly fiendish."

Judah P. Benjamin, Confederate Secretary of War and a former senator in Louisiana, described it perfectly. It wasn't so much what the North had done to the South, or even what it might one day do—it was the manner in which they acted, the moral arrogance with which they viewed and described the South. Southerners cared deeply about Northern opinion, as if to seek in it strains of their own legitimacy. The South was tired of inferiority.

William Kerr further took on the Union. "What does the record of the daily events show us? That this verily is a civil war waged by the North against the South, with all the barbarity of the Thirty Years' War. . . . It is a strife wherein the father meets his son at the point of the bayonet, and where the brother imbrues his hands in his brother's blood. It is a carnival of blood; and can it be wondered that man, drunk with the odor of carnage, should forget that he was framed after his Creator's image, and do deeds which bring him to the level of the wild beasts?"

Toussaint-Antoine-Rodolphe Laflamme, co-counsel for the defense, mocked the prosecutor's strategy to use bank clerks Breck and Bishop as the basis for extradition.

"Out of the whole of this expedition, the prosecution has thought it proper to single out the taking of Mr. Breck's money, the smallest incident in the whole transaction; a fact which cannot with any reason be abstracted or severed from the main project. . . . Clearly the Ashburton Treaty excludes the extradition of prisoners for political offenses."

Besides, Kerr went on to reason, Young was a mere patriot who risked his life to conspire against his enemy, and it was patriotism that impelled the raiders, nothing more. "In no other country, perhaps, but in the Southern Confederacy, would twenty young men be found who would be prepared to risk their lives to offer them to a certain almost ignominious death in taking possession of a town of four thousand inhabitants. All idea of personal profit, private plunder is excluded by the facts."

As for the question of neutrality, Laflamme summarily dismissed the notion that the raiders violated any such laws, as ambassadors needed to communicate when posted abroad. "If such a principle was affirmed, then England could not act through her ambassadors or her navy officers, when in neutral ground or neutral ports, to convey orders or instructions to those directly engaged in hostilities."

Then Laflamme invoked the inevitable "following orders" defense. He labored to establish that Young had had orders for special service, with Clay in the role of his immediate superior. The orders were to be taken as if they had come from the desk of President Jefferson Davis himself. These were orders not to be disputed or questioned. If Young and company refused to obey orders, they could have been tried and shot, Laflamme said. Now the prosecution insisted that the men be "delivered to their enemies to be tried as common criminals."

All players, save Clement Clay, who jumped into the role of a coward, admitted to the action and planning. Canada, however, chose to hide behind the Webster–Ashburton Treaty. Because Canada, via Great Britain, was still technically a neutral country, any plotting by raiders on her soil—and there of course was some—violated that principle. By that alone, the raiders should have been extradited to the United States to face a military tribunal.

However, the defense attorneys knew that their audience, at the local level, identified with the Southern Gentlemen regardless of the government's official line. So when they argued that extradition would mean certain death at the hands of the Federals, the judge believed it.

Bennett Young, taking the stand for the second time, flawlessly illustrated this point. The chestnut-haired lieutenant spoke of how he had ventured forth on this mission feeling somewhat reluctant, since he had always opposed "measures of retaliation"; but alas, he had "suffered so many hardships and endured so many privations in the cause of liberty and freedom, that my heart is steeled against sympathy for the invaders and oppressors of my beloved, my native land. Fresh from scenes of devastated firesides and ruined villages, and listening so lately to the wail of the widow and cry of the orphan; when I behold the ruin and devastation which marks the track of the Federal troops, can anyone wonder that the fires of revenge and retaliation should slumber within my bosom and only need the opportunity to burst into flames. . . . Truly in this War, civilization has been made to shudder, and demons to rejoice, in the backward march of all that is ennobling and worthy of the creatures made in God's own image and after his own likeness."

Either Young truly gloried in the notion of dying for the Stars and Bars, or he simply hungered for the dramatic as he told the courtroom: "I have faced death many times ere this; and should I, contrary to all precedent, be extradited, I am perfectly well aware what my fate shall be. I can die as a son of the South, and the agony of ten thousand deaths will never cause me to regret what I have done, and the part I have borne in this struggle of right against might."

But Young warned that if he were executed for the raid, "the day upon which I die will be one that will bring a wail to the best families in the Green Mountain State. My death shall be avenged, and that in the blood of Vermont officers."

Regardless of the degree of Young's sincerity in his willingness to hang for his action, he certainly voiced a common feeling among the Rebel party: that the St. Albans raid was just a small payback for perceived Union atrocities down South.

The defense's first attempt to locate proof that Richmond had officially ordered the raid yielded nothing, so Abbott called for another. This time the recess dragged on, with still no word as to whether copies of the orders could be found. The U.S. attorneys grew tired of waiting. They pushed Justice Smith to reopen the extradition proceedings. Smith wouldn't hear of it, and the waiting continued. Smith's refusal exemplified the obstacles that faced the United States legal team at every turn.

The defense had sent three teams of messengers on a journey south to retrieve this crucial bit of evidence. By this time in the war, many Southerners lived in Canada, and some of these refugees volunteered to retrieve documents from Richmond to prove the defense's case. The United States, however, turned down all requests that these Southerners be allowed to travel to Richmond under a white flag.

As far back as the first trial, Jacob Thompson had sent a messenger to Richmond requesting passage through Federal lines. Now, a Canadian attorney by the name of J. G. K. Houghton stepped in and called upon Lincoln to allow him to pass. But Lincoln wouldn't allow him passage through Union lines to get evidence for the prisoners' defense: "No. I will not. These men are Rebels. They go cutting and slashing around and I don't think it's any part of my business to help them."

During Houghton's testimony on February 11, 1865, he told the court how he tried to send a dispatch through generals Ulysses S. Grant and Robert E. Lee to Richmond. This request was denied. Lincoln said "You can see the Secretary of State," and gave Houghton a card to see Seward. Houghton testified how Seward refused an audience with him, sending only a curt note that explained that no foreign intervention would be needed if only the prisoners would come to the United States. Seward also told Houghton to leave the United States "without crossing military lines or attempting to enter the scene of insurrection, or to communicate with the insurgents."

Again, fate smiled on the defendants. As the proceedings resumed on a Montreal winter morning, all eyes in the courtroom were suddenly diverted to the back of the chamber. The open door framed a woman who claimed only to be a Kentucky widow. She had safely made the journey from Richmond to Montreal, concealing her cargo in her corset. She stood before the court with a large envelope clutched in her hand.

The woman handed the package to the Confederate counsel; inside it were copies of commissions and of the official sanction of the raid. The papers helped convince the court that the men were not mere ruffians, but rather agents acting on the lawful orders of their government.

Two days later, to further buttress the documents, Reverend Stephen F. Cameron arrived in Toronto with a duplicate set of copies of the raiders' orders given to him by Jefferson Davis, Judah Benjamin, and James Seddon.

Cameron lived in Maryland and had served as a chaplain in the Confederate States Army. While in Richmond, he obtained the necessary documents pertaining to Young and then asked Jefferson Davis himself for duplicates. Davis agreed but stopped short of taking full responsibility. With the materials in hand, Cameron crossed the Potomac dressed as a Catholic priest, accompanied by two female spies who were dressed as nuns. His skiff was nearly overturned by shells fired from a Union battery located on the western shore, but the party survived and the mission continued to its successful conclusion.

The papers showed three official orders from Seddon to Young, although not one specifically mentioned St. Albans. The first order instructed Young to "collect twenty escaped Confederate prisoners and execute such enterprises as may be indicated to you," and he was to make sure that there were enough monies, rations, clothing, and transportation for the crew. The second order told Young to report to Messrs. Clay and Thompson. The third order did not mention the commissioners, but said that "organization was under the direction of the Confederate War Department and as such could be disbanded at its pleasure. . . ."

Some people still question whether Richmond had falsified the orders to save the raiders' lives. But whether the papers were real or forged bore little consequence at the time; Young and his men were once again on the cusp of freedom.

But there was one more hurdle to jump for the defense: Clement Clay's role in the three sets of orders. These two issues posed a sticky problem for the defense to explain.

Prosecutor Bernard Devlin highlighted the fact that the orders were inconsistent, and he raised questions about how the raiders justified their actions based on the authority not of Seddon, but, rather "the mysterious C. C. Clay, whom nobody in Canada, except the prisoners and their Counsel, seems to have seen, known, or cared about."

Devlin demanded to know exactly who Clement Clay thought he was, to give himself "such extraordinary powers in a neutral territory." In his second round of testimony, George N. Sanders reiterated his and Clay's conversations regarding the raid.

"Now, if we are to believe Sanders, and I know of no reason why we should disbelieve his testimony upon this point, the prisoners had only the verbal authority of C. C. Clay, for their doings at St. Albans, upon the 19th of October," Devlin said.

Devlin asserted that the so-called October 6 letter was "undoubtedly written after the prisoners' visit to St. Albans, and in the month of December, a day or two before C. C. Clay withdrew himself from Canada. It is in evidence, that from the moment he set foot in this Province, he disregarded our neutrality laws, which, so long as he claimed an asylum in Canada, were as binding upon him as upon us." Without Clay to question, however, Devlin was on shaky ground at best.

Devlin implored the court to recognize the base motivations of the raiders: "Pray, what object had the prisoners in going to St. Albans? Was it not to steal? . . . Can it be reasonably pretended that when they stole from the banks $220,000 that they did not mean to do that either? Can it be believed that when Young and his party murdered Morrison, shot Huntington, and wounded several other citizens of St. Albans, they had no criminal intent?"

Devlin suspected that the trial would trifle with, as he put it, the nations' treaty engagements. He warned of the dangers of breaking the ties between the two countries, saying that it wasn't wise to tear asunder "the bond of friendship that has for so many years secured to us the blessings of peace and the enjoyment of an uninterrupted reign of prosperity between two countries so commercially and diplomatically entwined."

After six days of testimony, Justice James Smith delivered a two-day summation. The audience sat fixed in their seats. Little mumbling could be heard in the room.

In short, Smith said that, like Coursol previously, he had no grounds to extradite the raiders, who were commissioned officers in the Confederate States Army, which was currently at war with the United States. The Justice declared that the attack on St. Albans "must be regarded as a hostile expedition, undertaken and carried out under the authority of the so-called Confederate States, under the command of one of their officers."

At 11:40 P.M. on March 29, 1865, Secretary of State William Seward received a telegram: "Saint Albans raiders discharged. Have instructed Montreal consul to take no more steps in our behalf. If you desire otherwise, please inform me here."

An irate Seward fired off a telegram to Vermont. Five minutes later, at 11:45 P.M., Governor Gregory Smith received a telegram: "Telegram from our consul in Montreal says raiders discharged; their acts fully sustained. Have them arrested on another warrant."

After Judge John Smith freed the raiders, they hung around the city celebrating their release. They taunted the U.S. authorities, who would most definitely chase them down.

Bennett Young, William Huntley Hutchinson, and Squire Teavis sought the help of an old Irish coach driver. He drove the fugitives into the St. Francois parish, where the three principal roads leading out of Canada converge. They were detained there, yet again, just thirty miles from the border of New Brunswick where they would have finally been free from the law.

The other raiders fared better. After their release, Collins, Scott, Bruce, and Doty checked into an inn. At dawn, the four men, disguised as French peasants, found a sleigh loaded with furs and blankets waiting outside. David Têtu would be their guardian angel.

Têtu was a *courier-du-bois,* someone with strong links between the white community and the Canadian Indians. The thirty-six-year-old man knew his way around the woods, rivers, and people of the vast province of Quebec. With his large almond eyes, abundant moustache and beard, and thrusting chin, Têtu furnished the fleeing raiders with a strong sense of comfort.

As morning light crept across the sky, the sleigh traveled far and away. Hours after they started, they reached the Bay of Rocks, located twelve miles above the mouth of the Saguenay River. Têtu made camp for the small group there, nary a house or hut in sight. The men clustered around a fire and fell asleep.

At first light, the four raiders, with Têtu as their guide, resumed their trek. They were careful to remain concealed while they detoured around the village of Tadoussac. Têtu wanted to reach a fishing shack at Pointe-a-la-Cariole, situated on the northern bank of the St. Lawrence River.

Once at the shack, the plan was for the fugitives to hunker down until the spring thaw. But while they were out of the woods, they were not out of the woods; a detective named McNider had been searching for them on behalf of the American government.

Têtu, aware that McNider was on their trail, decided to appeal directly to McNider: "Why continue in the role of a spy? Believe me, it would be nobler of you to join with us in rescuing these men than to be at work toward their ruin. Instead of adding to their distress, you may as well become one of their deliverers."

In case that didn't persuade McNider, the *courier-du-bois* cautioned the detective of the raiders' skills as sharpshooters. He stressed that the men wouldn't be taken without a fight. Convinced, McNider did more than stand down; he helped Têtu and the fugitives. He carried a letter to a man named John Barry who lived near Pointe-a-la-Cariole. Barry invited the raiders to his home to wait for the river's ice to melt. Barry prepared a supper and a toast to the raiders as they sang Southern songs, played cards and chess. The raiders lodged with him for two months.

Finally, at the close of March, the ice began to melt. As the raiders bid adieu to Têtu, tears glistened in their eyes.

The issue of the raiders' violation of Canadian neutrality was something that the prosecution had constantly tried to highlight, but the defense successfully sidestepped it time and again. However, even after the trial was over, the United States refused to let the matter fade away.

The U.S. attorneys tried to convince the Canadian authorities that there should be no exception to the law that hostile action launched from neutral territory is illegal. Furthermore, Young and the others had spent far too much time in Canada to be considered belligerents in a war being conducted in the U.S.A. and

C.S.A., according to the prosecution: "As a matter of law, then, the prisoners, by making Canada an asylum, had ceased to be belligerents; and inasmuch as the expedition started from neutral territory, and returned thereto, with their spoil, immediately after its accomplishment, the expedition was absolutely unlawful."

The U.S. attorneys had gained some favor within Canada for this view. In December 1864, Edward Cardwell had encouraged Monck to understand that British and Canadian neutrality had been violated, since the Rebel raiders had used "the soil of Canada as the scene of their hostile plotting against the United States." Cardwell had said that the United States had a clear right to expect that Canadian law should not only punish the raiders, but should also suppress and prevent border raids.

Lord Monck in response informed Cardwell that if the Canadian tribunals found the raiders not guilty of any offense for which they could be extradited, he himself would consult legal advisers as to whether they had committed "an offense against the Sovereignty of the Queen, punishable by the laws of Canada."

Monck, hardly a fool, knew that prosecuting the raiders for breaching neutrality would help repair relations between the United States and Canada.

However, legislation moved too slowly for some U.S. congressmen, and so they decided to bid farewell to the Reciprocity Treaty on February 9, 1865, a treaty that had governed commerce and defense on the Great Lakes. The American legislators decided to use further sanctions as a means of punishing Canada for perceived violations of neutrality and for harboring and favoring the raiders.

On March 31, 1865, Secretary of State Seward informed the Canadian government that the United States would drop its proceedings if Canada detained the remaining raiders on their own charges. Inspired, Monck made sure that those remaining raiders who were rounded up after the Smith trial would face new charges of violating a new Neutrality Act.

On April 8, 1865, the few Confederate raiders left in Canada were arrested on the charge of breaking the Municipal Law of Canada. They were to be tried in Toronto.

"That they did accordingly receive from Mr. Clay, in Canada, instructions for the attack which they afterwards made upon St. Albans, and were furnished by him, in Canada, with money for that purpose; and they did, in fact, proceed from Canada to St. Albans on a belligerent expedition," Cardwell wrote. "If this be so, I am advised that the Attorney General of Canada is right in [that] the evidence discloses a gross deliberate violation of the neutrality of this country and that the prisoners, if discharged under the Warrant for their extradition, (together with Mr. Clay, if he can be found within the jurisdiction) to be put upon trial."

As Devlin argued, the raiders did not have the right to demand Canada's protection for their actions. "They have not the right to say, 'We will force ourselves into your Canadian territory; and though our guilt should involve you in war, we will still persist in demanding that you should assume all the responsibilities of our crimes, and, cost what it may, that you should shield us from the penalty due to our offenses."

Regardless of Canada's intent to rectify a deteriorating situation, however, there never would be a trial on the neutrality issue. The war was now all but over.

On April 10, 1865, all the remaining raiders in custody were freed. That month, the Canadian government paid $19,000 to The First National Bank, $20,000 to the St. Albans Bank, and $31,000 to the Franklin County Bank.

On April 14, 1865, Abraham Lincoln was shot.

A $25,000 price was put on the heads of Clement Clay, Jacob Thompson, George Sanders, and Beverly Tucker for their role in the Lincoln assassination. $100,000 was the reward offered for the capture of President Jefferson Davis, $10,000 for William Cleary.

Soon after the raiders were freed, Congress passed an act abrogating the Canadian reciprocity treaty; Congress also proposed to terminate the treaty about disarming the lakes. Seward refused to allow this to come to pass, but the situation lingered, fraught with tension, and Canadian and American troops remained on the frontier for many months.

Interestingly, much came to light regarding the plotting, execution, and aftermath of the St. Albans Raid during the trial of the Lincoln assassination conspirators.

One of the more fascinating bits of information to surface came on June 18, 1865, when Henry G. Edson took the stand as a witness for the prosecution. Edson practiced law in St. Albans and had acted as trial counsel on behalf of the banks and the U.S. government. Now he testified about a conversation he had overheard between George Sanders and some of the raiders during the St. Albans trial. The conversation must have impressed Edson, because he noted it in his diary: "In speaking of the St. Albans raid, George N. Sanders said he was ignorant of it before it occurred, but was satisfied with it. He said that it was not the last that would occur; but it would be followed up by the depleting of many other banks, and the burning of many other towns on the frontier, and that many Yankee sons of —— (using a coarse, vulgar expression) would be killed. He said that they had their plans perfectly organized, and men ready to sack and burn Buffalo, Detroit, New York, and other places, and had deferred them for a time, but would soon see the plans wholly executed; and any preparation that could be made by the Government to prevent them would not, though it might defer them for a time."

During the phase of the trial concerning Mary E. Surratt, who was executed for her part in the assassination, the extent of involvement that the Confederate commissioners in Canada had had with President Jefferson Davis became quite clear.

"That these persons named upon your record, Thompson, Sanders, Clay, Cleary and Tucker, were the agents of Jefferson Davis, is another fact established in this case beyond a doubt. They made affidavit of it themselves, of record here, upon the examination of their 'friends,' charged with the raid upon St. Albans, before Judge Smith, in Canada. The testimony, to which I have thus briefly referred, shows, by the letter of his agents, of the 13th of October, that Davis had before directed those agents to set his friends to work. By the letter of Clay it seems that his direction had been obeyed, and his friends had been set to work, in the burning and robbery and murder at St. Albans, in the attempt to burn the city of New York, and in the attempt to introduce pestilence into this capital and into the house of the President."

The Lincoln conspiracy trial also uncovered a bit more of the mystery surrounding Sarah Slater, who was believed to have been the "Kentucky Widow" who suddenly appeared with the documents that freed the raiders in their second trial. The spy had been given one last mission to carry out on April 1. The Confederates possessed considerable sums of money that they wanted to keep out of Federal hands, and the way to do that was to move it to Britain. While in Washington, D.C., on April 4, Slater called on John Wilkes Booth and then headed north, ostensibly carrying the money. While her husband Rowan survived the war, neither he nor anyone else ever heard from her or saw her again.

Testimony during the trial suggests that Sarah Slater wasn't just a bit player in the St. Albans Raid; she may in fact have had a hand in President Lincoln's assassination as well.

Had the shadowy figure been caught, she would of course have faced the death penalty, just like Mary Surratt, with whom she had crossed paths in March 1864. John Surratt, Mary's son and one of the four conspirators to hang for the assassination, escorted Sarah Slater on one of her trips from Montreal to Richmond. She had been carrying dispatches, and she spent two nights at the Surratt home.

"About the 17th of March last [1864], a Mrs. Slater came to Mrs. Surratt's house, and stopped there one night," said Louis J. Weichmann, a clerk in the office of Gen. Hoffman, Commissary-General of prisoners. "This lady went to Canada and Richmond. On Saturday, the 23rd of March, John Surratt drove her and Mrs. Surratt in the country in a buggy, leaving about 8 o'clock in the morning. He hired a two-horse team, white horses, from Howard's. Mrs. Surratt told me on her return that John had gone to Richmond with Mrs. Slater. Mrs. Slater, I understood, was to have met a man by the name of Howell, a blockade-runner; but he was captured on the 24th of March, so Surratt took her back to Richmond. Mrs. Slater, as I learned from Mrs. Surratt, was either a blockade-runner or a bearer of dispatches."

Further testimony placed her in a boat with another of the conspirators, George Atzerodt, who was apparently rather impressed with the young spy. "I had spoken to him [Captain Gleason] about this blockade runner, and about Mrs. Slater, but I can not fix the precise date," said Mr. Ewing during the trial. "Mrs. Slater went with Booth a good deal."

Still, there was more to the story of the St. Albans raiders from the Lincoln trial. On April 24, 1865, Secretary of War Stanton telegraphed Gen. Dix: "This Department has information that the President's murder was organized in Canada and approved at Richmond. One of the assassins now in prison, who attempted to kill Mr. Seward, is believed to be one of the St. Albans raiders."

★ ★ ★

After being detained in New Brunswick, Lt. Bennett H. Young finally had his freedom, but not his home. President Andrew Johnson denied him amnesty, thereby forcing the young man into a nomadic life.

He lived in forced exile in Europe until 1868, when he was finally granted amnesty and allowed to return to the United States. Young rarely spoke of his role in the raid, breaking his silence once in 1902: "My connection with the St. Albans Raid is shown by official documents, and legal decisions which I rely upon for my conduct in the matter. Acting under these orders, I have nothing to regret, explain or modify. With these official documents I think I can safely commend my conduct at St. Albans to the opinion of honorable men."

Epilogue

★ ★ ★ ★ ★ ★ ★ ★ ★ ★ ★ ★ ★ ★ ★ ★ ★ ★

In the autumn of 1864, the battlefields of the Civil War lived in the hearts, minds, letters, and newspapers of the citizens of St. Albans, Vermont, a quiet town just fifteen miles south of the Canadian border. While its men and boys were engaged in a fierce battle that would ultimately secure President Abraham Lincoln's second term, a flock of Rebel raiders swooped into the burgeoning village.

The town clerk had just rung three bells on the dismal afternoon of October 19 when twenty-one Confederate raiders simultaneously held up St. Albans's three banks. Thus, in the space of one blustery October afternoon, the whirlwind of war blew into town and robbed New Englanders of their sense of security for years to come.

The Confederate government had authorized the incursion with rather lofty aims. One, it was to be the first in a series of attacks along the northern border to secure needed money for the cash-poor Confederacy. Two, it would divert Union troops, in the interest of creating a two-front struggle. Three, the Southern government hoped to disrupt the presidential election of 1864. And lastly, of course, Richmond hoped desperately to find a way to force Washington to the peace table.

The St. Albans raid stands as the northernmost action of the Civil War, and as the largest bank robbery in Vermont's history. Although the men finally stood trial in Canada, they were ultimately acquitted. It can be argued that the presence of a known and active Confederate spy ring breached the neutral stand that Canada, and ultimately Great Britain, had taken.

The St. Albans raid revealed the extreme vulnerability of the United States' northern border. After the raid, citizens in northern New England lived in a state of fear and high alert. For the first time, Yankee soldiers clearly worried about those they left behind, sometimes even more than they worried about themselves.

In this tiny town and its single day of combat, the scope of the Civil War itself is revealed. Across borders, nations, the seas, and the states themselves, America struggled to save and to destroy itself, all at the same time. With great powers feuding and speculating over the war's outcome, and with any number of lesser ones profiting from it, the distinct characters of the nation were set against each other in an attempt to reconcile, among other things, the greatest disgrace the nation has ever brought upon itself. Young and his men, full of the romance that many still hold dear in the South to this day, were in their raid a great deal like their cause—desperate, fleeting, and too young to realize that greater virtue and glory lay ahead for the nation along a path different from theirs.

Lt. Bennett Hiram Young: After the war, Young moved to Ireland. He was made an "honorary general" of Confederate War Veterans. Half a century after the raid, he was a speaker at the Veterans' reunion at Gettysburg, Pennsylvania, in 1913 and the lead speaker at the dedication of the Confederate Monument at Arlington National Cemetery in Arlington, Virginia, in 1914. In

1908, St. Albans resident George P. Anderson, who had extensive correspondence with Young, and Cyrus N. Bishop, the bank clerk forced to take the oath of allegiance to the Confederacy, met with Young when he was on a business trip to Boston.

Bennett Young's tombstone reads: "I have kept the faith." He is buried in Cane Hill Cemetery in Louisville, Kentucky.

Charles Moore Swager: After the war, Swager studied law in Canada and went to Europe. He was in France at the time of the Franco–Prussian War and was killed in Paris when Germans were shelling it in 1871.

Capt. Thomas B. Collins: With the war over, but with no way to return to the United States, having been denied immunity, Collins departed for Europe, where he studied medicine in Brussels and at the University of Paris. He was interning at one of the clinics there when he contracted tuberculosis and died on April 12, 1869.

Charles Higbie: It is unknown whether he survived and recovered in Quebec, or if he died in Montreal.

Squire Turner Teavis: Donning women's clothing, he was the only raider to successfully sneak back across the border into the United States after the war.

Sarah Slater: She literally rode off into history. The Connecticut-Yankee-turned-Southern-spy was last seen heading toward Montreal just before Lincoln's assassination. On April 4, 1865, Sarah left Washington for New York. Based on testimony given at the Lincoln conspiracy trial, Federal authorities remained convinced that Slater was a vital link that connected Booth with Richmond and Canada. Sarah's husband, Rowan, survived the war and returned home but never saw Sarah again.

Jacob Thompson: Accused of taking part in the Lincoln assassination, Thompson fled to Europe for several years before returning to the United States and settling in Memphis, Tennessee. He died in 1885.

Clement C. Clay: After President Lincoln's assassination, Clay was accused of plotting both the assassination and the St. Albans raid. He surrendered, was held for one year without trial at Fort Monroe, and then was freed. He died in 1882.

George Nicholas Sanders: He had his fingerprints all over the assassination of President Abraham Lincoln, but as slick a man as he was, he eluded his would-be captors and never served time. Instead, Sanders fled to Canada—again, then on to Europe before returning to the United States. Sanders died in 1873 in New York; he is reportedly buried in Brooklyn.

Governor J. Gregory Smith: After serving two terms, he went back full-time to his duties as president of the Vermont Central Railroad. He died in 1891.

Anna Smith: After the war, she wrote religious-themed novels, lectured, and continued to write for local newspapers. She died in 1905.

Judge Charles-Joseph Coursol: A haunting? On the night of April 29, 1865, goes the legend, three Montreal detectives arrested a man named John Wilkes Booth. Yet Booth had been declared dead after being shot at a farm in Virginia on April 26! But some say he was actually staying at the Garneau Hotel in Montreal. Because Montreal had been a den of Confederate spies, the detectives, knowing Booth had been in Montreal, believed the man to be Booth. The detectives took the prisoner; according to the story, Coursol then ordered the man freed. So who was this man? Was he an impostor? A look-alike? Or was this story just another part of the conspiracy theories that took hold almost immediately upon Lincoln's murder?

Viscount Charles Stanley Monck and Lady Elizabeth Louise Mary Monck: They had seven children, four of whom lived to adulthood. After his term ended in 1868, Monck and his wife departed for Ireland, where he served as Lord Lieutenant of County Dublin from 1874 to 1892. Lady Monck died on June 16, 1892, and Lord Monck died on November 29, 1894.

The St. Albans banks: All three banks closed due to bankruptcy between 1864 and 1883.

★　★　★

It has been more than 140 years since Bennett H. Young and his fellow raiders sowed terror through St. Albans and the Northeast.

As the years passed, the anniversary of the raid was marked with sustained reverence for those who had fallen and for those terrorized. At one point, Bennett Young himself thought of going to St. Albans to mark the day, but withdrew after it was clear that his visit would rub nerves raw. Nevertheless, in 1911, Young visited Montreal and, rather than crossing the border into Vermont, a group of dignitaries from St. Albans called on him instead at the city's Ritz-Carlton Hotel.

Today, St. Albans town, with more than 5,000 residents according to the 2000 census, is surrounded by St. Albans city—both part of Franklin County. Still as green a Green Mountain town as any, the Vermont Maple Festival is held there each year.

Tourists can also visit the St. Albans Historical Society, open seasonally, which occupies the school where children once watched the raid unfold from upstairs windows, and they can read the marker that tells the story of the astonishing day.

The buildings where the banks resided still stand.

Bibliography

★ ★ ★ ★ ★ ★ ★ ★ ★ ★ ★ ★ ★ ★ ★ ★ ★ ★

UNPUBLISHED SOURCES

Bailey/Howe Library, Wilbur Collection, University of Vermont

"Correspondence relating to the Fenian invasion, and the Rebellion of the Southern States." Ottawa: Hunter, Rose & Co., 1869. [Cited as "Fenian" in endnotes.]

Devlin, Bernard. "St. Albans Raid: Speech of B. Devlin, Esquire, Counsel for the United States, in Support of their Demand for Extradition of Bennett H. Young, et al." 1865.

Davis Collection 1783–1868.

Fitch Family Papers.

Smith Family Papers.

William Wells Papers.

St. Albans Historical Society, St. Albans, Vermont

Branch, John, Sr. *St. Albans Raid*. In the *St. Albans Daily Messenger*. St. Albans, Vermont, 1935.

Johnson, Carl E. *The St. Albans Raid*. St. Albans, Vermont: Carl E. Johnson, 2001.

Letters

Sidney Parker to Friend David, December 18, 1862.

Bennett H. Young to George P. Anderson, June 13, 1906.

A. A. Simpkins to Dear Brother and Sister, Camp Griffin, February 16, 1862.
A. A. Simpkins to Sister and Children, USA General Hospital, n.d.
"Bennett Young Coming," *St. Albans Daily Messenger,* April 12, 1909.
White Family Papers

Filson Historical Society, Louisville, Kentucky

Bodley, Temple. Memoir, 1863.
Castleman, John Breckinridge Papers.
Clay, Clement Claiborne, Jr. Mss. 5–30.
Porter, John M. Papers.
Sprake, J. D. *Diary of a Confederate Soldier: 1 March 1863–13 Feb. 1865.*
Young, General Bennett Henderson Letters to General Marcus J. Wright, May 28, July 5, and July 8, 1912.
White, John Chester. *The War of the Union against Secession.* Manuscript (TS) Vol. IV, pp. 491–94.

Other

Holcombe, James P. "Richmond 1864," printed ephemera collection, Portfolio 187, Folder 26, Library of Congress. Digital ID: http://hdl.loc.gov/loc.rbc/rbpe.18702600.
Sanders, George N. "George N. Sanders on the Sequences of Southern Secession. New York, 30th October, 1860. To the Republicans of New York Who are For the Republic. [New York, 1860]." Portfolio 123, Folder 3, Library of Congress, http://hdl.loc.gov/loc.rbc/rbpe.12300300.

PUBLISHED SOURCES

Books

Aldridge, James. "The St. Albans Raid." Louisville *Courier-Journal,* Vol. 173, April 6, 1941.
American National Cemetery, www.arlingtoncemetery.net. "Julius Stahel, Major General, United States Army."
Ayer, I. Winslow. *The Great Treason Plot in the North during the War.* Chicago: U.S. Publishing, 1895.
Bakeless, John. *Spies of the Confederacy.* Mineola, New York: Dover Publications, 1970.
Barrett, John Gilchrist. *North Carolina as a Civil War Battleground 1861–1865.* Raleigh: Office of Archives and History, North Carolina Department of Cultural Resources, 2003.
Bélanger, Claude. *Canada, French Canadians and Franco-Americans in the*

Civil War Era (1861–1865). Montreal: Marianopolis College, Quebec, 2004.

Benedict, G. G. *Vermont in the Civil War: A History of the Part Taken by the Vermont Soldiers and Sailors in the War for the Union, 1861–1865.* Vols. 1, 2. Burlington: The Free Press Association, 1886. (Reprinted in Canada by Tony O'Connor, Vermont Civil War Enterprises.)

Benjamin, L. N. *The St. Albans Raid; or, Investigation into the Charges against Lieut. Bennett H. Young and Command, for their Acts at St. Albans, Vermont.* Montreal: John Lovell, 1865.

Billings, John D. *Hardtack & Coffee: or the Unwritten Story of Army Life.* Lincoln: First Bison Book, University of Nebraska Press, 1993. (Reprinted from the original 1887 edition by George M. Smith & Co., Boston.)

Blight, David W., ed. "When This Cruel War Is Over: The Civil War Letters of Charles Harvey Brewster." Amherst: University of Massachusetts Press, 1992. In Michael Perman, ed., *Major Problems in the Civil War and Reconstruction, Documents and Essays.* Boston and New York: Houghton Mifflin, 1998.

Butler, Lorine Letcher. *John Morgan and His Men.* Philadelphia: Dorrance, 1960.

Carpenter, George N. *History of the Eighth Regiment Vermont Volunteers, 1861–1865.* Boston: Press of Deland & Bara, 1886. (Reprinted in Canada by Tony O'Connor, Vermont Civil War Enterprises.)

Cheney, Cora. *Vermont: The State with the Storybook Past.* Shelburne, Vermont: New England Press, 1979.

Clay-Clopton, Virginia. *A Belle of the Fifties: Memoirs of Mrs. Clay of Alabama.* Garden City, New York, and London: Doubleday, Page, 1905. (Reprinted by the University of Alabama Press, Tuscaloosa, 1999.)

Cochran, Hamilton. *Blockade Runners of the Confederacy.* New York: Bobbs-Merrill, 1958.

Coffin, Howard. *Full Duty: Vermonters and the Civil War.* Woodstock, Vermont: Countryman Press, 1993.

Crocker, Howard W. *St. Albans Raid: An Incident in Canadian–American Relations.* Publication data not available, 1960.

Current, Richard Nelson. *Lincoln's Loyalists: Union Soldiers from the Confederacy.* Boston: Northeastern University Press, 1992.

Davis, Burke. "The Civil War, Strange and Fascinating Facts." New York: Wings, 1996. (First published as *Our Incredible Civil War.* New York: Holt, Rinehart, and Winston, 1960.)

Davis, Jefferson. *The Rise and Fall of the Confederate Government.* New York: 1882.

Davis, Kenneth C. *Don't Know Much about the Civil War.* New York: Harper Collins, 1997.

Davis, William C. *The Cause Lost: Myths and Realities of the Confederacy.* Lawrence: University Press of Kansas, 1996.

Douglas, John Borthwick. *History of the Montreal Prison, from A.D. 1784 to A.D. 1886: Containing a Complete Record of the Troubles of 1837–1838. Burning of Parliament Buildings, in 1849. The St. Albans Raiders, 1864. The Two Fenian Raids of 1866 and 1870.* Montreal: A. Periard, 1886.

Duke, Basil W. "A Romance of Morgan's Rough Riders: The Raid, the Capture, and the Escape." In [no editor listed], *Famous Adventures and Prison Escapes of the Civil War.* New York: DeVinne Press, The Century Co., 1893. (Later reprinted by Kessinger Publishing.)

Dutcher, L. L., with H. R. Whitney. *History of the Town of St. Albans: Civil, Religious, Biographical and Statistical.* St. Albans: S. E. Royce, 1872.

Fehrenbacher, Don E. "Kansas, Republicanism, and the Crisis of the Union." In Michael Perman, ed., *Major Problems in the Civil War and Reconstruction, Documents and Essays,* pp. 52–56. Boston and New York: Houghton Mifflin, 1998.

Ferris, Norman B. *The Trent Affair: A Diplomatic Crisis.* Austin: University of Texas Press, 1977.

Fisher, Ella Warner. "Reminiscence of the Civil War." *The Vermonter* 39: 141–2.

Foote, Shelby. *The Civil War.* New York: Vintage Books, USA, 1986.

Forsyth, General George A. *Thrilling Days In Army Life.* New York and London: Harper & Brothers, 1900.

Frohman, Charles E. *Rebels on Lake Erie.* Columbus: Ohio Historical Society, 1965.

Fry, James M. "Death of General John H. Morgan and What Led Up to It." Wills Point, Texas: Chronical (at Filson Historical Society this is a 20 page pamphlet)

Glatthaar, Joseph T. "Black Glory: The African-American Role in Union Victory." In Michael Perman, ed., *Major Problems in the Civil War and Reconstruction, Documents and Essays.* Boston and New York: Houghton Mifflin, 1998.

Gordon, Linda. "U.S. Women's History." In Eric Foner, ed., *The New American History,* revised and expanded edition. Philadelphia: Temple University Press, 1997.

Grant, R. G. *Battle: A Visual Journey through 5,000 Years of Combat.* New York: DK Publishing, 2005.

Great Britain, Foreign Office. *Correspondence Respecting the Attack on St. Albans, Vermont and Naval Force on the North American Lakes.* Presented to both Houses of Parliament by command of Her Majesty. London: Harrison, 1865.

Hardin, Bayless. *Brigadier General John Hunt Morgan of Kentucky: Thunderbolt of the Confederacy.* Frankfort: Kentucky State Historical Society, 1938.

Harris, William C. *North Carolina and the Coming of the Civil War.* Raleigh:

Division of Archives and History, North Carolina Department of Cultural Resources, 1988.

Haskell, Frank A., Col. *The Battle of Gettysburg: A Soldier's First-Hand Account.* Mineola, New York: Dover, 2003. (Unabridged reprint of the Wisconsin History Commission's *The Battle of Gettysburg,* 1908.)

Headley, John Williams. *Confederate Operations in Canada and New York.* New York: Neale, 1906. (Reprinted by Time-Life Books, Alexandria, Virginia, 1984.)

Heatwole, John L. *The Burning: Sheridan's Devastation of the Shenandoah Valley.* Charlottesville: Rockbridge, 1998.

Hendrickson, Robert. *The Road to Appomattox.* New York: Wiley, 1998.

Hertzog, Gary J. *Demise at Gettysburg: The Life and Final Hours of Elon John Farnsworth.* Civil War Interactive: www.civilwarinteractive.com

Hesseltine, William Best. *Civil War Prisons.* Kent, Ohio: Kent State University Press, 1972.

Hill, Herbert E., Col. *Campaign in the Shenandoah Valley, 1864.* A paper read before the Eighth Vermont Volunteers and First Vermont Cavalry, at their Annual Reunion in Montpelier, Vermont, November 2, 1886. Boston: Rand Avery, 1886.

Hines, Thomas Henry. *Thrilling Narrative of the Escape of General John H. Morgan from the Ohio Penitentiary. Century Magazine,* January 1891.

———. "The Escape." In *Famous Adventures and Prison Escapes of the Civil War.* New York: DeVinne, The Century Co., 1893.

Horan, James D. *Confederate Agent, A Discovery in History.* New York: Crown, 1954.

Hughes, Roger. "Recognition, Why Should We? The British Point of View." In *Camp Chase Gazette.* Morristown, Tennessee: September 1997.

Hunt, O. E., Capt., U.S. Army. "The Ordnance Department of the Federal Army." In Julian J. Landau and Frank Oppel, eds., *The Photographic History of the Civil War, Volume III, Forts and Artillery.* Edison, New Jersey: The Blue and Grey Press, a division of Book Sales, Inc., 1988.

Hutchinson, Jack T. *"Bluegrass and Mountain Laurel: The Story of Kentucky in the Civil War."* The Cincinnati Civil War Round Table, 1965: www.civilwarroundtable.com

Jackson, Donald Dale. *Twenty Million Yankees: The Northern Home Front.* Alexandria, Virginia: Time-Life Books, 1985.

Jones, Howard. *Under Peril: The Crisis over British Intervention in the Civil War.* Chapel Hill: North Carolina Press, 1992.

Kinchen, Oscar A. *Daredevils of the Confederate Army: The Story of the St. Albans Raid.* North Quincy, MA: Christopher, 1959.

———. *Confederate Operations in Canada and the North: A Little-Known Phase of the Civil War.* North Quincy, MA: Christopher, 1970.

———. *Women Who Spied for the Blue and the Gray.* Philadelphia: Dorrance, 1972.

————. *General Bennett H. Young, Confederate Raider and A Man of Many Adventures*. West Hanover, MA: Christopher, 1981.

Letcher, Butler Lorine. *John Morgan and His Men*. Philadelphia: Dorrance, 1960.

Lindeman, Jack. *The Conflict of Convictions: American Writers Report the Civil War: A Selection and Arrangement from the Journals, Correspondence, and Articles of the Major Men and Women of Letters Who Lived through the War*. Philadelphia: Chilton, 1968.

Ledoux, Tom. *Vermont in the Civil War: The Green Mountain Boys in the Wilderness: Their Bloodiest Day*. American Military University, Charles Town, West Virginia, August 2000.

Lindsey, David. "St. Albans Has Been Surprised." *American History,* January 1976.

Macdonald, Helen G. *Canadian Public Opinion on the American Civil War*. New York: Octagon, 1974.

Mallet, J. W., Lt.-Col., and O. E. Hunt. "The Ordnance of the Confederacy." In Julian J. Landau and Frank Oppel, eds. *The Photographic History of the Civil War, Vol. III, Forts and Artillery*. Edison, New Jersey: The Blue and Grey Press, a division of Book Sales, Inc., 1988.

Markle, Donald S. *Spies & Spymasters of the Civil War*. New York: Hippocrene, 1996.

Marshall, Jeffrey D. *A War of the People: Vermont Civil War Letters*. Hanover, NH: University Press of New England, 1999.

McFarland, Moses, Captain of Company A, Eighth Vt. Veteran Volunteers. *"The Eighth Vermont in the Battle of Cedar Creek."* Hyde Park, Vermont: Lamoille, 1897.

McPherson, James M. *Battle Cry of Freedom: The Civil War Era*. New York: Oxford University Press, 1988.

————. *Drawn with the Sword: Reflections on the American Civil War*. New York: Oxford University Press, 1996.

————. *For Cause and Comrades: Why Men Fought in the Civil War*. New York: Oxford University Press, 1997.

————. *Hallowed Ground: A Walk at Gettysburg*. New York: Crown Journeys, 2003.

Mountagne, Bernard. *A Historical Account of the Neutrality of Great Britain During the Civil War*. London: Longmans, 1877.

Murrin, John M. "Beneficiaries of Catastrophe." In Eric Foner, *The New American History*. Philadelphia: Temple University Press, 1997.

Nuremberger, Ruth Ketring. *The Clays of Alabama*. Lexington: University of Kentucky Press, 1958.

Perry, James M. *A Bohemian Brigade: The Civil War Correspondents*. New York: Wiley, 2000.

Pinkerton, Allan. *The Spy of the Rebellion: Being a True History of the Spy*

System of US Army During the Late Rebellion. New York: G.W. Carleton & Co., 1883.

Pitman, Benn, Recorder to the Commission, comp. and arr. *The Assassination of President Lincoln and the Trial of the Conspirators.* New York: Moore, Wilstach & Baldwin, 1865.

Rankin, David C. *Diary of a Christian Soldier: Rufus Kinsley and the Civil War.* Cambridge: Cambridge University Press, 2004.

Robertson, James I. *Tenting Tonight: The Soldier's Life.* Alexandria, Virginia: Time-Life Books, 1984.

Ross, David, Grant Tyler, and Rick Scollins. *Canadian Campaigns 1860–70. Men at Arms Series.* London: Osprey, 1992.

Royster, Charles. *The Destructive War: William Tecumseh Sherman, Stonewall Jackson, and the Americans.* New York: Knopf, 1991.

Senour, F., Rev. *Morgan and his Captors.* Cincinnati and Chicago: C. F. Vent, 1864.

Stern, Philip Van Doren. *Secret Missions of the Civil War: First Hand Accounts by Men and Women who Risked Their Lives in Underground Activities for the North and South.* Chicago: Rand MacNally, 1959.

Sullivan, George. *In the Wake of Battle: The Civil War Images of Mathew Brady.* Munich, Berlin, London, and New York: Prestel, 2004.

Taylor, John M. *William Henry Seward: Lincoln's Right Hand Man.* New York: Harper Collins, 1991.

Têtu, David. *David Têtu et Les Raiders de Saint Alban, Episode de la Guerre Americaine 1864–1865,* deuxieme edition. Quebec: N. S. Hardy, 1891.

Tidwell, William A. *Come Retribution: The Confederate Secret Service and the Assassination of Lincoln.* Jacksonville: University Press of Mississippi, 1988.

Trotter, William R. *Bushwhackers! The Civil War in North Carolina: The Mountains.* Winston-Salem: John F. Blair, 1988.

U.S. Government Printing Office. *The War of The Rebellion: A Compilation of the Official Records of the Union and Confederate Armies.* Washington, D.C.: U.S. Government Printing Office, 1880–1901. [Cited as "OR" in endnotes.]

Walker, Aldace F. *The Vermont Brigade in the Shenandoah Valley, 1864.* Burlington: Free Press Association, 1869. (Reprinted in Canada by Tony O'Connor, Vermont Civil War Enterprises.)

Warren, Gordon H. *Fountain of Discontent: The Trent Affair and the Freedom of the Seas.* Boston: Northeastern University Press, 1981.

Wert, Jeffry D. *From Winchester to Cedar Creek: The Shenandoah Campaign of 1864.* Mechanicsburg, PA: Stackpole, 1997.

Wickman, Donald H. *Letters to Vermont, from Her Civil War Soldier Correspondents to the Home Press. Vol. II.* Bennington, Vermont: Images from the Past, 1998.

Wiley, Bell Irvin. *The Life of Billy Yank, The Common Soldier of the Union*. Baton Rouge: Louisiana State University Press, 1952 and 1978.

————. *The Life of Johnny Reb, The Common Soldier of the Confederacy*. Baton Rouge: Louisiana State University Press, 1943 and 1978.

Winks, Robin W. *Canada and The United States; The Civil War Years*. Baltimore: Johns Hopkins Press, 1960.

Walsh, James. *Story of the St. Albans Raid October 19, 1864*. St. Albans: St. Albans Daily Messenger, 1939.

Wetherington, Mark. *Kentucky Joins the Confederacy*. For Kentucky Humanities Council Inc. Lexington, January 2005.

Wyatt-Brown, Bertram. *Yankee Saints and Southern Sinners*. Baton Rouge: Louisiana State University Press, 1985.

Vallandigham, Clement Laird. *The Great Civil War in America*. Washington: publisher not listed, 1863.

Vandiver, Frank Everson. *Blood Brothers: A Short History of the Civil War*. College Station: Texas A&M University Press, 1992.

Vandiver, Frank Everson. *Confederate Blockade Running Through Bermuda: 1861–1863 Letters and Cargo Manifests*. New York: Kraus, 1970.

Young, Bennett H. *Kentucky Eloquence Past & Present*. Louisville: Ben LaBree, Jr. (Filson Historical Society), 1907.

————. *Confederate Wizards of the Saddle*. Boston: Chapple, 1914. (First J. S. Sanders edition 1999, Nashville, Tennessee.)

————. "Secret History of the St. Albans Raid." *The Vermonter, A State Magazine*. Jan. 1902, Vol. 7, No. 6. Charles S. Forbes, ed. and pub. St. Albans (Filson Historical Society, Louisville).

Newspapers and Magazines

Civil War News. Historical Publications, Turnbridge, Vermont, October 2003.
Harper's Weekly
Montreal *Gazette*
New York Times
St. Albans Daily Messenger
The Vermonter
The *Times* of London

Endnotes

★ ★ ★ ★ ★ ★ ★ ★ ★ ★ ★ ★ ★ ★ ★ ★ ★ ★ ★

Prologue

p. 4. "If you stir or make any resistance . . . brains out": Benjamin, p. 23.

p. 5. "I take deposits": Benjamin, p. 23.

p. 5. "Not a word . . . as your soldiers are doing in the Shenandoah Valley": Benjamin, p. 28.

Chapter One

p. 7. All told . . . men than any other: Benedict, p. 2.

p. 7. Towns across Vermont . . . in the First Vermont Brigade: *Civil War News,* October 2003.

p. 8. "Often these fugitive slaves . . . 'Lord, don't let me freeze to death so near freedom!'": Cheney, p. 135.

p. 9. "Washington is in grave danger. What may we expect from Vermont?": Coffin, p. 21; Cheney, p. 137.

p. 9. "Vermont will do its full duty": Coffin, p. 21; Cheney, p. 137.

p. 10. According to state lore . . . from the gallery: Coffin, p. 25; Cheney, p. 137.

p. 11. "Notwithstanding my appeals . . . in a holy cause": *Rutland Herald,* June 6, 1862; Wickman, p. 62.

p. 11. Yet however . . . feel of a festival: Benedict, p. 30.

p. 11. Bands played . . . songs and cheering crowds: Blight, p. 136.

p. 11. "Sometimes the patriotism of such a gathering . . . less than an hour": Billings, p. 41.

p. 12. "Grant's scheme required . . . north was losing patience": Glatthaar, p. 298.

p. 13. "When this great national . . . die freemen": Joseph L. Perkins to his brother, Burlington, April 23, 1861.

p. 13–14. "On our journey from the Green Mountains . . . kisses at us": *Rutland Herald,* September 28, 1862; Wickman, p. 125.

p. 14. It's true that . . . "no means inconsiderable": Coffin, p. 319.

p. 14. "I am as safe . . . almost any time": Marshall, pp. 22–23.

p. 15. The troops complained that the tents . . . "pup tents": Sullivan, p. 133.

p. 15. Union camps looked like canvas towns . . . restaurants in inns from home: Billings, pp. 46–57

p. 16. "What a Godsend it seemed to us at times! . . . night's sound sleep!": Billings, p. 122.

p. 17. Production of weapons . . . arms and ammunition: Hunt, pp. 123–55.

p. 18. The Seventh Vermont . . . first year of duty alone: Wickman, p. 28.

p. 18. His mandate of 1860 no longer held . . . offer a better solution: Tidwell, p. 182.

p. 19. "I am just struck at the idea . . . they are fast pawning for despotism?": Wickman, p. 29.

p. 19. Women were thrust into jobs . . . troops in the field: Coffin, p. 281.

p. 20. Justin Morgan, a singing teacher . . . tiny horse to offer: Cheney, pp. 126–27.

p. 20. The horses were on average . . . forefoot and fore shoulder: Coffin, p. 99.

p. 21. Gloom for the Confederacy sat . . . like a fog: Horan, p. 67.

Chapter Two

p. 23. By the time the Union soldiers . . . Native Americans: Carpenter, p. 163.

p. 24. Indeed until the battles . . . push back the Confederates: Carpenter, p. 164.

p. 24. The Union Army . . . and about 5,900 Federals from the Middle Department: Wert, p. 22.

p. 24. At the time, the Confederates . . . beyond Cedar Creek: Wert, p. 170.

p. 25. For at least six weeks . . . the end of Sheridan's missions was, at the very least, in sight: McPherson 1988, p. 777.

p. 25. Whoever controlled the valley . . . fed the bellies of Northern Virginia: Hill, p. 3-4.

p. 25. "The character of the war . . . or be conquered by them": Letter, March 31, 1863 from General Henry W. Halleck to Maj. Gen. U. S. Grant, March 31, 1863; OR, Series 1, Vol. 24, Pt. III, p. 157. [EDITOR'S NOTE: For OR in the bibliography, see U.S. Government Printing Office, *Official Records.*]

p. 26. Lincoln went . . . when total war became the way: McPherson 1996, p. 66-86.

p. 26. Thickset and broad-shouldered . . . 120 pounds: Wert, p. 17.

p. 26. He had a misshapen head . . . bulldog: Hendrickson, p. 116.

p. 26. While Grant . . . command an entire army: Wert, p. 18.

p. 27. His true, warrior self . . . ranks thereafter: Wert, p. 16.

p. 28. "What was perhaps most important . . . against any enemy": Walker, pp. 122–123.

p. 29. "In pushing up the Shenandoah Valley . . . the course he takes": *OR,* Series 1, Vol. XLIII, Part 1, pp. 697-98; Wert, p. 29.

p. 29. Civilians suffered extensively . . . not always without compassion: Heatwole, p. 37.

p. 29. Federal troops . . . .let the house alone: Heatwole, p. 97.

p. 30. "The army again began . . . the valley had done heretofore": McFarland, p. 6.

p. 30. One soldier wrote . . . "conceived of to Whip us": Wiley, p. 311.

p. 30–31. In early October Sheridan . . . region's horses: Carpenter, pp. 165–67.

p. 31. The division of General Wesley Merritt . . . 3,300 head of livestock: Carpenter, p. 226-27; McFarland, pp. 18, 22; McPherson 1988, p. 778.

p. 31. "I therefore, on the morning . . . not to burn dwellings": *OR,* 43, Part I, pp. 40–57. p. 32 Some accounts point to Meigs . . . hole in his face: Heatwole, pp. 90–92.

p. 32. Sheridan ordered . . . be burned: Wert, p. 145.

p. 33. "This, every living soldier . . . heels with their throats cut": Heatwole, p. 93.

p. 34. "Although we had . . . driven away": Walker, p. 89.

p. 34. As he prepared . . . camped a few miles away: McPherson 1988, p. 779.

p. 35. "General—I enclose you . . . guarding against and resisting": Report of Maj. Gen. Philip H. Sheridan, U.S. Army, commanding Middle Military Division, including operations August 4, 1864–Feb. 27, 1865: *OR,* Vol. 43, Part I, in Walker, pp. 52–54. This letter is reprinted in Walker.

p. 35. During his stay . . . "Lieutenant-General Early . . . LONGSTREET": *OR,* XLII,1, 466; Wert, p. 172.

p. 35. "The cavalry is all ordered . . . everything that can be spared": Foote, p. 565; *OR,* XLIII, 1, p. 52.

p. 36. "So we all went to bed": Forsyth, p. 135.

p. 36. On the night . . . unable to sleep: Carpenter, p. 207.

p. 36. While on watch . . . on the Union lines: Carpenter, p. 207.

p. 36–37. "Surrender, you damned Yankee! . . . your request was not respectful": Carpenter, p. 208.

p. 38. From Winchester to New Market . . . littered the roadside: Wert, p. 142.

p. 38. Early's supplies . . . "early morning not many days thereafter": McFarland, p. 7.

p. 38. The spying on Union positions . . . a giant map: Carpenter, p. 206.

p. 38–39. From on high . . . artillery stood nearby: Carpenter, pp. 206–7.

p. 39–40. "Everything is confusion and dismay . . . in the wildest confusion": McFarland, p. 10.

p. 40. "The enemy captured the pickets . . . reckless dishabille": Walker, pp. 136–37.

p. 40. "My comrades! . . . lips are dumb": Hill, p. 8.

p. 40–41. "I do not expect to give you . . . infantry almost in a body": Wickman, pp. 183–184.

p. 41. McFarland reported . . . "six bullets inside a five inch circle": McFarland, p. 13.

p. 41. "That these men were brave . . . to survive": Walker, p. 137.

p. 41–42. "During my absence the enemy . . . little danger of attack": Sheridan's Report on the Shenandoah Campaign, *OR*, Vol. 43, Part 1, pp. 40–57.

p. 42. "For the Eighth Vermont . . . after the flag": McFarland, pp. 14–16; Wert, p. 190; Carpenter, pp. 215–17.

p. 42. As the fighting . . . "Take care of yourselves and the flag!": McFarland, p. 14; Carpenter, pp. 215–17.

p. 43. Sgt. Ethan P. Shores . . . "fired and killed him": McFarland, p. 14.

p. 43. Corporal George F. Blanchard . . . grabbing Old Glory: Benedict, pp. 163–64, 167; *National Tribune,* January 26, 1911; Carpenter, pp. 215–17.

p. 43. As he knelt down . . . despite the wound: Carpenter, p. 218; *National Tribune,* January 26, 1911; *OR,* Series XLIII, Part I, pp. 133, 308.

p. 43. Corporal Leonard C. Bemis . . . losing his numbers: Carpenter, pp. 216–17.

p. 43. "It was indeed . . . victorious foe": McFarland, pp. 17–18.

p. 44. "Wagons and ambulances lumbering . . . first Napoleon": Walker, pp. 139–40.

p. 44. His jubilant soldiers . . . wounded soldiers: McPherson 1988, p. 779.

p. 44. Around nine o'clock . . . two engineer officers: Forsyth, p. 137.

p. 45. "The sound of the artillery . . . and was off": Forsyth, p. 137.

p. 45. "Everywhere the dust . . . swirling behind us": Forsyth, p. 138.

p. 45. The small group . . . field hospital: Hendrickson, p. 118.

p. 45. "Then we came . . . the open field": Forsyth, p. 138.

p. 45. "Face the other way, boys! We are going back!": Forsyth, p. 138.

p. 45–46. "Taking twenty men from . . . their lost camp": Report of Maj. Gen. Philip H. Sheridan, U.S. Army, commanding Middle Military Division, including operations August 4, 1864–Februrary 27, 1865: *OR,* Vol. 43, Part I, in Walker, pp. 52–54. Walker included this in his book.

p. 46. One glance at . . . "by his encouraging words": Forsyth, p. 18.

p. 46. "fainting heart takes . . . by his encouraging words": McFarland, p. 18.

p. 46. "Up from the South . . . And Sheridan twenty miles away": from the poem "Sheridan's Ride" by Thomas Buchanan Read.

p. 46. "Sturdy, fiery Sheridan on . . . mad galloping": Benedict, p. 556.

p. 46. "No more doubt . . . and knew it": Benedict, p. 557; Walker, p. 148.

p. 46–47. "When the men saw . . . onward towards Cedar Creek": Wickman, p. 184.

p. 47. "Boys, if you don't . . . before four o'clock": *OR*, XLIII, 1, pp. 167, 174, 193, 209, 225, 261.

p. 47. "Caesar put on speed . . . by the cavalry": Caesar, *The Gallic War*, 7.88.3–88.3 in Grant, p. 46.

p. 47–48. A Vermont soldier . . . "as on a whirlwind": Walker, p. 155.

p. 48. "This attack was . . . very determined": Sheridan report, in Walker, pp. 170–91.

p. 48. Save for . . . failed to act: Wert, p. 226.

p. 48. Whatever the reason . . . the afternoon: Wert, p. 229.

p. 48. "Sheridan showed consummate... Cedar Creek": Hill, p. 11.

p. 49. "The blame rests upon himself . . . reprobates so bitterly": Walker, p. 145.

p. 49. "The very best troops . . . men was severe": Sheridan report, in Walker, pp. 170–91.

p. 49. Of the 175 Vermonters . . . or captured: Benedict, pp. 166–68.

p. 49. "The Eighth Vermont . . . of Cedar Creek": Hill, p. 10.

p. 49–50. "when, in the confusion and din . . . led on to victory": Hill, p. 10.

p. 50. Thirty-six-year-old . . . of his battered force: Wert, p. 208.

p. 50. One such soldier . . . "furniture in the subsequent advance": Walker, pp. 100-101.

p. 51–52. "Hurrah for Phil. Sheridan! . . . enthusiastic delight": *New York Tribune* October 20, 1864.

Chapter Three

p. 58. "There are many things . . . unpleasant for others": Aldis Brainerd letter to Anna Smith, June 13, 1862, Smith Family Papers.

p. 58. Yes, the tiny state . . . off to war: Rankin, p. 18.

p. 59. William White . . . Cedar Creek, Virginia: White Papers, Vermont Historical Society.

p. 60. "A Kentuckian born and bred . . . shines from his eyes": Young 1907, p. 411.

p. 60. In subsequent years . . . tilled the land: Kinchen 1959, p. 18.

p. 61. With secession . . . moment of its declaration: Royster, p. 176.

p. 61. When Kentucky voted . . . Stars and Bars in public: Young letters, Folder 1, 1843–1919, Filson Historical Society.

p. 61. "Esau and Jacob . . . John Hunt Morgan": Senour, p. 12.

p. 62. "The declaration . . . of the South": Butler, p. 17.

p. 62–63. "Your dispatch is received . . . Southern states": Senour, p. 14.

p. 63. Most people lived . . . telegraph lines: Trotter, p. 22.

p. 63. Reverend Robert J. Breckinridge . . . Confederate Army: Hutchinson (paper given for roundtable discussion).

p. 63–64. The fluctuating levels . . . vigilante sensibility: Trotter, p. 2.

p. 64. Abraham Lincoln . . . last man standing: Royster, p. 179.
p. 64. But the draft . . . in his stead: Trotter, p. 38.
p. 64. In some mountain . . . feared reciprocity: Trotter, p. 165.
p. 65. Morgan stood about . . . raised in Lexington, Kentucky: Butler, p. 8.
p. 66. The troops were feared . . . awe-inspiring cavalryman: Kinchen 1981, pp. 19–20.
p. 66. "General Morgan was a magnetic man . . . chivalry incarnate": Fry, pp. 9–10.
p. 66. "I wanted to be . . . And lettered C.S.A.": Butler, p. 119.
p. 66–67. General William S. Rosecrans . . . well worth taking: Butler, p. 79.
p. 67. "From every county . . . in Confederate circles": Butler, p. 52.
p. 67. Words used to describe . . . "always in doubt and apprehension": Duke, p. 118.
p. 67. "Its rank and file . . . 25 years of age": Hines, p. 117.
p. 68. "the young aristocrats . . . about Morgan's men": Butler, p. 52.
p. 68. "The highest commendation . . . long and trying march": Kinchen 1981, p. 31.
p. 70. The prison had been . . . thirty-one of them: www.civilwarhome.com.
p. 71. In 1862 the first . . . the African explorer: Prichett, C. B.: "To the memory," www.geocities.com/BourbonStreet/2757.
p. 71–72. While Camp Douglas . . . rats to stuff into pies: *Ibid.*
p. 72. "Sir, the amount of standing water . . . fire can cleanse them": *Chicago Tribune,* September 22, 1862.
p. 72. "Before entering the main . . . cutting of our hair": Hines 1893, p. 158.

Chapter Four

p. 76–77. As the events stemming . . . path to British favor: McPherson 1988, p. 387.
p. 78. Of course, the ruling . . . "the most hateful act of history . . . since Charles 2nd": Jones, p. 27.
p. 78–79. "We from that hour shall cease . . . Great Britain": Taylor, p. 170.
p. 79. In the months . . . realistic possibility: McPherson 1988, p. 546.
p. 81. News of Federal victories . . . "In effect . . . ray of sunshine": Têtu, pp. 35–36.
p. 83. It also served . . . Southern front: *Harper's Weekly,* Dec. 12, 1863.
p. 85. "an unusual number of persons . . . en route for Canada": Lyons dispatch to Seward, June 2, 1864, Fenian, p. 36-37. [EDITOR'S NOTE: For "Fenian" in the bibliography, see Unpublished Sources, Bailey/Howe Library, "Correspondence relating to the Fenian invasion."]
p. 85. "I trust your Grace . . . hospitality": Lord Monck dispatch to the Duke of Newcastle, Nov. 19, 1863; Fenian, p. 28.
p. 85. "Practices resorted to . . . the United States army": Lord Lyons dispatch to Viscount Monck, Aug. 8, 1864; Fenian, p. 8.

p. 85–86. "I cannot pretend to say . . . on the subject": Lord Lyons to Viscount Monck, Aug. 8, 1864; Fenian, pp. 7–8.

p. 86. Whatever prompted these . . . Congressional Medal of Honor: Mayers, p. 49.

p. 87. "Persons hostile to . . . mischievous plot": Lord Lyons dispatch to W. Seward, Nov. 11, 1863; Fenian, p. 29.

p. 87. Not willing . . . St. Albans and Swanton: Maj. Gen. Dix dispatch to Hon. E. A. Stanton, Nov. 25, 1863; Fenian, p. 35.

p. 88. "I sent a detective into Canada . . . international law?" Maj. Gen. Dix dispatch to Hon. E. A. Stanton, Nov. 25, 1863; Fenian, p. 35.

p. 88–89. "Sir, I beg leave . . . Nassau and Bermuda": Mr. J. T. Howard dispatch to Seward, May 26, 1864; Fenian, p. 36.

p. 89. The summer before, S. R. Mallory . . . "along the Northern frontier": *The Vermonter,* Jan. 1902.

p. 89. "The Confederate officers . . . homes of this region": *The Vermonter,* Jan. 1902.

p. 89. In July . . . "an attempt by . . . refugees to Niagara": Col. R. H. Hill dispatch to Captain C. H. Potter, July 30, 1864; Fenian, p. 37.

p. 90. The governor-general wanted . . . jail suspected Rebels: Mayer, p. 90.

p. 90. City leaders in Detroit . . . patrol the border: Mayer, p. 90.

p. 90–91. Yet Secretary of State Seward reported . . . "special attention in that direction": W. Seward dispatch to Lord Lyons, Nov. 30, 1863; Fenian, p. 34.

p. 91. "The public opinion grows . . . you came out": Castleman papers.

p. 91. "Do you know, I have got . . . goose cooked!" Harvie, Ronald T., "Behind the Scenes" Montreal, www.tourisme-montreal.org

p. 92. "The Queen's Hotel . . . on the course of events": John Y. Beall report as appears in Headley, p. 214–16.

Chapter Five

p. 94. "dispatches . . . by the aid of a powerful lens": Markle, p. xvi.

p. 94. Amateurs could, and did . . . professional colleagues: Markle, p. xvi.

p. 95. Just as the current Rebel soldiers . . . political career: Markle, p. xvii.

p. 95. Though a popular choice . . . *after* the deed, not before: Markle, p. 17.

p. 96. An investigation during . . . at their disposal: Mayer, p. 29.

p. 96. The doctor's bag . . . secrete information: Markle, p. 19; Bakeless, p. 127–28.

p. 96. Legend says . . . twenty-four hours: Markle, p. 20.

p. 98. Working as a spy . . . in the Northwest: Markle, p. 107.

p. 98. After his final meeting . . . and new places: Horan, p. 71.

p. 98. Aside from increasing . . . that would be on call: McPherson 1988, p. 763.

p. 98–99. From Canada, Hines . . . northern United States: Tidwell, p. 171.

p. 99. Throughout his tenure . . . Department of the Interior: Tidwell, p. 189.

p. 100. Thompson's remaining ties . . . Confederate employment: Mayer, p. 27.

p. 100. "Confiding special trust in your zeal . . . interests of the Confederates": Davis letter to Thompson, Filson Historical Society.

p. 101. Alabama Attorney Clement Claiborne Clay, Jr. . . . second in command: Clay-Clopton, p. ix.

p. 101. "Commissioner Clay's health . . . been charged": Hines page?

p. 101–2. "Early in the spring . . . succour, or yielding": Clay-Clopton, p. 204.

p. 102. "I am on my way . . . enjoy secret service": Nuremberger, p. 232.

p. 102. "When the parting came . . . kin in Georgia": Clay-Clopton, p. 205.

p. 102. As Mrs. Clay . . . "edible or wearable": Clay-Clopton, p. 222.

p. 102. "Delicately bred women . . . personal or family use": Clay-Clopton, p. 222.

p. 103. "Bring me at least two silk . . . books of fashions": Clay-Clopton, p. 226.

p. 103. Comforts were long gone . . . water and vinegar: Clay-Clopton, p. 227.

p. 103. "scarcely a smoke-house . . . deposited there": Clay-Clopton, p. 223.

p. 104. The blockade business . . . at which to anchor: Vandiver, p. xi to xlii.

p. 104. the people of Bermuda . . . they brought: Cochran, p. 46.

p. 104–5. "St. George's . . . became . . . Musson's warehouse": Vandiver, xxii.

p. 105. Most crews . . . inland rivers: Sullivan, p. 58.

p. 105. All told, about five hundred . . . to the Gulf of Mexico: Sullivan, p. 58.

p. 106. If a boat carried . . . Charleston, or Savannah: Tidwell, p. 174; McPherson 1988, p. 378.

p. 107. The Canadian network . . . materials to them: Tidwell, p. 174.

p. 107. The blockade never . . . for the military: Sullivan, p. 61.

p. 107. The arms and ammunition . . . depleted: Cochran, p. 43.

p. 107. According to Thompson . . . "naval stores": Horan, p. 86.

p. 108. To facilitate . . . in Toronto: Horan, p. 84.

p. 109. Once Cleary had procured . . . behind Union lines: Mayer, p. 56.

p. 109. Aside from Cleary . . . delayed-action fuses: Tidwell, p. 196.

p. 109. By the fall . . . manufacture and distribution: Kinchen, 1970, p. 18; Pitman

p. 109. "I have the assurance that 'Greek Fire' . . . through the lines": Col. R. H. Hill to Capt. G. H. Potter, Dec. 3, 1864; Fenian, p. 85.

p. 110. President James Buchanan . . . under Pierce: *Harper's Weekly*, vol. IX, no. 452, August 25, 1865.

p. 111. "Few of your party . . . will not be 'bullied'?": Sanders "On the sequences of Southern Secession: To the Republicans of New York who are for the Republic." New York, Oct. 30, 1860.

p. 111. "He [Sanders] sees everybody . . . the United States": London *Times* in Horan, p. 87.

p. 111. "George N. Sanders is at Niagara Falls . . . Asia or Africa": Clay letter to Benjamin, June 17, 1864, in Kinchen 1970, p. 47.

p. 113. "Sir: I desire to submit to you . . . catch Mr. Lincoln": Holcombe letter to Benjamin, Nov. 16, 1864. Library of Congress, Printed Ephemera Collection, Portfolio 187, Folder 26.

p. 114. Sarah Slater, nee Gilbert . . . Kate Thompson: Kinchen 1972, p. 3.

p. 115. As the summer of 1864 . . . armed faction: McPherson 1988, p. 762.

p. 115–116. Some Peace Democrats even took . . . anti-war faction in the South: McPherson 1988, p. 494.

p. 116. They wanted the Union . . . between the states: Jackson, p. 149.

p. 116. Between 1863 and 1864 . . . and even murder: Horan, pp. 15–16.

p. 116. Clement L. Vallandigham was the leader . . . Sons of Liberty in 1864: Stern, p. 198.

p. 116. From Canada . . . and forty thousand in Ohio: Froham, p. 48.

p. 117. "George Sanders has come . . . too many hands in it": Cameron Notes, Thompson letter to Clay, June 7, 1864. Confederate Museum, Richmond Virginia.

p. 117. "A great crowd gathering . . . favor of state sovereignty": Sprake Diary, Aug. 1864.

p. 118. Yet, for all . . . with its policies: McPherson 1988, p. 764.

p. 118. At the end of the summer . . . the old country: Stern, p. 197.

p. 118. The *Condor* had . . . Empress Eugénie: Cochran, p. 135.

p. 119. Augustus Charles Hobart-Hampden . . . slammed into a shoal: Cochran, p. 139.

p. 120. The secret agents . . . army-payroll funds: Stern, p. 198.

p. 120. Aside from using . . . sum of $25,000: Stern, p. 201.

Chapter Six

p. 123. As his ship fell . . . "under the guns of Fort Fisher": Wright Papers.

p. 124. Though of a different stock . . . young man: Benjamin, p. 206.

p. 124. "to proceed without . . . indicated to you": Benjamin, p. 206.

p. 124. For the Canadian continent . . . worth mentioning: Horan, p. 166.

p. 125. On August 20 . . . exposed to attack: Kinchen 1970, p. 128.

p. 125. "It is right . . . such warfare": U.S. Congress, House Judicial Committee Report, 39th Congress, 1st Session, Vol. 1, No. 104, cipher dispatch.

p. 125. After combing through . . . fighting the war: Tidwell, p. 200.

p. 126. "St. Albans will merely be . . . and be pillaged": *St. Albans Daily Messenger*, Oct. 26, 1864; Branch, p. 22.

p. 126. The very thought . . . "Burn the town and sack the banks": Benjamin, 217.

p. 127. He favored instead . . . the mission: Kinchen 1970, p. 129.

p. 127. Desperate to make . . . as well: Stern, p. 242.

p. 128. "I will see you probably . . . for 150 miles?": Clement C. Clay Papers, Young to Clay, Sept. 20, 1864.

p. 129. "I owe no allegiance . . . health and mind": Benjamin, p. 83
p. 129. With his strong military . . . ideal recruit: Têtu, pp. 96–97.
p. 129. "I wish to say . . . in its train": Pitman, p. 54.
p. 129. For the most part . . . impressed almost everyone: Têtu, p. 142.
p. 129–30. George Scott was a picture . . . common upbringing: Têtu, pp. 96–97.
p. 130. Quite taken with Young . . . "a nice mannered man": Smith Family Papers.
p. 130. "Their manners were . . . prominent residences": Smith Family Papers
p. 131. George Sanders . . . "with the best of revolvers": Branch, pp. 34–36.
p. 131. Higbie . . . "Sheridan gave us!": Benjamin, 77–79, 85–100.
p. 132. On October 6, Clay . . . of the border: Clement Clay Papers, Filson Historical Society.
p. 132. "This, I approved . . . the Confederate States": Clay letter to Benjamin, Nov. 1, 1864, Clement Clay Papers.
p. 132. Before descending into . . . traveled under assumed names: Benjamin, p. 220.
p. 133–34. While Young rehashed . . . pleasant: Davis, William, p. 380.
p. 134. Like many single . . . paying mills: Gordon, in Foner, p. 269.
p. 135. Samuel Colt of . . . a few days after Fort Sumter: www.homestead.com/homefront/ColonelColtsPlantation.

Chapter Seven

p. 139. "We have had a month . . . dark as every": Judge James Davis Diary.
p. 139. "Wood from the surrounding . . . ample sheds": Smith, "Personal Reflections," *St. Albans Daily Messenger,* Nov. 22, 1892.
p. 140. He then faced . . . midstep: Benjamin, pp. 22–25.
p. 141. "The citizens . . . a joke": Headley, 259; Headley in Stern, p. 243
p. 141. "I never saw . . . American House": Benjamin, p. 54.
p. 141. Roberts had been . . . ten minutes: Benjamin, p. 53.
p. 141–142. Four raiders who . . . in the streets: Benjamin, p. 53.
p. 142. Cyrus Newton Bishop . . . "your brains out": Benjamin, p. 23.
p. 142. At first he . . . men were customers: Benjamin, p. 70.
p. 143. "I take deposits . . . Confederate soldier": Benjamin, p. 28.
p. 143. "Not a word . . . Shenandoah Valley": Benjamin, pp. 28, 35.
p. 143. "They compelled him . . . remained": Benjamin, p. 25.
p.143–44. The robbers lustfully . . . fiends and funds: Benjamin, p. 134.
p. 144. "There was a rank . . . robbers": *St. Albans Daily Messenger,* Oct. 19, 1864.
p. 144. Before leaving the . . . Confederate States of America: Benjamin, pp. 24–25.
p. 144. "that government [the Confederacy] . . . had left": Benjamin, pp. 24–25.
p. 144. Once the bank . . . women and children: Benjamin, p. 25.

p. 144. "This party to which . . . of revolvers": Benjamin, p. 25.

p. 144–45. "The armed party all . . . as one party": Benjamin, p. 63.

p. 145. "We are Confederate soldiers . . . to do it!": Benjamin, pp. 53, 54.

p. 145. Inside, blissfully unaware . . . to raid the North: Benjamin, p. 61.

p. 146. "I will blow your brains . . . inch": Benjamin, p. 22; Sowles, p. 14.

p. 146. "You are treating . . . same manner": Benjamin, p. 61.

p. 147. "You are my prisoners . . . carry them out": Sowles, p. 16.

p. 147. At that very moment . . . his reading: Johnson, p. 19.

p. 148. "What is in here . . . cents": Johnson, p. 19.

p. 148. "What gentlemen . . . behavior": Johnson, p. 19.

p. 148. Standing across the street . . . discharged around them: Benjamin, p. 215.

p. 149. "What is going on? . . . the stable": Benjamin, pp. 142–43; Branch, p. 16.

p. 149. "Get with the other . . . let us catch them!": Benjamin, pp. 142–43, 215.

p. 149. Loren Downing raced . . . darted for cover: Benjamin, pp. 141–42.

p. 150. "If you don't . . . won't shoot me": Johnson, p. 25.

p. 150. Principal Taylor hurried . . . "quietly to your rooms": Johnson, p. 21.

p. 150. Leonard Leandre Cross . . . this day: Benjamin, p. 73.

p. 151–52. "What are you trying to celebrate here . . . into the street": Benjamin, p. 73.

p. 151. In the years . . . attending Phillips Andover Academy: Smith Family Papers.

p. 151. "His piercing black eyes . . . manner reassuring": Smith writing for *The Vermonter* vols. 3 and 4, December 1898 and January 1899.

p. 152. "Not very seriously . . . forced upon us": *The Vermonter* vols. 3 and 4, December 1898 and January 1899.

p. 152. "Ah, . . . I fear it is . . . tearful uncertainty": *The Vermonter* vols. 3 and 4, December 1898 and January 1899.

p. 152. "We have had . . . startling enough": Smith Family Papers.

p. 152. At the time . . . harvesting potatoes: Smith Family Papers

p. 152. "The Rebels are . . . burn your house": Smith Family Papers.

p. 153. "Our great danger . . . began to cry": Smith Family Papers.

p. 153. "My first impulse . . . I desisted": Smith Family Papers.

p. 153. She gave him . . . "Kill Them!": Smith Family Papers

p. 154. "Our little Ed's . . . return to St. Albans": Smith Family Papers

p. 154. Back in the heart . . . Nettleton said "No!": Benjamin, pp. 141–42.

p. 154. "Open your coat . . . obey": Benjamin, p. 141.

p. 155. You don't have . . . obey": Benjamin, p. 141.

p. 155. "Shoot the dammed . . . line!": Benjamin, p. 141.

p. 155. "Here's your hobby-horse, cap'n'": Benjamin, p. 142.

p. 159. Just then . . . slumped in his saddle: Headley, p. 259; Headley in Stern, p. 244; Sowles, p. 24.

Chapter Eight

p. 161. "We have a lot of rebel raiders here!" . . . Get your guns!": Branch, p. 11; Benjamin, p. 215.

p. 161. Young and his men . . . slumping body: Sowles, p. 24.

p. 163. Young and his men . . . pushing forward: Headley, p. 260-262; Headley in Stern, p. 244.

p. 164. "Put a discreet officer . . . destroy them": Headley, *Confederate Operations in Canada and New York* 1908, in Stern, p. 242.

p. 166. "I am their leader . . . command of the raid": Horan, p. 177.

p. 167. Captain George Conger . . . . toward Vermont: Horan, pp. 177–78, Sowles pp. 17–18.

p. 167. Perhaps he changed . . . in defense: Benjamin, pp. 107–108.

p. 167. Young's heart . . . British neutrality: Sowles, pp. 25–26.

p. 167. The officer handled . . . in Vermont: Headley, p. 262; Headley, *Confederate Operations in Canada and New York,* in Stern, p. 171.

p. 167. Nevertheless, Her Majesty's . . . most cordially: Stern, p. 246.

p. 168. While at the St. Johns . . . to jail: Benjamin, p. 40.

p. 168. James Alexander Doty . . . outer clothes: Benjamin, pp. 31–46.

p. 168. Sometime around . . . gold piece: Benjamin, pp. 42–44.

p. 169. Thomas Bronsdon Collins . . . dollars from him: Benjamin, pp. 31–46.

p. 169. Spurr and Bruce . . . the mattresses: Benjamin, pp. 31–46.

p. 169. A bit slow . . . at the border: Benjamin, pp. 31–46.

p. 170. Chief of Police Guillaume LaMothe . . . October 24: Benjamin, pp. 31–46.

p. 170. "I am no less . . . be attempted": Clay letter to Thompson, Oct. 22, 1864, in Kinchen 1970, p. 233.

p. 171. "My order to the officer . . . awaiting requisitions": Gleason dispatch to Seward, Oct. 20, 1864, St. Albans Historical Society.

p. 171. "I have been advised . . . and destroy them": Maj. Gen. Dix dispatch to Hon. E. A. Stanton, Oct. 19, 1864; Benjamin, pp. 134–35; Sowles, p. 18; Winks, p. 302.

p. 171–72. "Countermand the order . . . come back": Maj. F. N. Clarke dispatch to Maj. Gen. Dix, Oct. 20, 1864; Benjamin, pp. 134–35; *OR*, Series I, Vol. 43, Pt. 2, p. 421.

p. 172. One can only imagine . . . Southern arrogance: Royster, p. 38.

p. 172. "In realization for . . . its train": Pitman, p. 54.

p. 172–73. "The diabolical plot to burn . . . miserable failure": *New York Times,* Nov. 27, 1864.

p. 173. A military commission soon . . . "on the Canadian frontier": *New York Times,* Dec. 2, 1864.

p. 173. "It is feared that some . . . dastardly plot of last week": *New York Times,* Dec. 2, 1864.

Chapter Nine

p. 175. I worried very much . . . in these trying times": Anna Smith to J. G. Smith, Oct. 10, 1864, Smith Papers/St.Albans Historical Society.

p. 175–76. "The remains of Mr. Morrison . . . the building": Branch, pp. 15, 18; Judge Davis Diary.

p. 176–77. "I am feeling tonight . . . now write quick": Ann Pierce letter to Marshall Pierce, Oct. 19, 1864.

p. 177. "Southern raiders are . . . burning houses": Telegraph Message to Gov. Smith, Oct. 19, 1864, St. Albans Historical Society.

p. 178. As president . . . bureaucratic delay: Smith Family Papers

p. 178. "The excitement in the borough . . . left unfinished": Coffin, p. 325.

p. 179. "A large party . . . destroying property": Gov. Smith to Viscount Monck in *New York Times,* Oct. 21, 1864.

p. 179–80. "Two of our citizens . . . daring adventure": Gov. Smith dispatch to Maj. Gen. Dix, Oct. 20, 1864, St. Albans Historical Society.

p. 180. "What news . . . Advise him so": Maj. Gen. Dix telegram Oct. 20, 1864, St. Albans Historical Society.

p. 181. "If anyone attempts . . . on the spot": words on plaque of New Hampshire State House portrait of Gen. John A. Dix.

p. 182. "The excitement still continues . . . any emergency": Gov. Smith dispatch to Hon. E. A. Stanton, Oct. 22, 1864, St. Albans Historical Society.

p. 182. "The hours of the night . . . strongly guarded": Stanton in *The Vermonter,* vol. 1, 1867.

p. 183. "They board with . . . proper notice": Maj. Gen. Dix dispatch to Hon. E. A. Stanton, Nov. 22, 1864, Fenian, p. 40

p. 183. The regulation . . . enforced the orders: Seward dispatch to Consular Officers, Dec. 17, 1864; Fenian, p. 30.

p. 184. Secretary of State Seward . . . as a refuge: Seward dispatch to Lord Lyons, Nov. 3, 1864; Fenian, pp. 138–39.

p. 184. "unprovoked aggressions . . . fraternal national obligations": Seward to Lord Lyons, Nov. 3, 1864; Fenian, p. 139.

p. 184. "Information having been . . . lives and property": Benjamin, p. 134; General Dix, General Orders, No. 97, Headquarters, Dept. of the East, New York City, Dec. 14, 1864.

p. 185. "Allow me to suggest . . . under his command": Lt. Gen. U. S. Grant, War Dept., Washington, D.C., Oct. 23, 1864.

p. 185. "Madam, I am . . . for orders": Smith Family Papers.

p. 185. "My God . . . northern Vermont. Terrible": Smith Family Papers.

p. 186. "I shall never . . . the confusion": Smith Family Papers.

p. 186. "During all that time . . . my hand": Smith Family Papers.

p. 186. "Southern soldiers . . . in the dark ages." Anna Smith, *The Vermonter,* vol. 3, 1898.

p. 186. "It was the prevailing . . . our homes and firesides": Sowles, p. 19.

p. 187. "The whole length . . . "along the St. Clair River": J. T. Howard to Hon. E. A. Stanton, Dec. 2, 1864; Fenian, pp. 140–41.

p. 187. "The citizens were . . . of the attack": Major William Austine to Col. Van Buren, Oct. 23, 1864, St. Albans Historical Society.

p. 187. "We begin to realize . . . was shot, poor man!": Mrs. Henry E. Seymour letter to Miss I. C. Maybatt, Oct. 20, 1864, St. Albans Historical Society.

p. 188. "I assure you . . . of this department": Major-General Joseph Hooker letter to Sen. Zacharia Chandler, Dec. 19, 1864.

p. 188. "Vermont might submit . . . will not": Chandler address to U.S. Senate in Kinchen 1959, p. 77; Sowles, p. 21.

p. 188–89. "I am happy . . . of those States": Viscount Monck dispatch to E. Cardwell, Oct. 27, 1864.

p. 189. The militia . . . "has enjoined all her subjects": Lord Mocnk dispatch to Lt. Col. Walker Powel, Dec. 23, 1864.

p. 189. Yet rumors . . . further Rebel hostility: Tidwell, p. 205.

p. 190. "strong indication that . . . raiders effectual": Maj. Gen. Dix dispatch to Hon. E. A. Stanton, Dec. 10, 1864; Fenian, p. 42.

p. 190–91. "Dear Jacob, . . . there with you now": William White letter to Jacob Wead, St. Albans Historical Society.

p. 191. "Presume you have . . . Fraternally, Ben H. Dewey": William Wells Papers.

p. 191. In Vermont, newsboys . . . "St. Albans . . . Excited Today": *St. Albans Daily Messenger,* Oct. 19, 1864.

p. 192. "In the cold and no fire . . . grapevine!": Sprake Diary, Oct. 20, 1864 entry.

p. 192. It was highly . . . seems feasible: Tidwell, p. 207; McPherson 1996 p., 114–36.

p. 193. "Sir, I have . . . information to your Government": letter from D. Campbell McNab, County Carleton, West Canada to Stanton, March 14, 1865.

p. 193. "All I ask . . . the Atlantic.": Ibid.

p. 194. "I am no less . . . appearing in law": letter from Clay Cameron Notes, in Winks, pp. 312–13.

p. 194. In addition, Clay . . . been retained: Clay letter to Sec. J. P. Benjamin, Nov. 1, 1864; Fenian, pp. 43–46.

p. 195. "From reports which . . . to the Confederacy": Winks, p. 312.

p. 196. "We conceive . . . States Government": Clay letter to Sec. J. P. Benjamin, Nov. 1, 1864; Fenian, pp. 43–38.

p. 196. Abbott said Richmond... "struggle between the two sections": Benjamin, p. 115, 196.

Chapter Ten

p. 197. "It may termed . . . daring feat": Benjamin, p. 269.

p. 198. U.S. Attorney Edward . . . "table of a prince": Branch, p. 23; Sowles, p. 29.

p. 198. "To the editor of the St. Albans . . . Confederate States": Young letter to Wilber P. Davis, Nov. 20, 1864, in Branch, p. 43.

p. 199. "You will probably remember . . . your best bow. . . . ": Young letter to S. W. Skinner, Nov. 25, 1864, in Branch, pp. 55–56.

p. 199. At first, the United States . . . a Federal judge: Benjamin, p. 134; Branch, pp. 14, 50; Sowles, p. 37.

p. 199–200. At first . . . for the raiders: Winks, pp. 303–5, 309–11.

p. 200. He publicly described . . . "they were born": Kinchen 1970, p. 137.

p. 200. "I have ever done . . . that I did": Castleman Papers, Young letter to Clay, Nov. 21, 1864, Filson Historical Society.

p. 200. As for the money . . . "I won't do to serve them": Castleman Papers, Filson Historical Society.

p. 200–201. "I feel it be my duty . . . them justice": Castleman Papers, Young letter to Thompson, Nov. 29, 1864, Filson Historical Society.

p. 201. "He (McGinnis) offered . . . agreed to do": Castleman Papers, Clay to Thompson, Nov. 22, 1864, Filson Historical Society.

p. 201. But if Coursol . . . would have no jurisdiction: Benjamin, p. 125; Sowles, p. 33.

p. 202. Great Britain and the United States . . . surface once more: Benjamin, pp. 152–70, 226–27.

p. 202. Sanders furnished a letter . . . authorized the raid": Benjamin, pp. 209, 212–13, 236.

p. 203. "We all think . . . the Confederate States government": Kinchen 1970, p. 139.

p. 203. John Abbott knew . . . in Richmond: Benjamin, p. 195.

p. 203. Such proof . . . gather evidence: Benjamin, p. 163.

p. 203. At the prosecution . . . receive a fair trial: Benjamin, p. 176.

p. 203. "convinced that if . . . similar enterprises": Young, *The Vermonter,* vol. 7, 1902.

p. 204. "I am a native of Kentucky . . . for my own benefit": Benjamin, pp. 78–79.

p. 204. Young told the court . . . "upon to render": Benjamin, p. 80.

p. 204. "The strength of our position . . . Young and his party": Abbott to Clay, Oct. 25, 1864; Benjamin, pp. 115, 174–76, 191–93; Kinchen 1970, p. 139.

p. 204. Abbott had already written . . . " evidence in the pending trial": intercepted letter from Clay to Thompson, Nov. 1, 1864; Fenian, pp. 43–46.

p. 205. The frustration of the defense . . . "for the defense of the raiders": Benjamin, p. 211; Young 1902.

p. 205. Abbott made much . . . "of the Confederate States": Benjamin, pp. 241–42, 384–85; Kinchen 1959, p. 42.

p. 205. Abbott introduced letters . . . "soldier of the South": Clay letter to
   Thompson, November 1, 1864; *OR*, Series I, Vol. 43, Part II, p. 915.
p. 205. He recounted how . . . "distant from them": Benjamin, pp. 385–87.
p. 205–6. "If I made . . . brains out": Benjamin, p. 22.
p. 206. "I recognize two . . . of October last": Benjamin, p. 52.
p. 206. "dressed in ordinary . . . were a mob": Benjamin, p. 54.
p. 206–7. "I knew that Mr. Young . . . from the enemy": Benjamin, p. 204.
p. 207. William L. T. Price . . . on uniforms: Benjamin, pp. 199–200.
p. 207. "The advanced guards . . . clothes of citizens": Benjamin, p. 179.
p. 207. raiders "dressed as citizens . . . common robbery": Benjamin, p. 178.
p. 207–8. "When I arrested . . . agent at Montreal": Benjamin, p. 35.
p. 208. "I owe no allegiance . . . kindred plundered": Benjamin, p. 82.
p. 208. "Yankee plundering . . . mild retaliation": Benjamin, p. 85.
p. 208. "we would have been . . . into their power": Benjamin, p. 89.
p. 209. "The Yankees dragged . . . of Federal victories": Benjamin, pp. 95–96.
p. 209. "a war commenced . . . unwholesome to them": Benjamin, p. 96.
p. 210. In the meantime . . . and New York *News*: Clopton-Clay, p. 237.
p. 210. "Lest misunderstanding . . . may find necessary": Tucker letter to Clay,
   Dec. 9, 1864; Kinchen 1970, p. 143.
p. 210–11. A British boat carried Clay . . . of what happened: Clopton-Clay, p.
   241.
p. 211. "Consequently, I am bound . . . be discharged": Benjamin, pp. 125–26.
p. 213. "And thus richly . . . the United States": Seward dispatch to Adams,
   Dec. 24, 1864; Sowles, p. 32.
p. 213–14. "All military commanders . . . martial law": Benjamin, pp. 134–35.
p. 214. "inform him . . . Coursol's proceedings": *Toronto Globe,* January 6, 1865.
p. 215. "It would be difficult . . . become a cause célèbre": Benjamin, pp.
   274–75.
p. 216. "War is only war . . . treaty of extradition": *London Post,* Dec. 29, 1864.
p. 216–17. "We should expect . . . were our own": *London News,* Dec. 29, 1864.
p. 217. "We must, we repeat . . . that of savages": *Montreal Gazette,* Oct. 20,
   1864.
p. 218. " . . . in the handwriting . . . I know this from himself": Benjamin, p. 210.
p. 218. "about the eighth day . . . he was responsible": Benjamin, pp. 212–13.
p. 218. For the second . . . in Canada: Benjamin, p. 222.
p. 218–19. Kerr's points were . . . in neutral territory: Benjamin, p. 222.
p. 219. "man who has . . . be wrong!": Benjamin, p. 222.
p. 219. "They appear to . . . perfectly fiendish": Benjamin, pp. 241–42.
p. 219–20. It wasn't so much . . . tired of inferiority: Perman, pp. 52–56.
p. 220. "What does the record . . . wild beasts?": Benjamin, p. 242.
p. 220. "Out of the whole . . . political offenses": Benjamin, p. 246.
p. 220. Besides, Kerr . . . nothing more: Benjamin, p. 251.

p. 220. "In no other . . . by the facts": Benjamin, p. 253.

p. 220–21. "If such a principle . . . in hostilities": Benjamin, p. 265.

p. 221. He labored . . . Davis himself: Benjamin, p. 268.

p. 221. Now the prosecution . . . "as common criminals": Benjamin, p. 268.

p. 221–22. The chestnut-haired lieutenant . . . "after his own likeness": Benjamin, p. 170.

p. 222. "I have faced death . . . right against might": Benjamin, p. 170.

p. 222. But Young warned . . . "Vermont officers": Benjamin, p. 171.

p. 222. Regardless of the degree . . . atrocities down South: Benjamin, p. 172.

p. 223. The United States . . . white flag: Horan, p. 249.

p. 223. Now, a Canadian attorney . . . "business to help them": Benjamin, p. 191.

p. 223. "You can see . . . the insurgents": Benjamin, p. 191.

p. 224. Two days . . . James Seddon: Horan, p. 191.

p. 224. The papers showed three . . . "disbanded at its pleasure": Seddon letter to Young, June 16, 1864 in Benjamin, p. 206; Clay to Young, Oct. 6, 1864 in Benjamin, p. 209.

p. 225. "the mysterious C. C. Clay . . . cared about": Benjamin, p. 293.

p. 225. "Now, if we . . . of October": Benjamin, p. 293.

p. 225. Devlin asserted . . . "upon him as upon us": Benjamin, p. 293.

p. 225–26. "Pray what object . . . criminal intent?": Benjamin, p. 313.

p. 226. "the bond of friendship . . . and diplomatically entwined": Benjamin, p. 316.

p. 226. "a must be regarded . . . one of their officers": Benjamin, p. 469.

p. 226. "Saint Albans raiders . . . inform me here": George Edmunds to Seward, March 29, 1865, St. Albans Historical Society.

p. 226. "Telegram from . . . on another warrant": Smith dispatch to Seward, March 29, 1865, St. Albans Historical Society.

p. 227. After their release . . . blankets waiting outside: Têtu, p. 59.

p. 228. "Why continue . . . of their deliverers": Têtu, p. 90–91.

p. 228. Convinced, McNider did more . . . for two months: Têtu, p. 91.

p. 228. Finally . . . in their eyes: Têtu, pp. 123–124.

p. 228. The issue of . . . is illegal: Benjamin, p. 341.

p. 228–29. Furthermore, Young . . . "expedition was absolutely unlawful": Benjamin, p. 325.

p. 229. In December 1864 . . . "against the United States" E. Cardwell dispatch to Viscount Monck, Dec. 30, 1864; Fenian, p. 18.

p. 229. Lord Monck in response . . . "laws of Canada": Lord Monck dispatch to E. Cardwell, Dec. 30, 1864; Fenian, p. 121.

p. 229. Monck, hardly a fool . . . and Canada: Burnley to Viscount Monck, Feb. 25, 1864; Fenian, p. 126.

p. 230. On April 8, 1865 . . . tried in Toronto: *Philadelphia Inquirer,* April 8, 1865; Viscount Monck dispatch to E. Cardwell; Fenian, p. 126.

p. 230. "That they did . . . put upon trial": *Philadelphia Inquirer,* April 8, 1865; Viscount Monck dispatch to E. Cardwell; Fenian, p. 126.

p. 230. As Devlin argued. . . "due to our offences": Benjamin, p. 286.

p. 231. A $25,000 price . . . for William Cleary: *Harper's Weekly,* May 20, 1865.

p. 231. One of the more . . . noted it in his diary: Pitman, p. 53.

p. 231. "In speaking of the St. Albans raid . . . for a time": Pitman, p. 53.

p. 232. "That these persons named . . . of the President": Pitman, p. 376.

p. 233. John Surratt, Mary's son . . . at the Surratt home: Pitman, p. 376.

p. 233. "About the 17th of March . . . bearer of dispatches": Pitman, p. 113.

p. 233. "I had spoken . . . Booth a good deal": Pitman, p. 120.

p. 233. "This Department has . . . St. Albans raiders": Hon. E. A. Stanton to Maj. Gen. Dix, April 24, 1865, St. Albans Historical Society.

p. 234. "My connection with . . . honorable men": Young 1902.

Index

★ ★ ★ ★ ★ ★ ★ ★ ★ ★ ★ ★ ★ ★ ★ ★ ★ ★

About the Author

★ ★ ★ ★ ★ ★ ★ ★ ★ ★ ★ ★ ★ ★ ★ ★ ★ ★

Cathryn J. Prince has worked as a correspondent for *The Christian Science Monitor* in Switzerland and in New York, where she covered the United Nations. She writes a weekly column for *The Weston Forum* and is an op-ed contributor to *The Christian Science Monitor*. She is also the author of *Shot from the Sky: American POWs in Switzerland*. Prince and her husband live in Weston, Connecticut, and have two children.